FOOTLOOSE SCIENTIST
IN MAYAN AMERICA

FOOTLOOSE SCIENTIST IN MAYAN AMERICA

Sister Mary Corde Lorang

OF MARYKNOLL

Charles Scribner's Sons   New York

PICTURE ACKNOWLEDGMENTS

American Airlines: 40; Standard Oil Co. (N.J.): 10, 11, 14, 23; University Museum, Phila.: 15

Pages 190, 192, 196, 197, 198, and title page cut.
Reprinted from THE ANCIENT MAYA, Third Edition by Sylvanus G. Morley and George W. Brainerd with the permission of the publishers, Stanford University Press. © Copyright 1946, 1947, 1956 by the Board of Trustees of the Leland Stanford Junior University.

Photographs by the author unless otherwise credited.

197134

Printed in the United States of America
Library of Congress Catalog Card Number 66-16964

To my sister, Edna, and my brother, Vince,
in remembrance of wonder-filled explorations
we have had together

CONTENTS

LIST OF ILLUSTRATIONS

MAYAN AMERICA

PROLOGUE

There are many ways of visiting another country. Tourists zip into a city, run hither and thither with or without a guide, skim the surface and catch up with places of interest after they have passed, by looking out the rear window of the sightseeing bus. Because they do not understand the language of the country, even those who live and work in a foreign country tend to congregate into national ghettos and never learn to know the inner thoughts and feelings of their hosts.

Then there are the visitors who really try to understand the people of their host country. A long period of mutual getting acquainted must ensue before each pierces the surface of the other. This may take months or even years, dependent upon the temperaments of the individuals involved.

I was fortunate, most fortunate, in sidetracking all the above hurdles. I came to Mayan America as a member of a religious community, working, living and accepted by rich and poor alike. Immediately I was "one of the Sisters who know and love us." I was not considered a foreigner nor a tourist although I roamed around between teaching stints, laden with cameras and equipment. Even now I chuckle at the tourist who asked me directions in slowly spoken English, hoping I would understand. When I answered her in my mother-tongue, she looked amazed and blurted out, "My, you speak English well!"

And so, in one all-too-short year, I was able to learn much of the tremendous Mayan people and the folks who now live in Mayan America.

I wish to express my deep appreciation to Dr. Carlos Samayoa

Chinchilla, Director of the Institute of Anthropology and History in Guatemala City, for his exquisite courtesy in making available to me the facilities of the museum and his own large collection of books on things Mayan; to Dr. Gustavo Espinoza, Inspector General of Monuments, Guatemala, for sharing with me his vast knowledge of Mayan ruins and their excavation; to personnel of the University Museum, University of Pennsylvania, for information, photographs and permission to photograph their splendid collection of artifacts; to United Fruit Company for photographs and information regarding their restoration of Quirigua and Zaculeu; to Sister Jacinta Marie and Sister Mary Benigna for checking the manuscript and to Mr. Coley Taylor for permission to use copyrighted material from *The Dark Virgin*. I owe a deep debt of gratitude to Sister Maria del Rey who has made her professional skill available hour after hour, turning what might have been a dry account into a most readable book. And I am not only grateful but honored by the untiring labor of Sister Mary James Rogers in typing the whole manuscript.

Possibly my deepest gratitude goes to Mother Mary Colman and the Maryknoll Council who sent me to Guatemala as a substitute teacher. Had I not had this assignment, this book never could have been written.

THE AUTHOR

GUATEMALA

FROM HARBOR TO
MONTE MARIA

A night bird gave a muted cry and the waves patted our ship sleepily. They scarcely broke the velvet silence of Puerto Barrios harbor. The few lights on shore revealed no more of life in Guatemala than stars in heaven tell what goes on up there.

We had dropped anchor an hour before. Once the job was done in that neat and tidy way sailors have, the decks became deserted. My two traveling companions, Sisters destined to spend at least ten years—if not a lifetime—in Middle America, had yawned, excused themselves and gone downstairs. I was slated for only a year. This first night was precious; I'd waste little of it in sleep.

Guatemala was, for me, the end of a rainbow. I had been trudging along the rainbow for years, interested in just about everything man can know in sciences—botany, physics, geology, astronomy, archaeology and, especially, psychology. All my "ologies" pointed to a pot of gold to be found in Guatemala. There were volcanoes, sea shells, tropical flowers, odd fish, the southern constellations, mountains as well as humid lowlands, ancient Mayan ruins and present-day Indians. Every facet of this country fascinated me. A summer trip would never do. The psychologist in me wanted to know these people in their own environment, to dig deep, to know well. When the 1,100-student Colegio Monte Maria in Guatemala City needed a science teacher, luckily I was due for a sabbatical year anyway. I gladly took the assignment.

Maybe, as in Hawaii where I spent a year teaching in Kaneohe at the foot of the Oahu's Great Pali, a volcano would be kind enough to erupt for me.

Standing by the rail in the quiet darkness of Puerto Barrios, I thought of the night I saw a new crater a-borning on the island of Hawaii. For a month before, Kilauea Iki had thrown 1,700-foot fountains of lava into the sky in nightly spectaculars. Then the volcano seemed to tire of the fun, but rumbling still shook the earth. I hurried over from Oahu knowing that one of nature's major efforts would be staged. It was, and I had a front seat. The earth split open straight down Kilauea's flank, down to the ocean. Through the rent, a mile of small golden fountains played among the roaring columns of billowing steam. One by one, the small fountains died. Only one remained, that in what was once the little village of Kapoho.

I'll never forget that night. I watched the baby volcano toss flaming molten lava 700 and 800 feet into the black sky. As it fell not more than 200 feet from my camera, it started to shape into a crater. I was standing on Cemetery Hill; a few days later, undermined by flowing lava, the whole hill was carried down to the sea. Two months later, my baby crater was as big as Diamond Head, the famous landmark of Honolulu harbor. I always think of it as my crater; I was there the night it was born.

What would Guatemala give me? Judging from the events of that day, it promised to be a thrilling year. Just that morning at Puerto Cortes harbor in Honduras, we had been holed up in our cabins while a mob rioted over the ship's deck. Two weeks before, a full-scale revolution had shot up the town. Ignorant of this, we three Sisters had taken a taxi to church while the ship unloaded Detroit's shiniest cars onto the shabby dock. Going through the dismal streets in driving rain, our taxi driver had filled us in on the news.

"Just where your ship is now," he said in conspiratorial tones, "another ship had come in. Many people, yelling, fighting, screaming, tried to get on board. Why, I do not know, but this is the way in a revolution. The crew fought them off. Sixteen died; some were of the ship, some came from the town. Then many others were taken to that yellow building you see at the left. There they were shot. Fathers, brothers—they never came out. They died there."

A sobering reception to Middle America! But Padre Jaime Nadal's warm welcome to his ancient, shabby church dispelled the gloom. And hundreds of school children—they seemed hundreds anyway—came pelting through the mud puddles to get a glimpse of "las Madres." The lucky ones could hang onto our fingers; the rest could only troop behind, before and around us, as we entered the church.

Uneasy quiet filled the streets as we drove back to the ship. Soldiers stared at us on every corner. The town was under martial law, obviously. We climbed the gangplank and the officers on deck sighed their relief.

Later that morning, a crowd began to collect at the bottom of the gangplank. There were hucksters and loafers and girls of the town seeking customers. They began to get ugly; the carefree babble from dock to deck turned angry. Fists were raised. Yet off to one side, in the shadow of the dockhouse, a crippled girl leaned on her crude crutches. I was amazed to see Mr. O'Donnell, our Chief Engineer, dash down the gangplank, hurry through the crowd and hand the girl a brown paper bag. She smiled, bowed and turned toward the town. Mr. O'Donnell strode back on deck without wasting a second.

The situation was getting out of hand. "Go to your cabins," the Captain ordered us passengers, "and don't come out until you get the all-clear."

We went. The mob surged aboard. Hour after hour passed while the halls were filled with jostling bodies. Hands tried our doors. Shoulders heaved against them. Voices called for us to open. Then slowly the noise died out. The crew searched the ship from end to end, and eventually we were allowed on deck again.

I looked over the rail at the now-deserted pier. A lone soldier leaned on his antique rifle. He had the business end under his elbow.

"I hope that rifle doesn't go off accidentally," I said to Mr. O'Donnell.

"That thing couldn't go off accidentally or on purpose, unless it blew up," he smiled. "In the middle of the recent excitement, that poor fellow used the butt to kill a cockroach and the rifle split in half, right down the middle. He actually wept. I had to help him, so I put the rifle together again with a piece of wire."

And there he stood in his tattered uniform and bare feet as proudly as if his rifle were gleaming new. The words "Valley Forge" came to my lips. Less than two hundred years ago, the United States was "an emerging nation." May God help these nations as He helped us!

By four in the afternoon, we had sailed out of Puerto Cortes in

Honduras bound for Puerto Barrios, Guatemala's Caribbean port, almost 100 miles southwest. The sun threw a golden sheen over the Hawaii-like, eroded peaks. Somehow, in that soft glow, the three of us were less aware of the stark poverty, vice and suffering we were leaving behind. Tomorrow's hope for struggling people the world over gleamed just beyond the rough mountains of today.

Dark fell; we steamed into the harbor of Puerto Barrios, dropped anchor and here was I peering into darkness toward Guatemala's coastline.

The night my crater was born in Hawaii, I had walked the three miles back to the car (no vehicles were permitted so close to the eruption), guiding my steps by the Southern Cross and that great yellow star, Capella. Were these friends of the southern skies gleaming in Guatemala, too? I felt my way around the freighter's deck to the port side, and turned from the black sea to the blacker heavens.

Grus was there low in the west, marked by its two second-magnitude stars. Fomalhaut in the Southern Fish shone brighter than I had ever seen it in New York. Crux, the Southern Cross? No, of course not; it would not be visible in October. Maybe in December. Orion, well above the eastern horizon, again pursued red-eyed Taurus across the sky. And the river Eridanus traced a zigzag course down to Achernar, a brilliant star I had never seen before. Capella, the giant, was not up yet; in a few hours he would climb over the horizon to light the way for the mythical Argo Navis. In Hawaii, at 23° North Latitude, very little of the constellation had been visible. Guatemala, at 13°, would show more.

Trees and flowers of Hawaii—would I meet them again here? The same volcanic soil, same elevations. Would there be another Wilder Avenue flanked with brilliant Royal Poincianas as in Honolulu? The Jacaranda, the Cup of Gold, and mimosas? Pink and yellow shower trees? Plumerias, called in Hawaii the "maki-man flower" (dead man flower) because it grew so well in cemeteries? The huge, spreading banyan trees of Hawaii would not be here, I knew; would the ceiba be as big? Orchids! Would every poor home have orchids hanging in coconut husks from the porch as they did in Hawaii?

And the people! I had read much of economic injustice, social discrimination. Was it true? What were the facts? I wanted to hear both sides. And talking about people, did the Indians up in the mountains still practice their old pagan religion? The "costumbre" practices at Chichicastenango were pagan worship with a glaze of Christianity, reports said. The tale told to a Maryknoll Sister by an old man: "I remember years ago when our tribe threw a maiden into Santa Maria volcano, as propitiation."

Certainly I would see the old Mayan cities now being dug out of the earth. Temples, ball courts, palaces, roadways! The names were a litany; I had read every scrap written about them, ever since high school days—Tikal, Quirigua, Kaminaljuyu, Zaculeu. I would see them even if it meant crawling through the jungles to get to them.

I walked to the stern of the ship. The moon had come up, edging each wave with silver.

"Pretty late, don't you think?" It was Chief Engineer O'Donnell behind me, just coming off duty.

I demurred. "Tomorrow a dream comes true. So much has happened today. I'm not tired."

"You ought to be," he countered. "For a while there I thought hell had broken loose at Puerto Cortes."

"Yes," I said. "And you went through the mob to give something to the crippled girl with the sweet face."

"Oh, she! That's my little sweetheart, Elenita. I got to know her some months ago. She's like an angel in that riffraff at the pier. A cripple. Her mother sends her down when the ship comes in so that she can get a little money for food.

"I used to give her only money. Then one day, when we had a chance to talk a bit, she told me how much she loves apples. Now every time we come in, I manage to have a bag of apples for her, too."

I was silent. Then I said, "I never thought that men on ships ever got interested in the people of these poor little towns."

"Oh yes, some of us do," he said. "As for me, I've read the Maryknoll magazine for a long time and I send a bit now and then. Guess that has made me pay attention to the people I meet in these countries."

"I'll be getting off tomorrow to live with these people," I told him. "I know I'll like them. There probably will be unreconcilable contrasts screaming for resolution. There will be Christian pagans and pagan Christians, the tattered soldiers enforcing military law, the lovely child in the midst of prostitutes, the . . ."

"The fundamental good in spite of poverty, injustice, oppression and starvation," finished Mr. O'Donnell.

Up betimes next morning, in spite of the midnight watch! Sister Anne Regina and Sister Marisa said their early-morning prayers. I spent the time reveling in the glorious harbor before us. A half-circle of blue jagged peaks threw its arms around our ship—volcanic peaks, smoothed a bit by vegetation here and there. Large birds skimmed the water; they were pelicans diving for breakfast. We rocked gently at anchor two miles from shore as there was no room at the docks for us. Three large ships were tied up, one unloading, the other two filling up with bananas.

"Our good old *Sixaola* won't get to dock for three days," the First Mate told us. "But you can go as soon as the customs men are through."

The three of us piled into the little launch and were soon slapping the brisk waves to where white hankies fluttered on shore. A short time later we stood on Guatemalan land, embraced and welcomed by Sister Mildred and Sister Maria Carmen whose bright and happy faces we had not seen for years. There's something about meeting Maryknoll Sisters anywhere in the world which makes time melt away. For a few minutes we chatted of people we knew just as if we had parted yesterday.

A tall, elderly man with a crown of white hair stood alongside, happy because we were happy. He was Matt Molamphy, retired United Fruit executive, long-time resident of Guatemala and Welcomer Extraordinary for all Maryknoll Sisters. It is his job—so he thinks, and we welcome his aid—to make customs, immigration, baggage checks and hotel arrangements as smooth as possible. Travel, too.

"Too late to start driving back to Guatemala City," he cautioned now. "It's almost five hours' drive. I, for one, don't want to be on the road near the bandits' hideouts during late afternoon."

He brought us to the Texaco Guest House, a sort of stopover for the oil company's executives when traveling. Here Matt Molamphy gave us our first lesson in local pronunciations. He said, "Tex-ac'-co," and we found ourselves slipping into the Guatemalan way of saying very familiar words.

The five of us were soon bustling around the kitchen, getting up a dinner. We newcomers got primary lessons in health:

"Don't drink the faucet water. Use this bottled water."

"Never eat fruit skins."

"Don't eat lettuce or uncooked vegetables for the first three months. After that, you may eat them if you have built up an immunity."

Our "why's?" brought information on native fertilizers, unsanitary drainage and the sly way hepatitis and amoebic dysentery have of transferring from person to person. So we dutifully drank bottled water, peeled the tomatoes, skinned the pineapples and apples, avoided the tempting lettuce. A box of Spam and a cake from Monte Maria completed the meal. But not quite. We drank instant Incasa coffee, prepared and bottled in Guatemala. It was an event, an occasion, a revelation, a joyous beginning of a year of the most delicious coffee drinking in my whole life. Nothing, absolutely nothing, can hold a candle to Guatemala coffee.

Matt saw my ecstasy. "Guatemala keeps the third-grade coffee for domestic consumption," he said.

"If this is third-grade, I'd like to know what the others are like."

Matt smiled. "The second-grade goes to the United States to be mixed with other coffees and sold under brand names. Germany gets the first-grade; she is willing to pay for it."

"Third-grade coffee suits me," I said, cuddling my cup.

Matt soon left for his hotel and we toured around the port area. Actually, Guatemala has a scant sixty miles on the Caribbean. It shares historic Amatique Bay with Honduras on the south and Belice (which most of us know as British Honduras) on the north. On the tip of the bay is a new port, Matias de Galvez, where the entire Guatemalan Navy can dock at one time. Usually, however, only one third of that Navy—this amounts to one ship—is tied up at a time.

Just fifteen miles northwest of Barrios is a port with the most un-Spanish name of Livingston, most interesting of all. When that man of iron, Conquistador Hernando Cortez, led his army overland from Mexico, he reached the river Polochic, floated down to and across Lake Izabal to the short, wide Rio Dulce and on to what is now Livingston on the Bay of Amatique. Then he sailed across the bay and scaled the mountains to win Honduras for the Spanish crown.

Today, Livingston is little used as a seaport; it is, instead, a lovely natural park area. Tremendous trees, white sand beaches, waterfalls, and shaded spots under spreading vines make the town a tropical wonderland. The old fort, San Felipe, still stands guard, rising sheer out of Lake Izabal. Rather than fighting off foreigners, it welcomes them as hotel guests to lie in the shade of coconut palms.

This is tropical Guatemala at its loveliest. On the banks of the Rio Dulce monkeys chatter from the trees. The snout of a crocodile loafing in the water, a shark's dorsal fin, an occasional glimpse of a manatee nibbling the vegetation near the water's edge, the flash of iridescent birds—glowing yellows, reds and greens with long sweeping tails—these are memories of the Rio Dulce. On shore, peccary, tapir and jaguar roam the jungle for food. The anteater pushes aside the parasol ant hills and eats his fill. Bob-tailed cats lie lazily stretched along the tree branches. Small deer break a stick now and then as they glide through the underbrush. King of this country is the jaguar, commonly called the tiger. Feared for his relentless search for food, admired for his beauty, grace and cunning, the jaguar had his cult among the Mayas in the long centuries before Christian rule. Tiger-priest idols have been found over the length and breadth of Mayan America.

Next morning by 8 A.M. we were on the palm-lined road to Guatemala City, with Sister Maria Carmen at the wheel. The two-lane, hard-surface highway is the only such road in eastern Guatemala. Local people are not letting it go to waste. The farmers trudge along it; the women carry baskets on their heads as they walk on it; the dogs stretch out in sleep upon it; cats curl up and toast in the warm sunshine; cattle and horses cross it leisurely. Here and there, some thrifty soul has staked out a bit of it and spread his beans out to dry on it. He should build a cement drying floor when the government has generously spread out miles of concrete? In short, speed was impossible.

At about sixty miles, we reached the cut-off for Quirigua, ruins of one of the most ancient Mayan cities. The only transportation is via a small car on a railroad spur two miles long, operated by the United Fruit Company. It reminded me of the handcars used by section hands in the old railroad days in the States. But this had the body of an ancient automobile mounted on railway wheels.

"I suppose we *could* walk," Sister Mildred said, as we mounted this affair, "but it would be the longest two miles we ever walked. Tropical grasses grow up between the ties in just about twenty-four hours. One would need to be either a high jumper or a machete expert to get over and through it. Then, there are plenty of beasties—

the big ones run away but mosquitoes come to us as to a super-market sale."

Mowing down the grass as we rode along the hidden tracks, our little car plunged through a tropical paradise. Towering ceibas, regal mahoganies, tree ferns waving high above our heads, palms and the brown snake vine lined the railway.

"I'm glad I did not meet that snake vine in the dark," I remarked.

"If you were dying of thirst," Matt said, " it would be the most welcome sight in the world. That vine can yield a whole pint of clear, cool water. Somehow, it filters water and holds it for use later."

"Look at that tree," I called out. It was a tall tree with palm leaves in the center and some other kind on the outside branches.

"That's the matapalo, or 'kill-tree,'" Matt explained. "When young, it attaches itself to another tree for support. Then, as it grows, it gradually surrounds the host tree and strangles it to death."

Suddenly, I remembered having seen in Hawaii a banyan encircling a coconut palm. I had been amazed to see the two trees growing together in back of our convent in Nuuanu. The banyan was still young and apparently both it and the palm were thriving, but would it choke the palm as it grew older and bigger? Was the matapalo some type of banyan? I made a mental note to check the species someday.

At the end of the line, Matt led us down a path between rows of rich banana plants. A park opened before us—trees, grass, strange stones like tall, heavy columns. This was Quirigua, remnants of a powerful Mayan city which flourished over 1,200 years ago.

Matt turned us loose. "Look around but don't stay too long. We have a stiff drive ahead of us to Guatemala City," he cautioned.

I stood still a moment, feeling that I was on sacred soil. Here, in the early 1800's, had stood two remarkable men, John Stephens and Frederick Catherwood, cheerful victims of a sort of diplomatic comedy. Stephens had been appointed American ambassador to this part of the world; the countries had not yet been divided into nations. He roamed around for months trying to find a stable government to which he could present his credentials. He and his friend, Catherwood, were good horsemen; they thoroughly enjoyed all the sights they came upon between the towns they visited. I really think they forgot about the credentials as they followed rumors which led them to ruin after ruin throughout the length and breadth of Mayan America.

Quirigua had burst upon them unexpectedly as they rode through the almost impenetrable jungle. Indeed, Cortez passed very close in his march to Honduras in 1525. But he probably heard nothing about the ruins. Even then they had been buried 500 years in deep jungle.

While Stephens poked around, Catherwood, a draftsman, made line drawings of the intricate carvings on the stelae. Even today, Catherwood's work is preferred to photographs for clearness of detail. The photographer is plagued by light and shadow; Catherwood had no such difficulty.

In 1840 Stephens' book, *Incidents of Travel in Central America, Chiapas and Yucatan* burst on the world like a bombshell. America had its own Egypt, its own Assyria, its own aboriginal civilization. Not only a civilization but one advanced in art, mathematics, sciences and building.

The United Fruit Company acquired title to the site in 1909 and planted their ever-present bananas. But thirty acres of magnificent forest was left untouched as a setting for the ruins. Later, the company financed expeditions to repair and re-erect the stelae. I stood on what had been the Main Plaza, more than 2,000 feet long, scene of processions and ceremonies in ancient days. At either end of the plaza were great tree-grown mounds; buried in them were the temple pyramids, characteristic of Mayan architecture. Not much has been excavated yet.

We were at the northern end of the Main Plaza; three tall, red-brown stelae stood in a row there, spaced some forty feet apart. Most of the park is well marked and Sister Mildred remembered many interesting details from previous visits.

Stela A was nearest us, a huge monolith reaching up toward the sky. The four sides were covered with markings. North and south showed carvings of priests; east and west were filled with fascinating Mayan dates. On the side facing south was a strange figure which reminded me of an Egyptian Pharaoh or a Chinese mandarin with slanted eyes and small, pointed beard. It wore an elaborate headdress and covered the entire side.

"There are Indians in the highlands who look just like that," Matt said.

We walked around to the north side and came to a much-weathered carving of another priest. He was shown in profile, which is unusual, with a heavy face, square eyes and a protruding canine tooth.

"It seems to me," I said, "that the carvings found in Copan, Honduras, also show canine teeth. Can this be a representation of the 'tiger characteristics' associated with the priesthood?"

"Maybe," Matt replied. "A little further on is a zoomorph of a jaguar or tiger. Perhaps it was worshiped here."

Peering over the fence which protects the precious monuments, I examined the date glyphs on the eastern and western sides. Although I had studied up on Mayan dates, this was the first time I had seen the carvings wrought by some ancient stonecutter's hand to record for all posterity the exact time when this stela was erected. According to the Goodman-Martinez-Thompson correlation, the event took place in 775 A.D. The Spinden correlation places it 260 years earlier. This problem of placing Mayan dates in our calendar is still not solved to the satisfaction of scientists.

"If excavators find what they want at Dzibilchaltun in Yucatan, the matter of correlation may be settled," Sister Mildred said. "The Mayas lived there from long before Christ until after the Spanish conquest. It was a trade center; it may hold the key to dates for all the other Mayan cities."

Pointing to a large, double-spaced glyph, Sister Mildred gave a brief explanation of the dating system of these people who had devised a calendar even more precise than our own. They had a lunar calendar, a Venus calendar and a sacred calendar. The Metonic Cycle of the Greeks, in which they equated nineteen tropical years, 235 lunations or 6,940 days, was thought remarkable. But the Mayas discovered the same equation and, because they had a name for each day, were able to use it with much greater ease than the Greeks did. The following dates are based on the Mayan Calendar Round, which depends upon the Tzolkin, or sacred calendar.

"A double glyph," Sister Mildred explained, "introduces the date glyphs. It means the count of days since 4 Ahau 8 Cumhu. This 4 Ahau 8 Cumhu is something like the Birth of Christ in our calendar, a point from which we chronicle events before or after. However, no one seems to know what, if anything, happened at 4 Ahau 8 Cumhu. It means, literally, the day Ahau in the fourth place of the week and in the eighth position of the month Cumhu."

There was a date, maybe mythical, maybe real, when the day

Ahau fell on the fourth day of the week and the eighth of the month Cumhu. Maybe something special happened on that day; maybe it didn't. At any rate, all dating starts from that day. There doesn't seem to be anything equivalent to our B.C.; nothing is dated as before that date.

The difference of 260 years between the Goodman-Martinez-Thompson and the Spinden correlations is due to uncertainty in placing this basic date of 4 Ahau 8 Cumhu.

A sign near Stela A gave the date as 9.17.5.0.0. Sister Mildred explained. "It means 9 cycles, 17 katuns, 5 tuns, no uinals and no kin. A cycle is 144,000 days; seventeen katuns add up to 122,400 days. A tun is, roughly, a year—360 days; five tuns are 1,800 days. A uinal has twenty days; in this date we have none of them. Also, there are no kin, the Mayan word for a day. Adding all our days together, we have 1,420,200 days or 3,945 years after 4 Ahau 8 Cumhu. By involved calculations, this signifies that this stela was erected 6 Ahau 13 Kayab."

She pointed down to the glyphs following all these. "In case we did not add correctly," she noted, "the next glyph denoted 6 Ahau and—see?—further on is the one for 13 Kayab. However, between these are seven glyphs that cannot be read as yet. Probably they are variants for more commonly used glyphs. For instance, the sign for 'kin' or 'day' has at least two different glyphs when used in dates. When it appears here, on the breast of the priest, it looks rather like a Maltese cross, and the meaning changes from 'day' to 'sun.' We moderns do not have to wait centuries for a date to fall on the same day of the week, but the Mayas had three interlocking calendars."

"Definitely complicated!" I commented.

Stela C, standing next to Stela A, bore the same date and was very like its neighbor. Beyond that was Stela D, almost perfectly preserved; the sculptor might have just finished it and be around the corner taking off his apron. The figure he has just finished wears a tall headdress of three gargoyles, topped by a human face and finished off with a flourish of graceful feathers. The three gargoyles interested me because they all resembled the rain god, Chac, who has square eyes, an oblong mouth and a large curl for a nose. I always look for Chac in pictures of Guatemalan ruins; he's always lurking in a corner some place! The face which topped off the headdress was, again, very Egyptian in tone—cool, calculating and with a small, pointed beard. To meet this Egyptian gentleman in Quirigua was a surprise.

Sister Mildred, as usual, was poring over the date glyphs on the sides. "They're hard to read," she said. "Instead of using only heads as glyphs, this stela has full figures. Whoever carved this was celebrating in a big way. The date was finally determined as 9.16.15.0.0., or 7 Ahau 18 Pop. In other words, 766 A.D. or 506 A.D., according to which correlation you use."

Matt called, motioning us to the south. "Don't miss this zoomorph!"

Luckily, I knew what he was talking about. A zoomorph is a rounded boulder carved to represent a crouching animal, but so highly conventionalized that it is difficult to determine what animal is depicted. It usually has two heads; the eyes are represented by astronomical signs and the bodies are covered with hieroglyphs and decorations. For instance, a serpent may have two heads, feathers over his body, a mouth with curling fangs or human teeth and ornaments on forehead, nose and ears. Looking in a mirror, he would hardly recognize himself as a serpent.

Matt was looking at what seemed to be a two-headed frog with human incisor teeth in the upper jaw. The large, square eyes bore the "kin" or "day" sign, so it was connected with the priesthood in some way.

Sixty yards farther south, Stelae E and F reared their heights. Stela E is the largest Mayan stela yet discovered—a single stone, thirty-five feet high and weighing at least sixty-five tons.

"Don't tell me the Mayas floated that down the river!" I exclaimed.

"How else did they get it here?" Sister Mildred asked. "The only alternative would be human labor dragging it."

When found, Stela E was badly tilted and it fell to the ground in 1917. In 1934, the Fruit Company re-erected it with great care so as not to injure the carvings. Thick mattresses of dried banana leaves were lashed around it and a layer of split timbers was bound around that before the cables were placed in position to raise it by modern machinery. The Maya of 771 A.D. (or 511 according to Spinden) had no machinery and no beasts of burden—only human power and water flotation. They certainly must have been determined people. They wanted a 35-foot stela and they erected a 35-foot stela!

Stela F is considered the most beautiful. A 25-foot monolith dated 761 A.D., it shows a priest with a wealth of feathers in his headdress. They fall gracefully down the sides; one can imagine them moving in the faint, warm breeze. The stocky thighs and legs terminate in feet turned completely to the side. This position—impossible to anyone not double-jointed—keeps the stela from being too bulky. Perhaps for the same reason, the arms are not carved; only hands show in front of the breast. Often they hold a bar with the kin sign or some other sign of office. All figures wear a richly decorated loincloth hanging between the legs from waist to ankles. They always wear earplugs, bracelets, anklets and other decorations.

The priest on Stela F holds a manikin scepter, so called from the small human figure carved on the upright portion of the L-shaped scepter. An animal-man figure, he reminded me of the wily old wolf who pursued Red Riding Hood. The horizontal of the L ends in a serpent head with long incisor teeth and scalloped lips. Behind the head, he splits into two parts to form a handle so that the priest could grip the scepter. These manikin scepters are also found on Stelae D, E and K, and on Zoomorph P.

Zoomorph G, a few steps south, is said to be a jaguar; the nose, upper lip and paws are cat-like. However, the eye looks like a frog's eye to me. A human head is held between the animal's jaws. On the opposite side of this zoomorph, another human head can be seen in the carvings which also just might be a jaguar head. Date glyphs place its erection at 785 A.D.

Stela H, some 350 feet from this two-headed jaguar, is dated at 751 A.D., one of the earliest dates at Quirigua. Strangely, the glyphs on the north run diagonally in a mat design. Only on one other stela, which was found at Copan, Honduras, is this the case.

Called "The Dwarf," Stela K shows a short, pudgy figure with a flabby, vacant face. The eyes are baggy, the legs stubby; the plump right hand rests on a bar, or maybe a belt, bearing kin signs. Centered on the belt is a small human face much like the priest's own face. The Dwarf, dated 805 A.D. by Goodman-Martinez-Thompson, is the latest of the Quirigua stelae. The dull face, made even grosser by deterioration of the nose and the thick lips, disheartened me. It seemed to point to a decadent civilization.

We had crossed the Main Plaza, going from one stone monument to another. Now, on the southern edge of the plaza, we faced smaller relics of the past, many of them broken. Altar L is a flat, circular stone; Zoomorph M, the head of a small animal. Zoomorph N, broken, may have been a two-headed frog. Zoomorph O is large but very weatherworn. However, under the silt in front of it was found an altar in perfect condition, dated 790 A.D. On it, a masked dancer points a well-arched foot in ballet position.

We were then face to face with Zoomorph P, something I read about years ago.

A great stone, maybe six feet high, shaped like a turtle and weighing at least fifty tons, it is considered the finest illustration of aboriginal carving in all the Americas. Every single inch of the surface is carved; in places the sculpture penetrates the hard rock to the depth of a foot. The design is so complicated that, had I not read about it before, I could not have understood it. At each end is an animal head with jaws wide open. Between the jaws is a seated human figure with well-carved, muscular arms, dressed in priestly robes like those on the stelae. He is quite unperturbed by the fierce jaws and long teeth above and below. The "scalloped lips" which the Mayas carved on so many animals, and seen on the serpent of the little manikin scepter, are here too.

A Disney-like nightmare covers the rest of this huge turtle. On the eastern side, I found a little gem—a human head of rare beauty with curling hair and an ornamented forehead, placed in the mouth of a serpent.

An exquisitely carved altar, found buried in front of Zoomorph P, also shows a dancer.

"Did these people carve with obsidian?" I asked, thinking of the steel chisels sculptors use today.

"Possibly," Sister Mildred said. "They were very close to the veins of volcanic glass at Zacapa. We will pass through Zacapa this afternoon. However, they did have flint. A spear six inches long was found here at Quirigua."

Many mounds reared themselves behind us; they were once great buildings. Nearest was Structure 1 which Sylvanus Griswold Morley worked upon. I remembered having dug out a 1913 issue of the *National Geographic Magazine* years ago and read about this temple. Morley never did find the top of it; it had been too thoroughly digested by the great roots feeding on it. But he did make out a ground plan, 105 by 29 feet, and found traces of seven separate rooms inside. Now partially restored, it has three doorways, each leading to an inner chamber reached by steps decorated with hieroglyphs. The middle one of these chambers leads, in turn, to two inner chambers, again reached by more steps. The outer chambers on either side each lead to a single inner chamber. Torrential rains could not penetrate to these inner chambers.

The temple was made of sandstone. Quarried in the foothills a couple miles west of Quirigua, it could have been floated down the Motagua River on large rafts. Today, however, the stream has filled with stones and dirt and is no longer navigable. Dug-out canoes cross it from side to side; the swift, muddy Motagua is just about deep enough to float them.

Structure 2, called a palace, is much smaller than the temple and is partially enclosed in its foundation. It is thus supposed to have been earlier than the temple (810 or 550 A.D., depending on the correlation you use). I think it shows a woman's touch. At each doorway, a set of hooks is placed above and another set below. I can just see the prince's wife ordering those lower hooks set in the wall so that her curtains would not flap.

Thinking of this fussy housewife, I remembered something from that old 1913 *National Geographic.* "Say! Whatever happened to the effigy vase found in this palace?" I asked. "Morley himself took a picture of it—a beautiful little vase with longitudinal fluting on sides and back. The face intrigued me. Certainly not a Mayan face. Rather, the round eyes set in a full face reminded me of a good-natured Anglo-Saxon. And the pug nose was certainly that of a St. Patrick's Day marcher. But the stringy red beard and earplugs were not part of the Irish outfit. I can see that picture yet. There was a band around the head. . . ."

"Could it have been part of a cap?" Matt asked.

"Could be!" I agreed. "You know, I have a wild idea. I've heard so many people from Central America say that years and years ago, a white man visited these countries. He was credited with red hair, too. Do you suppose that, by any chance, this little effigy vase could have been a portrait of this mythical white man?" I have since inquired many places but can find nothing more of the present whereabouts of this mysterious effigy vase.

We were walking back over the Main Plaza to our little railroad-wheeled motor car. Matt warned us that we should be on our way so as to be out of the bandit-infested zone on the road before it got too late.

"How long was this site occupied?" I asked.

"Judging from the dates on the structures, not more than 87

years," Matt answered. "Surely there must have been a great deal of available labor to have completed so much construction in so short a time."

I looked at the stelae as we passed them and the high, tree-grown mounds nearby where Mayan temples lay buried, and nodded in agreement.

"What of Copan, over the mountains in Honduras?"

"A sister-city to Quirigua, yet different. They had their own techniques of construction and carving. The faces are different. And yet Copan is more like Quirigua than different."

I stepped into the car with regret. There was so much more I wanted to see. I promised myself to return, but I never did. As the months went by, this area became bandit-infested and no amount of prodding convinced United Fruit authorities that they should risk letting me prowl around Quirigua.

So we came back to Route 4 and headed for Guatemala City. The flat lands which extend along most of eastern Middle America began to rise and fall in hills. The altimeter near the windshield before me registered four hundred feet. After hanging around the early one hundreds for so long, this was quite an improvement. We were edging into the Sierra de las Minas, named for the mines where resources of lead, silver and possibly gold lie almost untapped. The feverish green of the tropics gave way to dusty, thirsty, low bushes along the roadside. Palms and tall cacti fought for living space; they tried to breathe through leaves encrusted with grey dust. The mountains on our right were bare of vegetation, but there seemed to be a sort of scalloped design on the slopes. One row of scallops arched from the tops of lower rows, in an all-over pattern reaching up the mountainside. I was later to see this same design many times on slopes in Guatemala.

"No one is quite certain why the Mayas made that design in so many places," Sister Mildred said. "It is certainly man-made; the design is too even and regular for nature to have executed it. The question is, why? An archaeologist told me he thought it might be a sort of amphitheater arrangement of rising seats so that many people could see the games and temple sacrifices. A sort of huge, out-of-doors bleachers.

"Could it be a crop planted that way?" I asked.

"None that we know about at present," she answered. "A little further on, you will see corn planted on the slopes. The people here painstakingly make each hole with a stick and deposit the seed in it. Even in Mayan days, it was done so. Other nations are more lavish; they scatter the seed widespread. For this reason, it's hard to explain to our farmers the parable of the seed falling on rocks, on pathways, on dry land and, finally, on the good soil. They make sure, personally, that each seed gets into as good soil as they have."

We had left the lowland State of Izabal which hugged the Caribbean shore and had now passed through the State of Zacapa. Passageway for the road has been dynamited through the mountains. As we went between the sheer rock walls, I could easily see the veins of obsidian from which the Mayas fashioned those surgically sharp knives they used for everything, from cutting the living heart out of a victim to carving dates in hard stone. Serpentine and slate were there, too. I picked up several hunks of obsidian which had fallen near the road. Some of it had a reddish tinge here and there which looked like garnet but probably was hematite.

The State of Progreso slid under the wheels. We gained altitude at every mile and vegetation changed to the Hawaii-type subtropical. Palms were no longer dry and dusty; there was adequate rainfall. Hardwood trees jostled the Hawaii-like brush for living space. The native huts of split bamboo had been doorless and flimsy down in the coastal region; here they became more substantial. Adobe filling between the bamboos kept out the winds; doors made them cozier.

Up, up! I kept my eyes on the altimeter. San Augustin 853 feet, Sanarata 2,821 feet.

The State of Guatemala, setting for Guatemala City, is a scenic gem. We looped around verdure-covered mountains overlooking fertile valleys below. Farms, or "milpahs," of growing corn reached to the very mountain peaks. To plant and harvest on a field standing at such an angle must be difficult.

"It is," Sister Mildred said. "More than once a farmer has fallen out of his farm and been killed."

"Back in New York, that would sound ridiculous," I chuckled. "Now I wonder it doesn't happen all the time."

We wound around the mountains on a road that was an engineering feat accomplished by American and Guatemalan know-how. We skirted many "barrancas," probably earthquake fissures, some of them 200 feet deep. It seemed odd to travel so far to get around a barranca when a simple suspension bridge would cut the mileage in half. Matt laughed.

"If American engineers had planned this road alone, there would be bridges. But Guatemaltecans don't rush. It's easier to keep roads in repair, and you must admit that the scenery would be spoiled by bridges."

He was right, of course.

"Do you notice the change in the air?" he asked. I glanced at the altimeter; it hovered around 5,000 feet.

"It's invigorating and crystal clear," I said.

"And therein lies a danger. You'll be so invigorated you'll want to go far beyond your strength. Then altitude sickness may catch up with you."

In Guatemala City's altitude, I later found out, some want to do nothing but sleep; others find it difficult to breathe. People like me, however, suffer no ill effects but find themselves yearning to do everything, all the time.

Along the road, Indians and Ladinos jogged along bent double with heavy loads on their backs. On level stretches, they kept up a trot. Even women balancing large baskets on their heads maintained a lively pace, pulling along small children whose little legs could hardly keep up. Babies were in bundles on their backs—big ones, wee ones, even husky two- and three-year-olds. Baby on back and basket of produce on head—neither impeded mama's trot along the road.

The paved road narrowed. One-story adobe houses squeezed together on both sides of the street. We dropped to a snail's pace and joined a stream of honking buses and carts and jay-walking pedestrians. We had reached Guatemala City.

Side streets on right and left were unpaved. Only this Roosevelt Carretera was unrutted and topped in this area. In residential Guatemala City, La Reforma is a beautiful street. The business section is modern. The city is such a mixture of old and new! Cadillacs pulled over to avoid a man-drawn cart; buses allowed a child and his dog to cross the street. A woman making tortillas at the street corner served them hot to passersby. Men leaned out of their "tienda" (shop) doors to watch the crowd go by, hoping to lure somebody in for a sale.

We turned off at the "trebol" (clover leaf), following a sign, AMATITLAN. Ahead of us loomed a tall cone of a mountain.

"That is Agua," Sister Mildred introduced me to a mountain I grew to love. "Agua is one of four volcanoes we can see from Monte Maria."

Suddenly things got familiar—we passed a Coca-Cola bottling factory, a John Deere tractor showroom (part of Coguma), an Esso gas station, and the Foremost Milk Company I had known in Hawaii. Also a chicken hatchery and a pen of Brahman bulls, stud animals to improve the breed of local cattle.

Then, the two-story Javier School for Boys, conducted by Jesuit Fathers, passed on the left and we turned into the grounds of Colegio Monte Maria. Of course, all sixteen Sisters stationed there were at the front door, all talking at once, all bubbling over with welcomes, all eager to show us everything at once.

Colegio Monte Maria is a special type of school. English is taught throughout to such an extent that graduates are thoroughly bilingual. Above and beyond this goal is that of inculcating social principles, so that the more fortunate people feel responsible for the less fortunate. They should know that the worker has a right to a living wage. They must want to become involved in teaching and giving medical aid to Guatemala's 80–90 per cent who have so little. Maryknoll Sisters have found the students generous and self-sacrificing once they see that others need help. It is this ability to see that so many lack.

The buildings, spread over a wide area and connected by a covered walk, are earthquake conscious. They can vibrate with the tremors. The one-story classrooms take off to right and left of the central walk.

In this set-up are 1,100 students, following the Guatemala system of education. Kindergarten is followed by a year of "preparatoria" and then by six years of "primaria," equivalent roughly to our grades. After that three years of "prevocational" give the girls a stiff course. In sciences alone, they cover chemistry, astronomy (they can identify every constellation), physics (they go into radio and TV waves), geology, botany, biology and anatomy (they memorize every muscle and bone in the human body). The students split into three divisions for the three years of "vocational." One group prepares for college work; a second, taking the "magisterio" course, becomes excellent primary teachers; and a third, after three years of "comercio," are bilingual secretaries and business women.

The faculty is mostly Guatemaltecan. Then there are the bus

drivers, gardeners, office workers, "muchachas" who cook for and serve the boarders and "muchachos" who clean the dormitories and classrooms. In all, nearly one hundred local people get salaries which raise living standards all around the area. Colegio Monte Maria is helping to build up a substantial middle class.

Besides the school itself, girls in the magisterio course assist in the Escuelita—"little school." The children come from nearby pueblos which cannot support their own schools.

In the bracing air, we walked through the dusk of a long, full day. "Just like spring!" I breathed.

"Guatemala is the Land of Eternal Spring," said Sister Benigna.

Black against the darkening sky were four volcanoes: Pacaya, Agua, Fuego and Acatenango, reading from south to northwest. And all around this mile-high plateau were mountains. Truly a good place to call home, be it only for a year.

KAMINALJUYU,
CITY OF THE DEAD

KAMINALJUYU, read the battered sign on the highway. An arrow pointed down a dirt road to the right.

"Hold everything!" I said to Sister Albert. "Here we drop deep into the Guatemala of 4,000 years ago!"

But this was no shock to Sister Albert. She was a missioner in China for nineteen years until the Chinese Reds pushed her out. Now she is rounding out fourteen years of service in Bolivia and other Latin American countries. Switching her civilizations is no trouble for Sister Albert. Kaminaljuyu of 4,000 years ago was just another milieu.

In the Indian dialect, "kaminal" means death, and "juyu" is a shortening of "juyup," a hill or mountain. This dirt road, then, would lead to the Hills of Death. More recently, it had been called the City of the Dead. A good name for the burial mounds of ancient Mayan Indians.

The old Volkswagen bumped up and down the rutted road, with Sister Albert and me aboard. I had heard of Kaminaljuyu for years. It was part of an area which should have been, geologically speaking, a flat plateau some 5,000 feet above sea level. From time immemorial, however, there had been hundreds of rounded mounds, twenty, thirty and forty feet high, scattered over twenty square miles.

Unlike Tikal in northern Peten province and Chichen Itza in Yucatan, there had been no startling moment of discovery, so far as I knew. Just gradually, people got the idea that these mounds were

man-made. Six years ago digging began and rich treasures, showing
the life and work of Guatemala's ancient peoples, were unearthed.
The work was difficult. Although the old Mayas knew how to work
with stone, still they preferred to build these tombs with clay. Every
part had to be extracted from the surrounding earth very carefully.

As always, there is little money for the work. In the meantime,
Guatemala City is spreading out; bulldozers are at work; a factory
for making adobe bricks is set up right in one of the mounds. Small
wonder that scientists are fearful lest some of their national heritage
be lost.

In the National Museum of Archaeology, I had seen the jade
necklaces and armbands, the pottery, obsidian knives and household
utensils extracted with such care from the mounds. Dr. Carlos
Samayoa Chinchilla, Director of the Instituto de Antropologia, had
told me much, and had given me a card of introduction to Dr.
Gustavo Espinoza, Inspector General de Monumentos. Dr. Espinoza
has an office in the museum but several calls had resulted in:

"I'm sorry. Dr. Espinoza is out at the diggings today."

Or:

"Dr. Espinoza is in the basement now, working with specimens
just brought in from Kaminaljuyu."

I knew he was a mine of information on Guatemaltecan ruins;
I determined to find him on the spot. Hopefully, this was one of his
days "at the diggings," and not in the museum basement.

To the right and left of the dirt road, bulldozers and tractors
were at work leveling the ancient mounds to provide space for
middle-class homes. I cringed to see it and yet even a scientist could
rejoice that good housing would be provided for Guatemala's
emerging middle class. However, part of the area has been declared
a national park and this is reserved for archaeological research. Even
so, the builders and Senor Espinoza maintain a running battle;
builders fight to enlarge the new age and the scientist struggles to
preserve valuable remnants of the old.

We skirted a huge hole. Sitting in the bottom of it was an ancient temple—or rather several temples built one upon another.
Only the thatched roof of the last temple would have showed above
ground, but this had rotted away long ago. Sister Albert and I hesitated; would we stop to see it? We decided to go on to what we
most wanted to see—an archaeological excavation in progress, and
the man who could tell us more about that temple than any other

human being now living. Fortunately, Dr. Espinoza himself later took us to see the temple.

The road ended at La Colonia Castillo Lara, a big name for a row of shacks. Entrance to the digging site was between two adobe dwellings. A wooden fence blocks it off, not very effectually. Many youngsters in the neighborhood find it exhilarating to scale the fence and walk along its precarious top.

A youngish man was clearing the mud steps near the street with a small whiskbroom.

"Will you give Senor Espinoza this card of introduction?" I asked, rummaging through my pockets and gadget bag for the precious card—and finding nothing. The absent-minded professor had proved herself once again!

I need not have bothered. From the rear of the site, a stocky man of medium height and medium age, with friendly, smiling eyes, came forward. He brushed the clay from his weathered hands and extended them in warm welcome. We were friends immediately. He opened the gate and closed it after us—a hopeful gesture to keep out the multitude of youngsters. But word had spread up and down the row of shacks that "las madres" were on the street. The youngsters came running from every direction.

We mounted some six or eight steps. Immediately we were face to face with antiquity.

On our right was a large clay altar built on three receding levels, all excavated most gently from the surrounding clay. The squarish base and two upper levels were severely decorated with a narrow, raised strip of smooth clay. Embedded in the front of the top level were oval pieces of obsidian, that dark volcanic glass which can be polished to mirror smoothness. Senor Espinoza thinks they were there to catch the rays of the sun and thus summon the people to the temple.

A huge human figure had been sculptured as sitting on the second level, for two objects faintly like legs, and what might have been a loincloth with five or six stripes on it, hung over the altar's front. A hand belonging to this figure lay flat on the second level. Pulling ourselves up two steps, each two feet high with narrow treads, we saw clay sculptures a little above the altar, still half embedded in the mud wall. Along the top was what appeared to be a serpent devouring a baby's body. Just beyond this was a representation of the rain god, still showing the original red paint. Near to us were two sculptures of human heads in the attitude of offering sacrifice. The features were formed so accurately that it seemed to me that they were, more than likely, masks of actual living beings. They were Mayan sculptures, surely, but so like the features of North American Indians! The Mayan faces carved on stone stelae in other ruins were not like these.

Here, too, we found four complete figures also in clay, some eighteen inches in height, beautiful in details of headdresses, necklaces, armbands and legbands. They held offerings to the gods in their hands; one held a small human head. The knees were bent and pulled up as if they had been seated on a low object, or sleeping up against a wall or something.

"These are exquisite in very fine details," I said to Senor Espinoza. "How did you ever excavate them from the dirt of thousands of years? They are only clay, and so delicate!"

In answer, he took me to the rear of the enclosure. "Watch Juan," he said. Juan was a young man working with a small trowel and a paintbrush. He scraped the earth with the trowel and gently brushed off the dust; then he scraped a bit more.

"All the temples which you saw on the road and the figures you see here were originally painted. By following this line of paint, we can disengage the sculptures from the surrounding dirt. See that narrow red line here and here and here?" He pointed to the wall-like side of the diggings. "That red line marks the outside of a temple on this end. By following it carefully, we may find even greater treasures.

"The small figures you admired so much were painted red, yellow and green. With patience, it was easy to bring them forth."

Easy? Now I knew why this work is progressing so slowly. It is like transferring an ocean with an eyedropper!

Juan—with his little trowel and paintbrush—was exposing a stairway hoping that it would lead to the tomb. It was almost certain that this mound did contain a tomb, because jadeite had been found there. This hard, tough, translucent silicate was one of the most common objects left with the dead as an offering. Already some of the mound had been removed; although the skeleton had not yet come to light many objects pointed to this being a burial place. Indeed, all along the stairway, pieces of pottery had been uncovered. They were all carefully catalogued so that the vessels might be reconstructed accurately.

What hands had placed these pottery pieces on the stairway thousands of years ago? What sort of mind directed those hands? Why did they dig into the earth, making steps down to the burial location and placing jars, vases, bowls, basins on each step? These are questions to plague an archaeologist, an anthropologist, an historian —even a psychologist!

At a depth of seven or eight feet, a large torso made of jadeite and wearing a loincloth had come to view. The head, arms and legs were missing. Perhaps an earthquake had broken the figure and sent the smaller pieces down further into the earth. It was possible, too, that the statue had been mutilated "to kill it." Primitive peoples sometimes do this to take away an image's power.

"How old do you think this tomb might be?" I asked.

"When the newspaper *El Imparcial* asked me that question," Dr. Espinoza said with a small grin, "I told them 'around 450 A.D.' But that is very conservative. It is very, very old, older than anything we have as yet encountered."

Indeed, it was conservative. Objects found at Kaminaljuyu have been scientifically appraised at 2,000 B.C. Somehow I got the impression that carbon dating, if possible, would place this statue long before Christ.

You see, the Mayas made a fetish of dating everything. Lines indicating fives and dots indicating ones are found in many stelae and buildings at Chichen Itza, Tikal and other places where ruins of the Mayan civilization remain. In fact, the reason for building seems to have been to make monuments to dates, or to something that could be dated. But at Kaminaljuyu, so far as I could see, there is not a single date.

Who built these temples? Who did this sculpture? No one is certain but most authorities agree that they were Mayas. "The work is Mayan without doubt," Senor Espinoza said. "The techniques, the ornamentation tell me that. But in this area there are records of an even earlier people—a pre-ceramic civilization which possibly dates back to 15,000 B.C."

This was news, indeed. "Do you think, Doctor," I asked, "that this area was occupied continuously from 15,000 B.C. up to the time this City of the Dead was built?"

He smiled and shrugged his shoulders. "It's a good question," he admitted.

Dr. Espinoza is now working on a book. It will be a gold mine of information, for this digging, working scientist knows the length and breadth of Mayan ruins in Guatemala. Just how they relate to the New Empire ruins in Yucatan is another field in which he excels. His book on Kaminaljuyu will be illustrated by Tatiana Prouskouriakoff of the Peabody Museum, noted throughout the archaeological world for her plans of the original temples, drawn from the ruins, and her drawings of what the restorations should be. I'm proud, too, to have a very small finger in this book; I inked in some of her original drawings.

Unfortunately, the tomb in this site (El Monticulo D-III-1 is its scientific name) may never be found. Shortly after Sister Albert and I were there, the meager funds gave out. Juan has stopped his patient digging and brushing; there is nothing available to pay his small salary. Other mounds, as yet untouched by scientists, are being bulldozed and incredible damage to the archaeological heritage of Guatemala results. Senor Espinoza, by sheer strength of personality and convictions, might be able to force them to desist, but he cannot be over the entire twenty square miles all at once. The National Park area is only a small part of the old City of the Dead. We have found obsidian knives and small heads even in our school grounds at Monte Maria, on the outskirts of Guatemala City itself. Mixco, a hamlet fourteen kilometers away, is part of the complex, too.

"How about my showing you the main temple? That large excavation down the road a bit?" Senor Espinoza offered. How about it? This was a windfall for us. To be shown an ancient temple by the very man who dug it out of the earth!

He lightly jumped into the Volkswagen with Sister Albert and me. We drove for ten minutes down the road, back toward the main highway. We parked the car and climbed a path between four untouched mounds. Children ran over them, laughing and shrieking in fun; their parents sat on hillocks, doing odd jobs, much as nursemaids take their charges to Central Park for an airing. Neither the youngsters nor they, I suppose, had any idea of their ancestors' ancient graves beneath them.

A stone frog, four feet in diameter, hollowed out to form a bowl, stopped our path, a huge squat thing that only a derrick could lift. The grey volcanic stone could have come from nearby; looking up, I could see four volcanoes ringing the horizon. Agua was dormant, but Fuego, Pacaya and Acatenango still belched forth lava now and then. Certainly the peoples of long ago had ready access to granite.

"Why are the temples in this area made of clay?" I asked Senor Espinoza.

"Well." He thought a moment. "There are many theories. One might be that, since they are burial temples, they were more fittingly made of clay. The Mayan version of 'Dust thou art and unto dust shalt thou return,' you know. And yet, Mayan temples in other places are also burial mounds and they are of stone.

"Another theory is that the builders felt that clay would withstand earthquakes better than stone. And it has. The stone cities the Spanish built were shattered; these clay structures, older by far, are still pretty much in one piece.

"Or, it could well be that the Kaminaljuyu people always built in clay. They certainly knew how to work stone; they could carve exquisite jade ornaments. Remember those opposite the front door at the museum? Yes, these people had stone and knew how to use it. But for some reason they did not build in stone."

We turned into a narrow opening between two high walls of earth, and found ourselves facing a rickety wooden door. Senor Espinoza inserted his hand through a convenient hole and loosened the latch on the inside. Then he flung open the door and we took one step; with this, we faced a civilization 4,000 years old.

We stood on the brink of an excavation fifty feet deep. A catwalk no more than four feet wide permitted one to walk around Temple Four which the old Mayas had built on Temple Three, which older Mayas had constructed on top of Temple Two, which the oldest Mayas built on the original Temple One.

I knew that fifteen men had worked five years on this excavation. This seemed very slow work until I stood on the catwalk overlooking this complex of temples and realized that the trowel-and-paintbrush technique had exposed every inch of it.

"Are you sure that only four temples were superimposed here?" I asked Senor Espinoza.

"Sure?" he answered. "No, we can't be sure. That is all we have found so far. If we ever get money, we certainly will investigate further." The same story—money giving out just when scientists are most anxious to continue! Lack of funds had locked up the secrets of civilizations thousands and thousands years old.

And at our left was modern Guatemala. Tomas, the guardian, had set up his household in what was probably the sacrificial area of the last temple. Here he cooks his tortillas and black beans, raises his chickens and beds down for the night with his wife and two children, Lupe and Miguel. As we came through the wooden door, Tomas unhurriedly and gently pushed chickens and their corn off the path before us. We greeted him, stopped to talk to lovely little Lupe and had a word for serious Miguel.

Ordinarily, Tomas would take visitors around. However, seeing Senor Espinoza with us, he pulled his bicycle aside out of our way and let his boss take over.

Senor Espinoza led off to the right.

"See the difference in these two slopes?" he said, pointing out the side of one temple and that of another. "This is where Temple Four was built on Temple Three. Those two little recessed places were probably intended as tombs. Whether they were used as such, we don't know."

He led us single file around the catwalk to a spot almost diagonally across from where we had entered.

"Look down here through this hole," he said. It was just about twelve feet in diameter, the right size to have held a ceiba trunk. "I believe that one of the wooden supports for this upper structure stood here and has completely disintegrated."

The size of a ceiba is something to marvel at. The entire town market at Palin is held in the shade of a single ceiba tree with a spread of 180 feet. Certainly a clay temple, held up by ceiba trunks, had solid support.

Senor Espinoza was pointing down this large hole.

"See the pottery bits protruding from the walls?" he said. "They record how long the temple has been occupied. The shards at the bottom are very old. Those at the top may have been made around 700 A.D."

"Does the pottery at the bottom date back to 2,000 B.C.?" I asked.

Senor Espinoza would not give a definite answer. "That has not yet been determined," he said. "Certainly it is very much older than that at the top."

Off we went on the catwalk circling the excavation. Again we stopped and Senor Espinoza looked toward the center on the opposite side.

"Note the clay, pipe-like structures running from the center off to the left and right. They are drains to carry off water from the upper flat area that had no roof. At first, we could not figure out why the drains ran in opposite directions. After study of the terrain, we realized that the exact center of the continental divide is right between the starting points of these two pipes. If they were to drain the water off this flat surface, they would have to go in two directions."

"Did these ancient people know this by a study of geography? Or was it by experimental work?"

"I wish I knew," said the man who probably knows most about the ancient Mayas.

We finished the circle on the catwalk, and walked over to a collection of artifacts, unearthed here but not yet taken to the museum in Guatemala City. There were parts of polychrome bowls, round planting tools, yokes, stone axes, clumsy things contrasting with delicate obsidian knives so straight and keen they could be used by surgeons. These were used to cut out the living heart from a victim so that it could be offered to the gods.

Some things like stone doughnuts intrigued us. Tomas told us they were used for planting corn. The farmer inserted a pointed stick through the hole as it lay on the ground. Then he withdrew the stick, dropped a kernel of corn, lifted the doughnut and closed the hole over with his foot. Today's poor farmers also plant every single grain by hand.

It is also thought that the doughnut-shaped stones were weights for digging sticks. They would be wedged onto the stick a foot or so above its point and would aid in driving the stick into the ground.

I kicked a yoke of stone which lay on the ground. It must have weighed fifty pounds. "And this?" I asked.

"Possibly the Mayan equivalent of handcuffs." The archaeologist smiled broadly. "A prisoner may have worn such a yoke just to keep him from running too far too fast."

"It must have been hard on the policemen, too, in those days," I thought. "Just carrying around accessories of their trade would tire them out!"

From the catwalk, we had seen the main areas of Temple Three, fifty feet below. Tomas, with Miguel and Lupe, decided to go down with Senor Espinoza and us.

Two steep stairways led from the upper level. Like all Mayan steps, they are narrow in tread and steep in riser. Wooden covers, one on each step, protected the ancient clay. Even so, it was too steep for Sister Albert and me, although Miguel and Lupe skipped up and down like mountain goats. Instead, we crawled over a low mound of earth, went down a narrow passage and walked across an ancient Mayan ball court which has not yet been excavated. From there a concrete stairway has been constructed for workmen and tourists, folk much less agile than the ancient Mayas.

At the bottom stair, we faced a narrow doorway with a pointed top. This was one of the trade-marks of Mayan architecture, the corbeled arch. Unable to construct a rounded arch, they placed each stone a little further across the opening until the last stones were close enough to be capped by a single stone. These pointed doorways are found all over the Mayan ruins. The arch, reconstructed here by modern workmen, started a narrow tunnel to the area we had viewed from the catwalk above.

Serious little Miguel handed us candles to light our way through the tunnel. These candles, I found later, are one more item in an archaeological budget which provides so little for so many things needed. On a later occasion when I returned to prowl around Kaminaljuyu by myself, a group of tourists arrived while I was talking to Tomas. They wanted to see the lower temples.

"Impossible," he said. "No, you may not do that."

This was surprising. Ordinarily he was gracious to everybody. Perhaps some support in the temple had become loose; maybe he knew of a danger down there. But when the group had left, he explained.

"Alas! I'm sorry. But we have no candles and no money to buy any."

But with Senor Espinoza, we took Miguel's candles and cautiously tip-toed through the tunnel. It seemed to be three or four feet wide and perhaps seven high. We emerged in the wide area we had seen from above. Boards covered an excavation in the center.

"We found the tomb there," Senor Espinoza said. "A priest must have been buried; rich jade and beautiful polychrome vases were left with him. Under the boards you see are two stairways leading down. On each step was left an offering—pottery, obsidian, a small sculpture. The flat space between the two bottom steps was the grave for the priest."

He led off to the left through another tunnel and emerged into another open space. Here was the skeleton of a slave; his social position was clear because he was buried face down. It was a Mayan practice to bury people and utensils with the dead so as to make the next life easier for them. Besides the slave, Senor Espinoza said, a baby was buried here. Possibly a beloved younger sister or brother, or the priest's own child.

"How do you know that a baby was buried here?" asked Sister Albert, her hand resting on a little shelf in the earthen wall. "I don't see any evidence of it."

"Move your hand a little, Sister," Senor Espinoza told her, "and take a second look at what you probably thought was a bit of clay."

Sister did. There was the skull of a baby beautifully preserved.

Continuing down the passageway, the archaeologist stopped and pointed out a distinct overlap in the clay walls. "This is where you can see the relationship of Temple Two to Temple Three." It was obvious that the third temple had been built right on top of the second. Still further on, by the light of our candles, we could see where Temple Two had been built on Temple One.

At the end of this passageway was a stone tigerhead; Miguel posed alongside for a picture. That started Lupe; she wanted to show how she looked beside a frog sacrificial bowl. Tomas liked the corbeled arch as background.

Thus we retraced our steps up to the top level again. "You must see the sacrifice-form," Tomas insisted, taking us farther up the hill. Carved from volcanic rock, a hard granite substance, it stands about four feet high. The victim bent over this backwards, his hand grasping small knobs at the sides, his breast protruding. Probably the priest slit the torso—chest near the breastbone—and reached up under the ribs to wrench the living, beating heart loose from its vessels. Then he pulled it out of the body and offered it to the gods. Tomas bent backwards over the form. Suddenly, seeing a living man so placed, the horror of such a sacrifice flooded us. Not everyone agrees that this is a sacrificial form, but the human body fits it so perfectly that it is hard to believe otherwise.

I have heard often enough that Mayas did not have human sacrifices until the Aztecs came down from Mexico some time after 900 A.D. Then why this sacrifice-form at Kaminaljuyu? There was no other Aztec influence in any carving or structure that I could see. There were tiger men, rain gods, little squat gods, but no Quetzalcoatl. Perhaps traders had brought the sacrifice-form from a Yucatan temple. While most of these temples were built after the people had migrated from Guatemala and settled there, at least one city, Dzibilchaltun near Merida, was flourishing while Kaminaljuyu was in existence. We are certain that Dzibilchaltun traded with Tikal, and Tikal is only a hundred miles from Kaminaljuyu. Kaminaljuyal trade pieces are also found at Teotihuacan and vice versa. In the Fall 1965 number of *Expedition* (Vol. 8, No. 1) Dr. William Coe of the University of Pennsylvania speculates that the Teotihuacan influence may have come to Tikal by way of Kaminaljuyu. He has found Teotihuacan-type pottery, decorations and figures in fifth century Tikal.

You and I would not think of moving by man power a huge stone, weighing perhaps two or three tons, over a hundred miles of jungle land except perhaps as a physical-fitness stunt. Yet modern Guatemalan Indians do carry heavy things for long distances as a matter of course. Perhaps their ancestors lugged this sacrificial form from Tikal or Mexico. Did they roll it on tree trunks all the way? Did they devise a sort of sling so that teams of men could carry it in relays?

Questions in archaeology can tie one in knots. They are asked of people long dead who had no idea that anybody would want to ask such questions. One calls over the vast void of centuries to men on the other brink. In answer they hold up a bit of pottery, a broken wheel, an arrowhead or fragment of iron. These must do for words.

Once more we boarded our trusty Volkswagen, and turned back to Monticulo D-III-1. By the road was an "adobe factory" where large sun-baked clay bricks, which make up most homes around here, were produced. The brickyard, anyone could see, was a half-demolished mound. I called Senor Espinoza's attention to it.

"The brickmaker there is Senor Rodolfo Urrutia," he explained. "He has a provisional limited permission to use the clay. But if he comes upon any indication of ancient construction, he must advise the Instituto de Antropologia e Historia."

It might be a good thing to do a little digging around that adobe factory; I decided to try my archaeological luck there soon.

A week later, I took another Maryknoll Sister for a Volkswagen jaunt. We stopped at the adobe factory. Senor Urrutia gave us carte blanche and even goaded on his two small sons to give us a guided tour.

Francisco and Jose needed little goading. Almost twins, they both wore tattered straw hats turned up rakishly at the sides. Jose's chin strap was intact; Francisco's was broken, and looped the right ear. Their bare feet were encased in the mud they wander through most of their free time. Clay was their bread and butter, so to speak; it lay on faces, hands and nails. Each carried a five-gallon gasoline tin; their job in the family business was to carry water for Rodolfo to mix with clay.

The father was on top of the mound now, throwing down clay with his shovel. Bits of pottery were all through it. None of the Urrutias were interested in the shards. The boys pulled us over to the wooden forms to show us how adobe bricks are made.

"First you get all the junk out of the clay. Then you put a little water into it. You make it smooth and pat it into this wooden form. You leave it here until it dries a bit. Then . . ." and here the boys carefully lifted a frame that had been filled the day before, "you have a brick!"

Sure enough! Francisco pointed with delight to a still damp adobe brick, fourteen inches square and four inches thick.

Yes, yes, but we were there to dig around in a burial mound. Francisco took us off to one side where we would not be pelted by his father's shovelfuls, and we went to work examining bits of pottery and obsidian, feeling around for those painted clay walls which might indicate statues or even temple walls in this mound.

Sister Jacinta Marie is a fairly young Sister with a yen for archaeology. She had come down from her small school higher in the mountains. She had poked around up there for evidences of the Mayan ruins, for certainly there are man-made hills and small mounds in her vicinity.

She could hardly restrain herself now. Plainly visible were pieces of thin orange pottery, black pottery, parts of pot legs—made hollow probably to contain a few stones which rattled—why, I can't say. There were round handles and pointed handles, pieces of utensils with carved designs. A tug at my arm brought me back to the present, and Jose. From some nook, he had brought out a battered, headless plaster statue from Spanish times. Once painted red and green and brown, it might have been Santiago, complete with sword. No doubt it was several centuries old. But I was living back around 2000 B.C.; I brushed Santiago aside with little interest. One look at Jose's downcast face brought me to my senses. I admired the little broken thing extravagantly. Too extravagantly.

"You want to buy?" was his next move.

I declined and went back to picking up fragments of his ancestors' civilization. Jose looked me over for a long, long time. Then he thrust the treasure into my hands with a smile.

Both boys became scouts. They dug up corn grinders, large pieces of obsidian, small statues, parts of bowls, pots, flat plates. Jose spotted a nest of beautifully thin, curved obsidian blades. Even after centuries, the blades were still so sharp I had to hold them carefully to avoid a nasty cut.

The boys and we took the loot to the Volkswagen. I felt sure there was jadeite in this mound and I did so want to find a piece all by myself. The boys were intrigued by Sister Jacinta Marie by now; I could slip away. "Green, green! Oh, Lord, show me green," I prayed, pacing back and forth with my eyes glued to the ground. There it was—a tiny fragment of green jadeite. Ancient hands had flattened one side and the edge was razor sharp. No doubt it is a fragment of something still buried in the mound, perhaps broken off by Rodolfo's shovel. Worthless to anybody else, it is precious to me. My own souvenir from the men of long ago.

Back at the Volkswagen, comedy was going on. Rodolfo was still on top of the mound tossing clay over the small cliff he had made. As each shovelful fell, Sister Jacinta Marie darted in to pick up bits of obsidian and pottery. Poor Rodolfo, afraid of burying her alive, bellowed at her at every new heave to stand back. She shouted up to him that all was clear and he could heave away. It was a good system but what with the noise from the street and the thud of falling earth, neither could hear the other. We took pity on Rodolfo and moved away from his workplace.

Quite a pile of what Jose called junk, the stuff picked out of the clay destined for brickmaking, lay close at hand.

"Look!" said Sister Jacinta Marie, snatching up a pottery shard. It was the rim of a small bowl. On the edge of it was a design sculptured in the clay, showing—I am sure—coffee beans.

"I found a design like that on something I picked up in the mountains," Sister Jacinta Marie said. "Coffee, isn't it?"

"What else could it be?" I countered.

We sat down on a little mound to think of all the seeds likely to have grown in that area thousands of years ago. Which was used for the design?

Cacao? No.

Beans? No.

Maize? No.

Then I passed in review the extensive collection of tropical and subtropical seeds I had amassed while in Hawaii in 1960. Any of Hawaii's trees, bushes or vines could grow in Guatemala because of its varied climate. None of their seeds could have been the model for this design. After all, nothing I have ever seen has the form of the coffee bean except the coffee bean itself.

"Why do you hesitate to admit it is a coffee bean design?" Sister Jacinta Marie asked.

I groaned. "What will it do to all the histories of coffee that have been written?"

She admitted it would be fatal. "But it won't be the first time that books have made mistakes about coffee. Remember those supplementary readers we got from the States? My class burst out laughing at the idea of picking brown coffee berries. Maria Carmen's father owns a coffee 'finca.' 'Don't they know in the States that it takes nine washings, three days' drying, hours of abrasion to get off the upper coats and then a roasting to turn red berries into brown ones?' she asked.

"So," she concluded reasonably, "if some writers don't know that much about coffee picking, possibly others are wrong on its history too."

It is puzzling. Encyclopedias tell us coffee was first used in Arabia at the beginning of the thirteenth century and was brought to Europe and America in the sixteenth and seventeenth centuries. But I wonder. Perhaps twenty centuries ago, people in Guatemala so loved coffee that they fashioned berries of clay to decorate their bowls. Could this have been a beloved coffee pot? Ah, one nip of the brew makes all ages kin!

Suddenly we came to. We were loaded down with Jose and Francisco's donations. How ever did that nineteen-pound half-of-a-corn-grinder get on my lap without my noticing it? Besides, there were lumps of obsidian, miscellaneous shards, handles and pot legs. Sister also had as much, if not more. The youngsters stood leaning on an empty oil drum waiting for us to show our gratitude.

It was getting late. The boys helped us carry our treasures to the car. Washed from mud, graded, appraised, labeled—they would be added to the small archaeological collection we had started at Monte

Maria in Guatemala City. As for our clothes—they were ready for the laundry, if not the rag bag. We drove back to the city, asking ourselves questions the whole way.

By the roadside, a large stone female figure had been uncovered by bulldozers; a snake was looped around her neck. Who was she—a goddess? She reminded me of India. Who made her? Why?

Farther on was what might have been the belly of a great fat somebody with a hand resting placidly on its granitic front. Was this part of a Buddha-like statue?

We asked ourselves again the burning question, asked by anyone interested in Mayan civilization: Why, in the 700's A.D., did the people leave these old flourishing cities and go off to found the New Empire in Yucatan? They had obsidian and jade right here, enough to trade for anything else they needed. For there probably was trading throughout Central America—pottery from El Salvador, Peten and Mexico has been found in these mounds.

Did fear of earthquakes drive them away? They had many, but none seem to have toppled their buildings. Maybe Kaminaljuyu was a burial place for tribes from a wide area around. Did they come here only to honor their dead? Was this why the pottery from distant countries is found here? Not that there was commercial trading? Was it that each tribe brought its own precious offerings to bury its dead?

We have no end of questions on these ancient Mayan people. I wish I knew just a few of the answers. A great many other people wish they did, too.

WATER COMES
TO CASTANAS

Amoebic dysentery, hepatitis, diarrhea, chemical poisoning. . . .
The list of ailments seemed endless as I watched Dr. Gerardo
Tanchez's work at the Saturday morning clinic held in Monte
Maria's Escuelita, the little school for poor children. The doctor
comes out from Guatemala City bringing supplies and instruments
in a mobile unit given by the Alliance for Progress. The Red Cross
donates the services of two nurses; the Maryknoll Sisters at Monte
Maria provide the room and non-medical equipment. One of the
Sisters, a nurse, carries on during the week, giving injections and
medications prescribed by the doctor. I had helped to set up the
place with clean sheets, tables, chairs and desks. Now I tried to be
helpful in any way at all as the poor came through—women with
dusty, dirty faces, in clothes that were stained from the very washing water, bringing children with dry, parched skins often broken
by sores. A harsh judgment was easy: soap and water is all they need!

Soap and water, indeed!

Dr. Tanchez finished with one patient. He turned to the sink,
washed his hands up to the elbows, dried them and pulled the plug
from the drain. We all heard a gasp—"Don't!" His next patient was
standing in the doorway with her hand over her mouth.

"Don't what?" the nurse asked her.

The woman was terribly embarrassed. She could say only "yes"
and "no" to questions about her ailment. She kept staring at the sink
as if the shining faucets had hypnotized her. I glanced at the clinic
card she handed to the nurse:

Name: Margarita Bautista
Address: Castanas
Ailment: Boil on her arm

As soon as she could, she gathered her wide skirts around her and went toward the exit door. But just on the sill, she turned and paused, fascinated as Dr. Tanchez once more went to the sink to wash.

"Yes?" said the Red Cross nurse, thinking that the woman had forgotten something.

"That water, where does it come from?"

"From these pipes." The nurse pointed to the small pipes along the wall.

"And from where before that?"

The nurse smiled pleasantly. "From bigger pipes which get it from still bigger ones which are connected to the city's water mains."

Just then the doctor pulled the plug and the water gurgled down the drain. Pain flashed across Margarita's face. She reached forward as if to snatch the water back again. Then, flustered at having talked so much, she turned quickly and went. I saw her talking with Sister Alma Jude later.

"What's the story?" I asked.

"I'll take you up to the third-floor back porch," she said, "and tell you."

The back porch faced south. Three volcanoes, Agua, Fuego and Acatenango, dominated the western horizon. The perfect cone of Agua stood stark against the afternoon sun. Fuego and Acatenango, a little to the northwest, were lopsided. They had probably erupted in a strong wind and all the lava had blown to one side. In the distance the two lopsided volcano twins seemed to be one mass. Only a jet of smoke rising into the clear air from Fuego let us know that things were still cooking inside.

Between us and those distant volcanoes was a range of worn peaks, once fiery young volcanoes. They too had humps near the craters, just like Fuego and Acatenango; the same wind must have been blowing when they spouted lava. Now, the side we saw was in blue shade, but at the foot of one peak, still bright with sunlight, lay a small pueblo. It might have been a mile and a half or two miles away.

"That is Castanas," Sister said.

"Beautiful! All golden in the sun!" I replied.

She handed me binoculars. "Look at reality," she said tersely.

The binoculars told a different story. One rutted dirt road wound up a hill between the adobe huts. Cows and pigs, chickens and turkeys, ragged children, laden men and bent old people trudged the road. A bus, detouring through the village in hopes of a passenger, coated the children, the men, the pigs, the huts, the choking green things, with another layer of dirt. The golden haze which looked so pretty from a distance was this cloud of dust from the bus.

"That is Castanas," said Sister Alma Jude. "Margarita walked from there this morning for the clinic."

"Why not take the bus?"

"You do not understand! We're talking about Castanas people. They can't afford buses."

I looked again at the dirt road, the huts, the few women working outside their homes, the bus and the cloud of dirt.

"How many people live in that place?"

"A thousand. Maybe more."

"What do they do for a living?"

"Whatever they can find to do. Some raise flowers and sell them along the road or in the market. It's a backbreaking job because, as yet, they have no water."

"No water?" I said. "Not more than six miles from the city limits, and no water? Then they have no sewage, either."

"Right! No sewage. Any water used in Castanas has to be carried by the women from a stream at the bottom of that dusty hill. It was once a clear little stream."

"Once?"

"Yes, not now. The chemical wastes from a factory are now dumped into it. You remember that smelly brook a mile or so down the road from here? That's the stream Castanas people have to use; it pollutes even the clothing they wash in it. As for drinking . . ."

She paused.

"Yes?"

"If they have the money, they can buy it for five cents a bottle."

"How big a bottle?"

"Oh, about the size of a large coke bottle."

This took some thinking over. The air is dry in Guatemala; it made me thirsty much of the time.

"Most cannot afford it, of course," Sister Alma Jude continued.

"When a man makes sixty or eighty cents a day and has a wife and several children, nobody in that house can buy drinking water."

Things were getting clearer in my mind. "Small wonder Margarita cringed when she saw good drinking water going down the drain!" I said. "Even though the doctor had washed his hands, it could have been used to water plants or wash clothes. The women have to carry every drop of that foul water up the hill, I suppose. I see it all—diarrhea, amoebic dysentery, chemical poisoning . . ."

"That is what happens. Most of the patients in the clinic today were Castanas people with just those diseases. I go to the pueblo often with one thing or another. If they were sick just every now and then, as we are, it would not be so bad. But they are always ill; they don't have the strength to throw off disease. Here, where fruits, vegetables, coconuts, you-name-it, grow in abundance, these Castanas people have an eternal diet of tortillas and black beans. No wonder they're spindly and old before their time! Their ancestors were a tall, straight, strong people."

True. Carvings in the old Mayan temples show beautifully proportioned men, muscular and solid. At Bonampak in Chiapas are murals painted on temple walls depicting the torture of prisoners. A dead figure in the center shows exquisite development; certainly the artist was familiar with beautiful bodies. Why should the present race be so haggard?

Without good food, a child's bone structure cannot mature; he cannot grow properly or resist disease. Without water, intestines and glands do not function normally. No matter how willing a man may be, he does not have the strength to work.

Below us Cheppy was mowing grass with a machete roped to a long pole. After every swing, he rested. He had no strength to swing, swing, swing; it had to be swing, rest, swing, rest, swing. Cheppy had not a lazy bone in his body.

This lack of proper nourishment is a problem, not only of the area near the city, but of nearly every inch of Guatemala. Those employed at Monte Maria receive a living wage. Slowly they build up to strength and vigor. Jaime, for instance, after ten years was able to make the first payment on a nice house and buy an automobile. Guillermo did the same thing last year. Both of them, simple laborers, have moved up to the middle-class bracket.

Sister Alma Jude took up her story.

"A few years ago, the women of Castanas pleaded with the men to negotiate with the city water company to put a pipe into their village. After all, city water comes out here to Monte Maria; it would not be much to extend it two miles farther. All the women asked for was a single faucet in the middle of the hamlet so that they would not have to carry water all the way up the hill. It would be clean water, too.

"Francisco Lopez is head man of Castanas. He got an estimate from the water company. It was high. They would have to save, penny by penny, to get it together. I think the men would rather have used the money for things like shoes, clothes, food—things that the children needed. But the women persuaded them that nothing was more important than water for drinking, washing and cooking. So the entire pueblo started saving for the water.

"It took well over a year. Then, just when they had almost all they needed, the money was stolen. They may have their suspicions, but they don't talk much about it.

"It broke their spirits completely. As usual, there was plenty of rear-view wisdom. They should have put it in the bank. Yes, of course, but each week's total was so small, they hated to pay bus fare to take it to Guatemala City."

"Did they start saving again?"

"Not for some years. Then two of us Maryknoll Sisters started going there to teach religion and try to lift the level of their living. We tried to inspire them to start collecting again. They did, after a lot of prodding and encouraging."

"Where do they stand now?"

"Now?" she said. "Now, at this very moment, last-minute preparations are going on out there for a great ceremony. The water company has laid the pipe; the valve is installed; and this afternoon the water will be turned on. It's a great day. Want to come?"

"Camera and all!" I answered.

As Sister drove the Volkswagen up the dusty, rutted hill, a half-completed building of hollow tile stood out from among the small huts lining the road. People going by toward the center of town looked at it with pride, even with smug satisfaction—a solid building for Castanas!

"It's the new church," Sister explained. "Over there on your right is the present church."

I looked. There was nothing but a small store, a sort of out-house and an adobe hut.

"Wait, I'll show you." She stopped before the outhouse and unlocked the door. Sure enough, there was an altar and room for not more than six inches of Father's head under the roof. The rest of him would have to be out in the weather with his kneeling flock. Castanas certainly needed a church.

"I'll tell you later how they got the church," Sister said.

Around the corner, we negotiated another road, bumpier and dustier.

"It wouldn't take much to get seasick on this road," I grumbled.

Francisco ran to meet us as we neared the meeting place.

"We couldn't start without you. But oh, has it been hard to keep the youngsters from turning on the valve!"

We took our places in the circle. Margarita, her arm tied up in white bandage, made space for us. Little Miguel handed us programs printed for the occasion.

On the front was:

WATER FOR CASTANAS.

Simple statement for epic rejoicing!

Programs were only for adults, but the youngsters pleaded for them. Mothers held their babies and the babies held the programs. Since the mothers could not read any better than the babies, it was all the same. I held my program long enough to see that it listed refreshments, dancing, marimba music—all the makings for a town fiesta. Then a grinning ragamuffin begged for it and got it.

A speech, of course. Francisco thanked everyone for cooperating and working to make this pipe-dream become a real pipe. There was a pause. He advanced slowly to the pipe, reached up dramatically, grasped the valve and turned it.

Water gushed out. It drenched the people standing in front. The youngsters pushed between the legs of the men to see this marvel. Toddlers peered around their mothers' skirts. A few skidded on the mud. The women breathed deep and feasted their eyes. The dogs—practical souls!—lapped up what they could get from the fast-forming pool.

But even the plenitude of water did not make Francisco waste it. He turned the big valve off and the dogs moved in to drink their bottomless fill before the pool had soaked into the thirsty earth. A smile of deep content played around the lips of many women. This water meant relief from so much weariness!

Ting! Tong! Zing! Hammers fell on the marimbas as eight players set to earning their pay. The spell was broken. Women started to make tortillas, flattening the dough between their hands and tossing them to cook on a grill over the fire. Children ran back to the house for this or that forgotten ingredient. Black beans rattled into the big black pots. With a joyous whoop, the cooks dragged the pots to the new pipe and saw the marvelous water fill them at the mere turn of a handle. This was a village meal.

A dance area was roped off. A shelter of palms and vines stood in one corner and young fellows were up on chairs stringing crepe paper around. But, so long as the marimba played, people danced in and out of the area.

As the 25-watt bulbs glowed in the dusk, Sister Alma Jude turned to go. It took a few minutes to free her rosary, skirt, arms and fingers from the children. It was their right to hang onto her, they felt, and she agreed. We picked our way to the Volkswagen, stepping over the dogs stretched out in bliss, still lazily licking their chops after the first full drink since the rainy season.

Marimba music grew fainter in the background as once again we passed the half-finished hollow tile church.

"And that?" I asked.

"Ah yes, that!" Sister Alma Jude smiled. "Well, once money for water had been collected, the people saw what team action can do. They all knew they needed a church; they all wanted an adequate building. Something the town would be proud of.

"But tile, cement, wood, glass—these cost money. It took some talking before they agreed that they could do the work themselves and buy only the absolute necessaries.

"Once agreed to go ahead, however, they were surprised to see how others came to help them. I talked to my fourth grade class at Monte Maria and asked them to pray. They did that and more. They carried the word home. One father donated wood. Several mothers held suppers and rummage sales for us. I was able to get the pick-up truck from Monte Maria to haul supplies, so that saved transportation costs. A group of business men offered to lend money without a set date for repayment; it would be gradually canceled by small payments. The interest would be pretty high to compensate for the slow return, but Francisco and the other men put their heads together one night and concluded that it was the only way to start.

"Start they did. As soon as the first spadeful of earth was

turned, everybody in Castanas became vitally interested. Many men, after working a twelve-hour day for someone else, came over to volunteer a couple hours at the church.

"But to lay the grey tile for the floor, we had to hire a professional; he gets $1.25 a day, about twice what many village men get. Francisco and the others agreed, however, that this was necessary; otherwise the tiles might crack and be a total waste. I used to lay tiles myself back in the States, but here there is no wooden floor under them. The whole foundation has to be built up with sand and gravel which should be pretty level. Each tile is put down and wiggled into place until it is secure. An amateur can bungle the job."

"How soon will it be finished?"

"In two weeks, we hope. They invited the Apostolic Nuncio— no less!— to dedicate it. I nearly collapsed when he said he was coming. 'It's just a small place, Your Excellency,' I demurred, 'and very poor.' He's a dear; he smiled, 'That's what I surmised from the first.'"

She sighed the happy sigh of an energetic person over one hump and facing another.

"Heaven knows what we'll do to furnish the place! I think the Jesuits will lend us benches from Javier School. And we can borrow vestments from Monte Maria. There's a portable organ I can lay my hands on and I can round up some girls to sing. But I'm still stumped on what we can get for an altar."

She laughed confidently. "By that time, God will provide!"

197134

TIKAL, CITY IN THE JUNGLE

Tikal! I was a high school senior when I first heard of Tikal. As our DC-3 flew over the jungles where the ancient Mayan city had lain buried in greenery for a thousand years, I strained at the small window to catch a glimpse of its temples and playing fields, its tombs and reservoirs.

Sister Anthony Mary and I were two of a dozen passengers who had risen long before dawn, hurried over to the small Aviateca wing of Guatemala's L-shaped airport and were whisked off the ground at 7:45 A.M. The twice-weekly plane is the lifeline for University of Pennsylvania scientists who have spent years untangling 225 square miles of a fabulous civilization from the choking growth around. In the center of our plane crates and cartons were stacked; food, clothes, instruments, household utensils, even drinking water, must come by plane. A road as far as Flores, capital of the State of Peten and a good fifty miles from Tikal, has been projected for years. It is still projected.

So this was the Peten! The rolling sea of green below looked nothing like the sharp, box-like shape of Guatemala's northernmost state. Sparsely inhabited, unscarred by roads, threaded by snaky rivers, it's a primeval wilderness almost untouched by mankind. Yet here was the center of a highly intelligent, artistic, religious people who used a calendar more precise than our own, and had figured out the orbit of Venus to the last decimal point. The Peten, almost 166 miles square, is landlocked. Mexico on the west closes it off from the Pacific; British Honduras, which Guatemala names Belice and claims as part of her territory, blocks off the Caribbean on the east.

The Peten must steam in its own jungle, unable to dangle its legs into either sea.

This might change soon. There is oil in the Peten and the world market knows it. Foreign companies have prospected the area and staked their claims. But for the present, its chief product is chicle used for making chewing gum—of all things! The "chicleros" beat their way in and out of the jungle in the wet season, tapping the sapodilla trees and bringing back tales of Mayan ruins, panthers, pumas, tigers, bobcats and monkeys.

I looked at the other passengers. Mostly Americans. They too had heard of Tikal's story and wanted to see it. Some of the temples were more than 200 feet high, equal to a twenty-story building; surely, I thought, they would show above the treacherous green mass, threaded by meandering rivers.

I closed my eyes and could see them again as I had first seen them on the pages of an old *Geographic Magazine* in our high school library. The pyramids with steep stairways up the sides; the impertinent trees forcing their roots into the half-crumbling walls; the graves rich with jade and obsidian; pottery used by housewives 1,500 years ago; stelae with carvings done by no bungling amateurs, all carefully dated by that extraordinary calendar—these pictures were as fresh in my mind as yesterday's newspaper.

The text had told me how Tikal was first seen. Father Andres Avendano in 1695 was fleeing through the jungle because the Chichen Itza people who had penetrated to Flores on Lake Peten threatened his life. After two weeks wandering through the forest, he came upon "a number of ancient buildings. Some I recognized as living places and although they were very high and my strength very little, I climbed them." After incredible hardships, he reached New Mexico and told his story.

More than 150 years later, Colonel Modesto Mendes set out from Flores to find Tikal. Wandering Indians had confirmed Father Avendano's story. He and his party of twenty-three men from Flores made maps and measurements. This set off the exploration and excavation of this fantastic city. Begun around Christ's time, it grew tremendously in the 700's, flourished in the 800's and, like the other Mayan cities, died abruptly in the 900's. Why, no one knows.

Still the green sea below was unperturbed. The hawks and buzzards, the bright jungle birds wheeling above, could have seen nothing of the ancient city smothered in leaves. Yet I knew that down there somewhere were 85 large masonry structures, a great plaza, a causeway wide enough for an eight-lane highway more than two miles long, reservoirs which held forty million gallons of water for thousands of people, and a built-up ceremonial platform 500 feet long, 650 feet wide and thirty feet high. How could such a city lie buried for a thousand years? Yet here I was almost directly above it and as yet I could see nothing.

It was 9:00 A.M. now. A few minutes before, we had seen the blue, blue waters of Lake Peten gleaming in the jungle green. We had seen a doll city on a doll island in the southern bend of the lake. Tiny white houses lined a tiny street. That would have been Flores, a city of 7,500 people. Tikal must be close.

Suddenly the white top of a temple pyramid reared above the dense jungle. I focused the camera. Just then the wing of our plane dipped in salute and I had a perfect shot. The window was dirty; the slide is messy as a result. But it was my first view of Tikal, the reality of a dream that had haunted me since high school days.

Sister and I kept looking for the landing strip we knew must be there. The tree tops became bigger as we lost altitude; we could distinguish the sapodilla, mahogany, logwood, ceiba, Spanish cedar, palms and Tzol trees with light grey bark dotting the jungle like ghosts. Without warning and absolutely bumpless, we were rolling along the airstrip, a grassy bit of mowed lawn. It takes a keen-sighted pilot to contact ground at Tikal!

As the cabin doors opened, blinding tropical sunshine and steaming heat hit us. The Peten lies between fifteen and eighteen degrees north latitude; the elevation is about 200 feet. The plane lost no time whipping off into the sky again and we passengers turned to see a pick-up truck ready to take us to the small hotel, Pasada de la Selva ("Passage in the Jungle"). Clean and well-equipped as possible in this isolated spot, the hotel featured rest rooms which were "down a little path to the left," and sleeping rooms in the building "just beyond the row of philodendrons." The "sala," where both hard and soft drinks were served, was palm-roofed.

Jose Ortiz, his wife and youngsters, and his brother Antonio, were hosts, guides, bartenders and soda jerks. The wife and children drifted over to Sister Anthony Mary and me. There is a school on the grounds. And lots of fun playing around the ruins.

"When you grow up, will you take people around to see the ancient temples, as your father does?" I asked.

Well, no, said young Jose. It would be much nicer to do what the scientists do. "They find things," he said with shining eyes, "not just show them to visitors."

"But your father and uncle guided the scientists through the jungle," Sister Anthony Mary countered. "How could they have found anything, if your father hadn't showed them where to look?"

"And Antonio found a new complex of temples, didn't he?" I stood up for the uncle.

"I guess so," conceded the boy in a half-convinced tone.

In a few minutes, the sturdy truck came again to take us to the excavation sites. There's something about sitting on the rim of a truck which makes the whole world kin. Up to that point, we twelve visitors to Tikal had been a disorganized group. But with women scrambling to hoist themselves up four feet to the truck floor, and men exerting chivalry to haul them aboard, the ice melted fast. I was perhaps the least agile. With two cameras in my hands and a good bit of arthritis in my knees I was helpless until a Mr. Wilson from California gave me a push and a pull where needed. From then on, we sat around the rim of the truck body with jokes and quips. Two men mounted the cab roof and others saw that we did not slide off the back. The rest of us as we bounced down the short road looked up at tall trees and marveled to see ahead of us the topless pyramids of Complex E.

Thirty years ago, Sylvanus Griswold Morley divided the area into nine groups of buildings, now called complexes and labeled with the letters of the alphabet. Each complex was built on a high platform of earth and stone; each was composed of temples, palaces, stelae and altar stones. Six complexes contain twin, flat-topped pyramids with no evidence of construction on the upper level. This is rare in Mayan architecture; nearly all of the huge stepped-pyramids are crowned with temples at the top.

Complex E is built on a giant platform, eight to thirty feet high according to irregularities in the earth's surface. From north to south, it is 650 feet; from east to west, 500 feet. It took at least 6,000,000 cubic feet of fill to build this platform. This is a lot of fill in any man's language. Where did it come from? Possibly from the far side of the complex where we were shown a water course, a channel several hundred feet wide and so deep that we could look at the tops of trees growing on the bottom. Possibly the fill came from the thirteen large reservoirs scooped out by the Tikal inhabitants to supply their water needs. One of these, restored by the scientists working the site, to provide their own water in the dry season, holds 5,000,000 gallons. Another was twice as large. But, no matter where the earth and stones came from which filled this tremendous platform, it certainly took a lot of man-hours to dig and carry 6,000,000 cubic feet of it.

One of many buildings on the platform is a flat-topped temple, Structure 36. Its five terraces are set one on the other and the visitor expects to find the top one crowned with an ornate little temple. But, climbing the thirty-nine huge steps up, one finds nothing to indicate there was ever any structure on the broad, flat fifth—no holes for posts, no beginning of stone walls. The entire pyramid is without a single decoration and the nine crystalline limestone stelae standing before it are also uncarved.

"Why are there no carvings on the temple and stelae?" I asked Jose Ortiz, our guide.

"We are not certain," he answered, "but we think that they were originally painted, instead of carved. Throughout the centuries, the paint has worn off, although we do find tiny flecks of red in the rough places."

Red paint! My mind went back to the red line of paint at Kaminaljuyu.

Why red? When the Mayas painted the outside of their temples, it was fairly easy to get red dye. Hematite is abundant in iron-rich volcanic soil and rocks. Was this the only reason? I think not, because they also used cinnabar as a red dye. Perhaps they liked the cherry red of hematite and the scarlet of cinnabar—and, liking them, they associated them with religious meaning.

I looked to the east. The sun, already high, blazed down on a building known scientifically and unromantically as Structure 39. It is simply a large, oblong, unroofed room. Coming closer, we saw that along the base of the wall are small drains where stones had been omitted to let the water run out.

"Those drains prove that this room never had and was never intended to have a roof."

Right in the center of Structure 39, and facing the corbeled, arched doorway, stands a solid piece of limestone about six feet high, almost four feet wide and about twenty inches thick. This is Stela 22, bearing the Mayan pictographical date 9.17.0.0.0, which, according to Thompson's correlation, may be 771 A.D. Carved in bas-relief scarcely an inch high is a human figure, known as the corn god. With one hand he sows corn; with the other he holds a ceremonial scepter. The headdress is made up of masks and quetzal feathers. A bag with the Tlaloc, or "rain god," motif hangs from his left wrist. In the rear something that is either a large human mask or a head is attached to his clothing. Jaguar skins cover him in front and in back; shell decorations dangle from his belt completely around him. He wears jade earplugs and a jade collar.

The corn god's face had been originally carved in profile but it had been deliberately disfigured. Why?

"Possibly the people were getting ready to add to this room, or to start building an upper structure which would mean that this room would have to be filled with earth," Jose explained. "Ordinarily, when they planned to stop using a place for sacrifice, they 'killed' the god there, by scratching out his face. This took away his power. Then they could use the stela upon which he was carved as fill for the temple built upon the old one.

"Possibly, too, the epidemic or war or whatever caused the Mayas to abandon this place and migrate to Yucatan to set up the New Empire came before this new temple could be built. What reason? Well, no one knows."

Immediately in front of the corn god stela was a huge round stone, maybe four feet in diameter and twenty inches high. The bas-reliefs around the side showed four men, facing north, south, east and west. Each was seated differently; three faces were front view, the fourth a profile. But in all, the hands were bound behind their backs and a double rope looped them together. This is puzzling, for the Mayas, according to some writers, depicted prisoners full-face and gods in profile. Thus three of the figures here would seem to be captives and the fourth a god. Yet all four are bound together. A woven mat design which reminded me somewhat of the Celtic cross was interposed between the four captives. On the top of the stone was carved a figure lying on his belly with hands bound behind his back.

"Was this stone the altar of sacrifice?" asked Mr. Jones, one of our group.

"We think it was," Jose said. "Or it might have been a sort of table upon which the priests placed objects being offered to the god.

"This altar is especially interesting," he went on. "It is perfectly round, a fact that refutes those who say the Mayas never had a wheel. They did. Any people who have made a perfectly round object could not avoid finding out that it will roll. What the Mayas never had was the axle. However, they did have hardwood; they used it for supports and lintels. But we have no evidence that they ever made round wooden wheels."

I asked, "Could it be that the Mayas did use wooden wheels and no remains of them are left? It would have been so simple to cut a slice from a large trunk of, say, a ceiba tree and use it. Somehow, I cannot believe that so intelligent a people could not see the possibilities of a wheel. Even their dates follow a sort of intermeshing, geared wheel plan."

Jose agreed. "Some researchers feel the same way," he said, "but they need evidence and, to date, it has not been found."

The prone figure carved on top of this round stone caught my eye. "Do you suppose that the bodies of victims, after the hearts had been torn out, were thrown face down upon this altar?" I asked. "The blood could thus have been caught on the altar."

Mr. Wilson, who had helped me into the truck, added an idea. "These temples and altars were built before the Aztec influence brought in human sacrifice. But later, the Aztecs might have used them as you say."

As we left Structure 39, we looked back. Through the doorway we could see the altar and stela directly in line with it. Jose noted, "This made it possible for all the people working in this area to see what was going on—or, it would have been possible for the priest at his prayers to keep an eye on all the workers."

Within a stone's throw of Temple 36 and facing it across the road is its twin, Temple 38. It has not been touched by the excavators. The top is rounded and crumbling; trees grow on it; tropical growth is matted on the great temple's sides. What a job it will be to dig out this ancient building and carefully restore each stone to its right place—stones that have been pushed out by the roots of centuries-old trees and vines! I appreciated more than ever the work, perseverance and dedication that University of Pennsylvania archaeologists have put into this restoration of an ancient city since 1956.

A bit south of Temple 38 is the palace, Structure 37. It is a long, narrow building with broken columns four and a half feet high. When it was discovered, so much masonry was lying around that scientists thought there had been vaulted doorways. Sure enough!

When the building was excavated in 1957, the vault stones for nine doorways were found, and the drab name of Structure 37 was embellished to read, the "Palace of the Nine Doorways."

Leaving the twin pyramid complex of Group E, we came, without knowing it, to the next one. Without a guide we would have passed by these heaps as being merely sharp hills. But they are Pyramids 40 and 42, as yet totally unexcavated. Besides these, there is a building with doorways, Structure 41, and an enclosure like the unroofed building in Group E. In this latter is a stela very much like the corn god of Stela 22 bearing the Mayan date 9.8.0.0.0, equivalent to 791 A.D. Again, a round stone altar stands before it. A figure lying face down is carved on top. The four figures carved on the sides are not captives but gods; their bodies are front view but the faces are in profile, turned over the right shoulders. As in the other altar stone, woven mat designs alternate with the figures around the stone, but the ropes are missing.

As others of the party walked around the area, I watched Jose Ortiz. With a faraway look in his eyes, he stared at the tree-grown Pyramids 40 and 42. "This is how the whole place was when I first saw it," he said. "Just a cluster of odd-shaped hills."

Jose Ortiz and his brother Antonio in 1937 guided Dr. Samuel B. Eckert who made the first aerial photographs of Tikal from the Wrigley Chewing Gum camp's airstrip at Uaxactun. Then, on muleback, the brothers had guided the scientists through the jungle. Antonio, indeed, is credited with discovering the whole complex of Group I in 1951. It is complete with a huge temple, stela, altar and a very large plaza, a full half-mile further into the jungle away from the highly concentrated Groups A, B, C, D and G.

Jose and Antonio Ortiz know Tikal; they have watched it emerge from the green shrouds of the jungle and begin to square its shoulders and face the sun like the proud city it once was.

Our group walked slowly over to the pick-up truck, and clambered up to sit once more on the rim. Poor me! Mr. Wilson pulled from above; Sister Anthony Mary pushed from below. I made it, cameras and all. Before he swung up into the driver's seat, Jose told us what to expect.

"We're going up to the old Mayan causeway, a sort of broad highway that connects nearly all the temple complexes. So far, we have cleared only a narrow, two-lane road, but the original causeway was an eight-lane highway at least two miles long. It was built carefully. A stone road bed was laid, then it was paved with a two-inch layer of lime mortar. Even with the deterioration of a thousand years' jungle growth, it is still a solid road. It needs only to be cleared to be used."

We made a wide left turn from the jungle pathway into the broad causeway. In a sense, it was like coming out of the Hudson Tubes into the shining city of New York. Far in front of us, we saw the towers of temples, some reaching into the sky, others still bearing their crowns of jungle growth, as a lovely Spanish woman conceals her face under a mantilla and high comb.

The jungle had encroached upon the grand roadway elevated from the earth, so that trees hemmed us in as the truck drove slowly down the twenty-foot road. Nevertheless, I could see in my mind the gayly dressed processional, the proud warriors with flowing feather headdresses, the priests in ceremonial robes, the victims dragged along roped together. I could hear the plaintive conch horns, the flutes and the chant of religious people rising as they walked forward to the "Temple of the Giant Jaguar," greatest of the huge structures of Group A. We approached the Jaguar Temple from the rear; on this side it has been practically untouched. Its 145 feet rear into the sky; the perfectly restored top temple crowns the steep tree-grown slope like a pointed-nosed wolfhound shaking itself free from encumbering bed coverings. I was glad we saw the back door of this astounding temple before we approached it in all its restored glory. In the rear, the 23-foot-high platform on which rest all the complex of Group A is clearly visible. I could not separate its nine sequences of construction, but I knew they were there, helping to support the tremendous weight of an acropolis of temples and to make a level area for the Mayan ball court.

Our truck mounted a steep climb, turned to the right and there we were in the center of the Grand Plaza. This was the Tikal I had dreamed of for many years. This was the Tikal Padre Andres Avendano found as he fled for his life through the jungle in 1695. Those steps up to the high platform, 145 feet up in the air, on which rests the crowning structure of Temple I, had known the tread of Modesto Mendes in 1848. He found the steep stairs covered with verdure but still negotiable. Mendes was the second white man ever to see Tikal.

In the years since then, every archaeologist of note has climbed to the top of Temple I at Tikal. Bernouilli of Switzerland who took the carved wooden lintel from the temple doorway to Basle in 1877; Maudslay and Charnay in 1881; Maler in 1895; Tozzer and Merwin in 1918; Sylvanus Morley in 1914 and again in 1937; and in the '20's, Fernando Cruz, Thomas Gann and the English team of Robson, Jolly and Heron. Since then many others have come from all over the world to puzzle out the meaning of the hieroglyphic inscriptions. Perhaps the ones most remembered are John Dimick who restored Zaculeu near Huehuetenango, a project financed by the United Fruit Company (the Tikal excavations, it is estimated, will cost $6,000,000), Edwin M. Shook, a veteran in Mayan restorations, who actually began the present work in 1956 and Dr. William Coe, director of the Tikal project. The Guatemalan government built the airstrip and ferried in men and supplies without charge.

For a thrilling moment, I saw in my imagination the procession of famous archaeologists mount that great stairway of Temple I, reach the summit, survey the site and then descend—even as we were to do that day.

In Tikal, Temple I is central; everything is measured from it. The latitude is 17° 13.5′ north; the longitude 89° 37.9′ west; the elevation 200 some feet above sea level. Tikal National Park also centers on Temple I. Within its 576 square kilometers are more than 2,000 known "structures," a generic term for temples, palaces, ball courts, stelae, or anything constructed by the Mayas. Six of these structures are the highest Mayan temples ever found. An average of 235 structures dot every square kilometer. In one area, labeled "6E," the average is 640 structures per square kilometer. They did a lot of building, those Mayas.

We stood on the Grand Plaza, facing north. At our right rose the rugged majesty of Temple I; on our left was Temple II, 143 feet high, just emerging from its leafy veils. It is known as the "Temple of the Masks." Before us were two rows of stelae, some with altar stones in front. The space between Temple I and Temple II is estimated roughly as four city blocks. Spanning the full distance were five steps leading to the Northern Acropolis, a great platform holding sixteen temples of different sizes. Like all Mayan steps, the treads are narrow, the risers high.

We examined the stelae before us first. Judging from the spacing of those that remain, possibly twenty were once ranged in the row nearest the steps, and eight round altar stones stood before them. In the row immediately before us there were half as many stelae and six stones. Most of them were highly ornamented with engravings and bore dates on the sides or backs.

We mounted the high steps to the Northern Acropolis. Four large temples, 32 to 35 inclusive, faced us in a row. They are ninety feet high, equal to a nine-story building, but in comparison to the majesty of Temples I and II they seem low. They stand in a row. A dozen or so stelae and altar stones, placed at random, stand before them.

Behind the row of ninety-footers is a cluster of four more temples, each facing a cardinal point of the compass, and with their backs forming the sides of a central square. These are Temples 36-39, inclusive. Other smaller ones are placed in any unfilled corner.

Although not much has been done on these temples to consolidate and restore them, shafts have been dug through the solid interiors in search of tombs. Precious jades, carved bones, pottery, obsidian and human skeletons have been found.

Digging through Temple 33, excavators found that it enclosed an earlier structure. A tunnel through the center uncovered two tombs, one from the early classic era, the other from a later period. The early tomb, decorated with hieroglyphics on white-washed walls, is dated March 15, 457 A.D. The later tomb is dated 758 A.D. In it lies the skeleton of a young priest, 4' 5" tall. The bones are red, probably due to dye in the jaguar-skin shroud he wore. The tomb seems to have been closed hurriedly; a splash of mortar on the wall was smoothed with an unknown workman's fingers. Both fingerprints and footprints remain in the mortar. It seems as though the tomb had to be used before it was finished.

"Why was there such a rush?" I asked Jose Ortiz. "Have the scientists proposed any theories?"

"No, so far no one thinks he knows the answer," he said. "It is just one more of Tikal's mysteries."

On the outside of the sealed door, a brilliant red dot had been found. Was it to mark the center of the temple? Or did it designate something about the burial?

The crowd of us started into Temple 34. When I say "into" I mean exactly that, for these temples are all solid, packed with stones, mud, rocks, old masonry, whatever could be found to pack it solid. To penetrate into this in order to discover what older temples had been covered by the newer ones, scientists must dig ever so carefully through the solid mass. Can you imagine 225 square miles, liberally sprinkled with buildings from six to twenty stories high, each filled completely with earth and stones? Furthermore, clusters of these solid buildings are set on massive level platforms which are also built solid. The amount of fill needed for such an operation is staggering to think of. Small wonder the Mayas "killed" the gods on stelae and used them to help fill up the other buildings and platforms. The only hollow spaces in these temples are the three-room temples proper, set up on the highest step, and surmounted by a "comb" of heavy, decorated limestone.

We now began to penetrate Temple 34, the "Temple of the Red Stela." It was the first one excavated at Tikal by Field Director Edwin M. Shook of the University of Pennsylvania team. Boring through the large pyramid, he found an earlier temple which had been filled with rubble when the vaster temple was built. Now, the three rooms have been cleared; we reached the first by going down some slippery steps after Jose Ortiz who carried a strong flashlight. The rooms were built in a series, one behind the other, each with a central doorway. Judging from the debris still on the floor, they originally had vaulted ceilings and the walls were decorated with molded stucco, painted red.

In the last room Jose's flashlight suddenly illuminated Stela 26, also painted red. It seems to have been deliberately broken into two main pieces and several small fragments. What a pity! It was exquisitely carved. The front shows an elaborately costumed figure; the sides are engraved with two rows of hieroglyphics. Oddly enough, the stone from which this stela was made is not from the area; its source is unknown.

Secret hiding places have been found in the floors of all three rooms. They were filled with jade ornaments, sponges, coral, seaweeds, sea shells, sting ray spines and imitation sting ray spines, fish vertebrae, incised and eccentric obsidian, flints, crystalline hematite, mother-of-pearl, obsidian blades, jade offerings and a crystalline vessel covered with jade mosaic. There is also the head of a Mayan god.

In the bedrock under this old three-room temple, the excavators found an opening which led into a tomb. The date seems to be 400 A.D. Here are buried a male skeleton, a five-foot-long alligator and two turtles. Truly strange burial companions!

We came out of Temple 34 into the bright sunshine, only to plunge again into darkness in a tunnel in the rear of Temple 33. At the end of it, in the garish light of Jose's giant flashlight, was a stela which was "killed" when the face was obliterated, and was used as fill for the temple being built above it. Eight rows of dates are marked in 213 hieroglyphics on it; the initial one is 445 A.D. Even without a face, the figure is so arresting I paused in wonder before it.

In his right hand, the figure holds aloft the first large ring of a chain encircling his hand. The links grow smaller as they fall from his hand and end in a snake's head. The flamboyant headdress, too, terminates in a series of serpents' heads. His earrings are formed like birds; they are not the usual round plugs the Mayas depict. Two other figures are on the stela's sides but they seem to have been carved by another Mayan artist.

Could it be that this fury of serpents' heads and the long chain ending in a serpent were carved by an original artist, and later Mexican artists added the bird figures and the other serpents? Or was the whole thing carved first by a pre-Mayan people, unknown to us?

The upraised arm is strong and grasps the chain so firmly, I could feel the tension. It could have been the arm of a Greek warrior or Apollo. Speculation ran rife in my mind. The Mayan mounds are very like the mounds at Stonehenge, England. A Mycenaean dagger carved on the large stones there lends credence to the theory of Greek influence. Does this Medusa-like headdress and beautifully carved arm also indicate Greek influence? Or was there a people who were common ancestors to Greeks, Mayas and the builders of Stonehenge?

Between Temples 33 and 34 and a little to the rear is the oldest dated tomb. Found under fifty feet of construction, it bears the inscription, 16 A.D. In the same area are Stelae 1 and 2 showing the same art as the Leyden Plate displayed. This was a small jade carving found at Puerto Barrios in 1864. It showed a captive which resembles those at Tikal. Dated at 320 A.D., it may have been brought from the City of Temples to this port on the Caribbean 250 miles away, over the excellent, raised roadways which connected the Mayan empire.

On the walls of this same old tomb, dated in Christ's lifetime, is a mask some twenty feet above the ground. It is an ancient god, adored in those long past years. Two holes for eyes, a bump for a nose and an oblong bump for the mouth complete this very primitive deity. Just below it, there is an altar. It was evidently too high for ordinary use, so another altar one could reach from the ground had been carved out of the rock below. Like the one above, it is simply a shelf upon which offerings could be left.

Standing once more on the top step in the sunshine flooding the Great Plaza, we could look back on the Northern Acropolis. Sixteen structures are here but most of them have not yet been excavated, and the stones torn loose by burrowing roots have not been replaced.

We descended the five steps to the Grand Plaza and walked over to Temple II at the right. This is, even now, in the consolidation stage, but only the comb top and upper chamber are free from vegetation. Consolidation of these huge buildings is a gradual, careful process, planned as much as possible to restore each stone to its original place. It will be years before all 143 feet of this temple are fully restored.

The most splendid of these structures I have left for the last—Temple I, the Temple of the Jaguar. Jose Ortiz pointed to the base of the temple where a tunnel was closed by a wooden door.

"That opening leads to the tomb of the young priest found seven years ago. *Life* magazine wrote a feature story speculating on the origins of the young man."

"May we see this tomb now?" I asked.

Jose smiled. "It would be possible if the men were not digging there now, looking for another tomb which may be to the side. They have found more obsidian fragments, usually a sign that a burial place is near."

Even outside, we could hear the pounding and noise, so we knew we would not be welcome at the digging site just then. But Jose told us all about this strange tomb.

"Usually in these pyramids, the burial spot is right in the center. But this in Temple I was not. A tunnel bored from front to back missed it completely. However in the digging, obsidian was noted in the wall. Digging in that direction, they found the tomb.

"It must have been a very important gentleman buried there. Maybe a priest; maybe a leader. An eight-pound jade necklace had been thrown over the body, rather carelessly. It was so heavy, it could only have been a ceremonial necklace. Many other jade ornaments and shells, monkey and other animal bones delicately carved with hieroglyphics, beautiful polychrome pottery and other treasures attest to the importance of this young man."

"Is the jade still here?" someone asked.

"It certainly is," Jose responded quickly. "We have started a museum which I plan to show you this afternoon. A small place so far, but we hope to enlarge it."

To really see Temple I, we backed off a hundred feet from it. Rising 145 feet above the filled-in platform which is the Grand Plaza, it is built in nine levels up to the crowning structure. High on the topmost level is a squarish stone building with a wooden lintel over the door and a thirty-foot roof comb. The north side of Temple I has been almost fully restored and so has the roof comb. The south side has been consolidated but has not yet been faced with the cut limestone which gave these temples their white, gleaming beauty. From the south, Temple I presents an appearance of rough stone.

Scaling the beautiful north side are the steps, more than a hundred of them, cleared and climbable in the center and on the upper right side. Like all Mayan steps I ever saw, they were steep. I am five-foot-three and the fifth step was over my head! Of course nothing like hand-railings were there to help a softie like me. It's laborious to climb up, but frightening to come down. Many tourists who go up like gazelles come down in fear and trembling. After all, States-side people don't usually go up and down ladder-like steps scaling a sixteen-story building! Looking down, you feel that you are a human fly.

Jose Ortiz put the proposition to us. "If you think you can make it to the top, it will be well worth your try. But if you get dizzy at heights, don't try it. We like live visitors, not dead ones."

The view from the top, I found, is well worth the effort to reach it. Directly across the Grand Plaza is the "Temple of the Mask," (II) and to the right is the Northern Acropolis with its cluster of structures, even more impressive from the height than from the ground.

To the west is that giant among Tikal's giants, Temple IV, 212 feet high, rearing its crested head, bedecked with waving trees, high above the jungle. To the south is another cluster, known as the Southern Acropolis.

Craning our necks to look up, we saw the high roof comb of Temple I, a huge, erect piece of limestone, rising into the sky. Upon it is carved a figure, seated on a throne, royally dressed and decorated with a fabulous headdress and large earplugs. On either side are serpent motifs.

The rooms below this roof comb make up the temple proper;

all the rest of the structure exists merely to lift it skyward. The temple has three rooms—long and narrow here because the corbeled arch would not permit any wider opening. Had the Mayan builders ever found the true arch, their rooms would have been tremendous, judging from their usual majestic style of operation. Their motto was "Think big!"

Carved zapote beams serve as lintels. Bernouilli took those from the third room to the Museum of Ethnology in Basle, Switzerland, a hundred years ago. A reproduction of the original, placed in the original position, shows an intricate carving of the giant jaguar; this gives the name to Temple I. Bernouilli also took to Switzerland lintels from Temple III. Copies of these now hang in the museum in Guatemala City. The beauty of these carvings is amazing. Today, to do similar work, wood-carvers would need steel instruments with a variety of tips and curves. The Mayas had nothing but pressure-flaked obsidian blades. They were surgically sharp, but only glass-like. Wonderful people, those Mayas!

With the exception of crystalline limestone which we will talk about later, all the materials used in the Grand Plaza and its buildings were found at hand. Lintels and supports were made of zapote (*Archras zapota*) and logwood (*Haematoxylum campechianum*) —trees which grow in the area. The limestone blocks could have been quarried from the rock base upon which Tikal stands.

However, the man-hours of work required is staggering to think of. The pyramids are, for the most part, solid structures, filled with rubble to enable them to support the top sacrificial rooms and the huge roof combs. Possibly more than 25,000 man-hours were required to build up the central core of a temple 140 feet in height. Then, the outside of the entire building had to be covered with cut, set and finished limestone. The making of lime mortar by reducing limestone to cement by burning was another staggering job. A great amount of wood had to be cut with stone axes; the wood growing around Tikal is so hard that it dulls steel saws today. To obtain one cubic meter of cement, experts say a cord of wood would be needed. With acres of surface to cover on each building, one cubic meter would be a mere drop in the bucket. Tikal has eight giant pyramids, possibly ten times that number of lesser palaces and other buildings. A thousand stelae and altar stones are placed on the grounds. While these last did not require fill and cement, they were usually covered with glyphs. The stone and wooden carvings on practically everything could not have been dashed off between breaths. It is too perfectly done—and done with uncooperating tools, unfitted for delicate, artistic work.

We face another amazing fact if we believe the dates on the temples and other structures. The guide told us that 80 per cent of Tikal's buildings were erected between 720 and 771 A.D. Indeed, it is thought that probably the whole 145 feet of Temple I was reared within two years; the date at the top is just two years later than that at the bottom.

By its own records in stone, Tikal flourished from 416 A.D. until 869 A.D. Therefore all of the buildings above ground must have been done in this 450-year period. And yet—like the old tomb dated 16 A.D. and the Leyden Plate of 320 A.D.—there have been indications of far earlier occupation. As diggings go on, it is becoming apparent that the Northern Acropolis stands on the top of eight earlier platforms, the first of which has been carbon-dated at first century B.C.

Some investigators think the Itza people occupied Tikal in the fourteenth century A.D., adding a few of their serpent symbols here and there, carving a figure on a blank side of a stela or building a small shelter. But for the most part, they just cleared and used the major buildings vacated by the Mayas when they had left 600 years before.

By now, it was almost high noon. We visitors to Tikal sat or stood in the shade, talking. Mr. Jones put into words the question that plagued me and, I found out afterwards, Sister Anthony Mary as well.

"Why did the Mayas leave all their cities of the old empire, those tremendous places like Copan, Quirigua, Zaculeu, Uaxactun and this Tikal where we are now? Why were they abandoned between 700 and 900 A.D.?"

We mulled over some guesses. Was it need for farm land? Looking out over the expanse of luxurious growth around Tikal, we decided the answer must be "No." Could it have been an epidemic? Well, so far no mass burial places have been found; from this, one would judge that they did not all die off in large numbers at once. Was it a revolt against the priesthood and its demand for human sacrifice? Mrs. Maler thought so. "Could be!" she said. "Remember how the Indians left with all their possessions when the Spanish oppressed them in Iximche? They disappeared into the night, bag and baggage, and started to build another city after the Spanish had given up the chase."

Jose summed up the discussion. "Your guesses are as good as anyone's. So far, no one knows or even thinks he has a good clue. We all hope some time that some stela or building will give us the answer. Until then, we keep checking one possibility against another."

We climbed aboard the pick-up truck once more, for the half-mile drive to Temple IV. This is another leg of the right triangle which the Great Causeway describes, connecting the largest and most important temple complexes. Group A, where we were, sits at the right angle. Group D and Temple IV are at one of the points of the triangle; Group H is at the third point.

"This causeway is just a small part of the road system in the Mayan Empire," Jose told us. "If you care to drive to Uaxactun thirty-five miles away, this road goes all the way." He admitted, however, that it might be best to get a horse for such a trip; the road might be in need of repairs after a thousand years. None of us took him up on it, there was still too much to see right where we were. Besides, snakes, tigers, jaguars and tapirs roam the jungle between these two ancient cities.

The causeway zigzagged a bit around the 178-foot Temple III and Structure 69. Passing the tree-grown mound which holds the base of this great temple buried, we recalled the superb lintels that Bernouilli took from it as trophies to Switzerland. They reached Europe in 1877, and ever since have been considered among the finest examples of wood carving in the world.

Near Temple III is structure 16, perfectly round and dated 711 A.D. Made of crystalline limestone, it has stood unprotected from the weather these twelve centuries. Just where the stone came from has not yet been determined. Certainly it was not taken from any of the local limestone deposits. The Lanquin Caves, halfway to Guatemala City from Tikal, are filled with crystalline limestone; the vein extends, according to hearsay, all the way to Mexico. Guides at Lanquin Caves told me they had found a large underground lake on the fourteenth day of a long exploration trip through the caves. Judging from my own difficulty in crawling over and around limestone blocks, treacherous drops, fallen stalactites and other debris, I don't think they got very far in any day. This could well have been a source of the crystalline limestone used at Tikal. Of course, it would have taken considerable man power to transport it 125 miles if there is no secret entrance to the caves closer than Lanquin, but it would seem that the Mayas had plenty of man power available.

At the foot of a short, steep incline, we again left the truck and climbed up to a flat spot in front of Temple IV, the 212-foot giant. Clinging lianas, large philodendrons, wild orchids and air plants made of it one huge, wild bouquet. Only the limestone top pushed above the mass of tropical flowers.

The sturdier members of our party forged ahead to climb to the top, but I had to concede defeat. The Mayas had me frazzled. With a few others in the same condition I stood aside in the shade of the tropical growth and let the brave ones climb over the gnarled roots of mahogany and chicle trees to start their courageous ascent.

Presently, a chattering broke out in the trees above us. We looked up. Overhead, monkeys scrambled from limb to limb and cocked their pert grey heads to get a look at these invaders of their domain. Then a game started; they threw small branches at us. Their aim was poor; a dodge now and then kept us from a direct hit. But, judging from the chattering above us, the monkeys thought it great sport. They don't get a chance at living targets too often.

The game was going well—for their side—when whoops and yells came from on high. It was the scouts of our party up on top of Temple IV calling down to us about the wide vista open before them. The monkeys, hearing yells above and below them, thought themselves surrounded and beat a quick retreat, scampering from limb to limb, swinging back into the greenery.

By this time, it was past 1:00 P.M. We were all hot, tired, thirsty and hungry. With relief, we piled on to the truck and drove back to the lodge for lunch. We passed all the gorgeous temples and stelae of Group H. But to me, the Mayas are heady stuff and in the morning I had seen enough to keep me thinking and wondering for a long, long time. I could take no more just then.

Sister Anthony Mary and I had been so busy absorbing impressions all morning that we hardly had a chance to talk together. It was good to clean up, and sit with her in a corner of the wide sala and open the lunch we had brought. The other visitors planned to eat in the dining room. Mr. Wilson came over and brought us soft drinks. Then he turned his kindly deed to good advantage by boasting about buying drinks for the Sisters at the bar. He kept it up all afternoon; the story grew taller with each telling.

Downing the chicken sandwiches, Sister Anthony Mary and I put the Mayan character on the couch and tried to analyze it. A thankless task. What a jumble of conflicting traits they—like every people on the face of the globe—show to the generations following them! However, as the last of the cookies and drink went down, we had enumerated some few of their achievements.

They were experts in the delicate modeling of stucco. Their wood carvings can scarcely be equaled today. Their ceramics were in exact proportion. While not as delicate as Limoges china, they were lovely in shape and polychrome decoration. Their paintings as evidenced on the tomb walls at Bonampak were anatomically correct. At Palenque, freedom from constraint in portraying the human figure resulted in a naturalness of pose akin to that found in early Grecian art. They knew the art of mosaics, not only turquoise mosaics, but the more painstaking feather mosaic work such as the Hawaiians did.

In weaving, their matching of colors and perfection of patterns are not equaled by any peoples of the New World, with the possible exception of the Incas.

In the abstract sciences of astronomy, mathematics and chronology, they had few if any peers among their contemporaries of the Old or New World. Their calendar was more accurate than any used in Europe, Asia or Africa before Gregory XIII revised the Julian calendar. In fact, the Mayan calendar was actually more correct than the one used by the Western world today. It was correct to the fifth decimal point in comparison to sidereal time; ours is correct to the fourth decimal point.

Their agriculture was and is an ingenious method of taming wild, hostile mountains. They had no open spaces like our Middle West. They had few valleys. Their farm land, for the most part, consisted of sheer mountain slopes covered by only inches of fertile soil. No machinery could be used on those slopes. Today, experts concede that the Mayas discovered the only feasible method of working their lands. They did not have commercial fertilizers for bigger and better crops but they did know how to plant and how to harvest.

These Mayas were an intelligent people. Why then were they so illogical in their religion? Why did they worship stones they themselves had carved and could "kill?" Why did they try to take power away from these stones by defacing them? Why were they under a compulsion to build every certain number of years? Why? Why? Why?

Refreshed and energized again, Sister and I rushed out to see one of the reservoirs the Mayas had paved in order to store water. The natural ravines and perhaps old stone quarries were used for this. Thirteen reservoirs with a total capacity of 40,770,000 gallons are known so far. Filled to the top in the rainy season, they lasted through the dry. From this, scientists gather some vague idea of Tikal's population. Also, the amount of building accomplished in a short time presupposes a tremendous number of people living in the city. I wonder what Mayan executive organized the work force. What architects planned the temples. Who gauged the amount of water needed. How many of our top executives now could get this city built with the materials, tools and labor available then.

In the embryonic museum Jose had spoken about, I photographed the jade, the gargoyle-ish incense pot, the black pottery, some redware vessels from Burial Spot 85, dated 110 B.C., and other things. We all went to the airfield then, just as our plane put down on the grassy strip. It took only a few minutes to mount the steps, buckle seat belts and be airborne.

Mr. Wilson, from across the aisle, called, "If you want a last shot of Tikal, give me your camera." I passed it to him hurriedly; he clicked the shutter as we circled the white temple tops. It was a "good-bye" slide—good-bye to a dream come true.

We made a stop at Flores, that toy town on a toy island in a blue lake, capital of the province of Peten. Most of us escaped from the stifling plane to get a little air. When we returned, the ten double seats in the plane's center had been folded up and the space filled with burlap-wrapped rectangles of chicle—2,000 pounds of it, enough to set America's jaws a-chewing for quite a while. We arranged ourselves before and behind the "chewing gum makings."

"Now I've seen everything!" I gasped to Sister Anthony Mary. "Ancient temples all morning and American chewing gum in the afternoon!"

The plane turned around practically on a dime and, in a flash, was airborne again. If any of those pilots fly into Kennedy Airport, the control tower will find itself in a dither.

FOUR ATTEMPTS TO
FOUND A CAPITAL

The rocky, narrow street of Tecpan, perched in the mountains at 7,218 feet above sea level, is lined with one-story, brightly painted adobe buildings. Sure-footed Indians plod the mountain paths to sell their corn in its market. The more affluent lead mules with carts filled with wood to sell; the less affluent are content with dried corn-stalks which they hope someone will buy to stuff in the cracks of aging adobe walls.

Like most Spanish towns, the blank walls which face the street tell you nothing of the people who may live there. Some—a few—enclose lovely gardens; others are one of the four walls which make up a one-room dwelling. Tecpan is to our way of thinking dead asleep. Over the town towers the big Spanish church, the sole reminder that here, 440 years ago men of Spain, the greatest nation on earth at the time, set up the first capital of Guatemala.

They were wise to do so. Included in the town limits of Tecpan, now a city of fewer than 4,000 people, are the ancient ruins of Iximche, chief city of the Cakchiquele Indians and a thriving center of trade when the Spanish came to Guatemala.

We drove down the village street slowly. Barefooted women, balancing baskets on their heads, walked alongside the car or in front of it with complete indifference. Dogs loped languidly after their masters or lay in supine bliss on the dusty road. Babies bobbed in loose bundles on their mothers' backs. Sister Kristin Marie, who had come with me on this historical pilgrimage to Tecpan, remarked,

"I guess not much has happened here since Pedro Alvarado at

the head of his company cantered down this street, stuck his halberd into the soil and said, 'Here, men, we set up our capital.' "

She was wrong. A great deal of blood, thunder, earthquakes, floods, cruelty, intrigue and oppression has happened. Also, much of compassion, joy, kindness, art and beauty have stemmed from the conquest. One week, let alone four and a half centuries, cannot pass in the international scene nowadays but that some nation is forced to drink a full cup of suffering. So it is now; so was it in Assyrian times; so has it been all the years between.

Just to get to Tecpan—or Iximche, as it was known then—was a triumph for Alvarado. We had just scrambled up a mountain road, skirting the narrow edges of the earthquake fissures, or barrancas. Hairpin turns so narrow that only one car can make it at a time; blind spots made horn-blowing as commonplace as braking. Many a time I prayed for a truck which had pulled over to within a hairline of a hundred-foot drop, to let us pass. Even if the engineering had been perfect, slight tremors in earthquake country like this can dislodge stones and weaken the road bed.

Fortunately for Alvarado, the Mayas had causeways connecting their important cities. Although he marched through hostile country, at least he had a substantial road under his feet. But he was marching into the face of a powerful Indian combine. The Cakchiquele Indians were in a confederacy with the Quiches who held the rich lands to the west, and the Tzutuhiles around Lake Atitlan to the southeast. However, civil war among the three tribes weakened them. A sixty-year war had broken out in 1440 among the confederates and another internal war followed it among the Cakchiqueles. These left the Quiches on top but gasping for breath. Their man power and wealth had been decimated.

The Quiches are an interesting people. They held the land where Santa Cruz Quiche and Quetzaltenango now stand. Some years ago I was able to read the Popol-Vuh, the sacred book of the Quiches, their ancient tradition. It has been translated into English. I was amazed at the many ideas it has in common with the Bible. I dimly saw a triune God, Creation, Cain killing Abel, the battle of the angels—all these formed a background upon which was woven a fantastic worship.

I thought then of a story which Francisco, our driver, had told us on the long drive to Tecpan from Guatemala City that morning. I have heard it many times since from Central Americans—

Mexicans, Guatemaltecans and others—but Francisco's words stay in my mind.

"Sometime in the distant past," he said, "a blond man in a long flowing garment came among us. This man immediately became one with our people; he spoke our languages and understood our thoughts. He taught us charity, kindness, brotherhood. That is why, before the Aztecs came, human sacrifice was unknown. This man taught us to make just laws and codify them. He improved our cultivation of maize and showed us the best methods of agriculture possible on our rocky land.

"Our people loved him with a deep love. When he told them he must go to other peoples as he had come to us, they wept and tried to hold him. He promised to return." Here Francisco paused. "Up to the present, he has not," he ended simply.

Francisco is one of Monte Maria's bus drivers; we knew him well. Seeing the old town loosened up some spring in him; Sister Kristin Marie and I urged him on with questions.

"When the Spanish came, did the people think that their friend was returning?"

"So people say," he said. "But I have heard another story. Around the year 1500, a Cakchiquele war prisoner was killed by the Quiches. Just before he died, he told the Quiches,

" 'There will soon appear in your land, men clothed and armored, not naked as we are. They will destroy your great city, Utatlan.' The prophecy was written down and many must have known it. So it is possible that from the beginning they recognized the Spanish as enemies."

We will never know just how the Quiches felt when they saw Alvarado and his men, haggard but hard, with dusty beards and dulled armor, appear in their capital. We will never know because, by his own account, Pedro Alvarado's policy was to kill or crush every Indian he saw. They were not encouraged to say what they thought about the conquest.

To avoid death, the Indians became Christian, but they kept on with their pagan worship in the hills and, later, even in the churches. They incensed the statues, burnt candles, knelt and prayed as they had done to their idols in the great white temples before the Spanish wrecked them. In some places, few though they were, heroic Catholics were made by the saintly Franciscans. Such was Juan Diego and his village—Juan who saw Our Lady at Guadalupe.

Most, however, embraced the new religion as a matter of expediency. Now, three hundred years later, many Indians go through the motions but they are not Christians in either mind or heart. I have seen them performing the "costumbre," or pagan worship, in the cathedral at the heart of Guatemala City. In rural areas where teachers have not penetrated, paganism is still more deeply entrenched.

Francisco filled us in with a running account of the Spanish conquest:—Alvarado made quick work of Utatlan's pitiful defenses. On April 4, 1524, he had the last Quiche rulers burned alive and their fortress capital destroyed. Naked, armed only with stones and obsidian knives, the Indians resisted bravely. The Spanish were mounted on horses, fully armed and protected by armor. They not only shot the Indians but crushed the life out of them under their horses' hoofs.

The Quiches were soon devastated; Alvarado turned to the Cakchiqueles' capital at Iximche. The quaking Cakchiqueles quickly decided, "If you can't fight them, join them." They agreed to help the Spaniards subdue the next tribe on Alvarado's list, the Tzutuhiles. Ever since the confederation had broken up they had been enemies.

Alvarado did not stop with the Tzutuhiles. He killed and burnt until all the tribes in the south and southwest were crushed. Then he returned to Iximche and, on July 25, 1524, founded his first capital there, calling the city Santiago de Guatemala. It was a massive four months' work.

The Cakchiqueles paid heavily for becoming Alvarado's allies to save their own skins. They were branded and sold as slaves at public auctions. Taxes and tributes were unbearable. They were beaten and killed as just other animals used by the conquerors. They would have bided their time for revenge had life been livable, but it was not. They resorted to an old trick which Indians have used from time to time—the fly-by-night.

On August 26, just a month after the capital was founded, they silently fled the city under cover of darkness. In the morning, not an Indian remained. Alvarado sent runners to beg them to return, but they would not. Infuriated, the conquistador began an insane war to wipe out every tribe that had affronted him. From Iximche to Xapau, from Melactan to— But the carnage was halted suddenly; Cortez, chief Spanish officer in Central America, commanded Alvarado to report to him in Honduras.

"As you tell it, Francisco," Sister Kristin Marie said, "it seems like steam rollers crushing ant hills. The Indians must be bitter against all white people when they think of the injustices of 400 years ago."

Francisco shrugged. "Perhaps—but there are very few full-blooded Indians left. Intermarriage has made us all part white and part Indian. We are both conquerors and conquered."

We were through the main street of Tecpan by then and out into the bare fields. It was about as level a place as possible in those mountains. Soon the road, such as it was, dwindled to a footpath. We left the car on the grassy field to walk down toward the poor ruins of a once-proud city.

There was a low, filled-in platform, maybe six or seven feet high, shored up with limestone, and at one corner of it a temple. It was about thirty feet high in all, made up of four levels with a central stairway. Beyond were several tall, rounded mounds untouched by excavators; these probably contained other temples also of modest size. We mounted to the platform, once a ball court; grasses and weeds fed on the limestone blocks and forced them apart. From the top of the temple hung a mat of vines and a tree waved its foliage proudly on the highest level.

"They started to repair this place," Sister Kristin Marie said, "but the money gave out and weeds have taken over again. This paving of the ball court under our feet is actually part of the original limestone. Gives you an eerie feeling, doesn't it?"

Yes, it did. On the sun-baked ball court overgrown with high grasses, lithe players had raced to catch the hard rubber ball they used. They were to toss it through a stone ring with the center hole maybe thirty inches in diameter; only elbows, hips or knees might touch the ball. At Iximche the uprights, the viewing stands, the rings themselves were gone. But we stood on the very limestone paving over which their bare feet had run. Or was that right? In many ancient carvings, players wear sandals, as well as pads on elbows, hips and knees.

"Not much left," I thought as we walked back to the car. It had acquired a guard. A solemn little tike, not more than seven, had appeared from nowhere and taken his stance. Not necessary, of course, for no one lived within eyesight, but it might net him five centavos for a tip. Francisco presented him with ten centavos. He got double the smile usually given.

"What is your name?"

"Santiago, Senor."

"Very fitting!" Sister Kristin Marie said. "Santiago in Santiago de Guatemala, the Spanish name for this first capital."

The Indian boy set her right. "Oh no, Madre. I am Santiago in Tecpan."

I wondered if he had any idea what the ruins here at Iximche had meant to his people. "Do you know who lived here?" I asked.

"Lived here? In that bunch of stones?" He pushed his torn brown hat farther back on his head to ventilate his thoughts. "Nobody lived here. There are no houses!" The look on his face said plainer than words, "One certainly meets queer people in this car-guarding business!"

Sister Kristin Marie whisked us off to a finca. It's an odd word —finca. It usually means a large farm for a cash crop where an owner lives in a spacious house and the workers are scattered in a settlement around it. In the Philippines they call it a "hacienda," in Chile it's a "fundo." In Ceylon they grow tea on "estates." In our own South, there were cotton "plantations."

We went to Marta's finca. Not that Marta owns it; a German family does. But Marta is major domo and had often welcomed Sister Kristin Marie and her Girl Scouts when they camped in the mountains. Marta's finca is a bit different from most; it is a flour mill set in the middle of mountains covered with wheat fields, something that I, from the flat Middle West, could hardly believe.

Marta is Indian and German. She did not approve of the lunch we had brought. Far too skimpy. She added a dish of squab, a plate of tortillas, some hot rolls, fresh cold milk, hot coffee and lemonade.

The German touch was evident in both house and mill. Well built, the house had high ceilings and solid floors. The flour mill was spotless and efficient. A young Italian, Giovanni, took us around the plant.

"Me? I came with the machinery from Italy," he said.

"Why from Italy?" I asked.

"Lower duty, that's why," he said.

Guatemala charges much higher duty on United States imports. "Rich American," they called me in the shops and markets of Guatemala, Honduras, El Salvador and Mexico! I just might get a bargain, if I could pass for anything other than American!

To a Midwesterner like me, wheat grown on terraced mountainsides is ridiculous. I knew wheat fields in Iowa and Kansas. As a child, I stood to one side while the combine worked a path around the great field. I used to fear that the machine had got lost or wandered off into some other field, when it took what seemed years to come around that corner to me again. It was flat, flat country— nothing to meet the eye for twenty miles in either direction except the waving wheat. And the sight of it from the air! Meandering streams added their green banks as a design on the tawny background. Wheat on mountains just did not seem right, but, as Francisco said,

"If you need wheat and all you have are mountains, it's logical to use mountains to grow wheat."

Logical but difficult. Every grain must be planted by hand, every head cut by hand, every bunch of stalks carried down the treacherous slope on a man's back. There the bundles are stacked to a man's height and threshed beside the road by hitting the stack with a broad paddle. Grass brooms sweep up the grains and they are carried off to a wheat mill.

"Guatemala grows one-third of the wheat it uses," Giovanni told us. "The other two-thirds comes from the United States. While corn is the staple for Indians and Ladinos, Europeans and Americans live here and want wheat." He smiled in explanation. "You are here and I am here. And many tourists come through."

Looking back at Iximche, I wondered if any wheat had been grown before the Spanish came. There was certainly corn. And Alvarado claimed that part of his trouble in subduing the Indians was their habit of hiding from him in the cacao plantations. These two crops at least were cultivated.

We started off to see Guatemala's second capital, a fascinating place called Ciudad Vieja—"Old City"—on the lower slopes of Agua volcano. It is about twenty miles from Tecpan as the crow flies. Crows need not wind down mountain roads and they have a neat trick of flying across earthquake fissures, so we did a bit more mileage on the trip to the Old City. On the way, we caught up with the Adventures of Wild Boy Alvarado.

Word of his bloody campaigns reached Spain and Alvarado was recalled to give a report. Charges were brought against him and he was sent to Mexico City for trial. However, just at that point, the king of Spain saw fit to lavish new honors and privileges on our hero. Yellow gold covereth a multitude of sins. The situation was helped by the fact that Alvarado had married Dona Francesca de la Cueva, niece of the Duke of Albuquerque.

Meanwhile, Jorge Alvarado, left in charge during his brother's absence, moved the capital from Iximche to the fertile valley of Almolonga in 1527; the palace was built in what is now known as Ciudad Vieja. He chose a lovely site for the town on the slopes of Agua volcano, almost a perfect cone. Ringing the horizon were other volcanoes, Fuego, Pacaya, Acatenango and Santa Maria. Dainty patterns of smoke from them tinged the blue heavens.

When brother Pedro returned in April, 1528, the influential Francesca sickened and died. Seven years later, Pedro went back to Spain and married her sister, Beatriz de la Cueva. And this is where his troubles began.

Beatriz needed several ships to convey her twenty ladies-in-waiting and an army of servants, as well as her furnishings, draperies, costumes, wigs, jewelry and what-nots to the primitive new capital. She had a great palace constructed; it was to be a regal setting for her regal self. On the top floor she had her chapel, hung with rich brocades, crimson velvets and oil paintings. It was more an art museum than a place of worship.

It was scarcely done when Alvarado took off in 1541. The king wanted him to find the Spice Islands but he was sidetracked by the viceroy of Mexico into helping a friend who was getting the worst of it in a fracas with the Indians in Nueva Galicia.

On a rocky mountain slope, his secretary's horse slipped, rolled Alvarado off his horse and crushed him in his heavy armor. As he lay dying, a soldier asked him,

"Where does Your Grace feel the most pain?"

Alvarado answered—as well he might—"in my soul."

When she got the news at the end of August, Beatriz went wild. She had the palace painted black from top to bottom. She seized the power, overrode everyone's judgment and tried to set up a dictatorship as well as plunge the whole country into deepest mourning. A plot was hatched to arrest her; she got wind of it and threw into prison everyone involved and even those who knew of it in some far distant way. She signed the order, "La Sin Ventura Dona Beatriz," or "The Unfortunate One." Many muttered, rather, "The unfortunate country!"

The annual rains had started. At first no one was alarmed; it was only the usual downpour. But there was no let up. Soon, not even the sloping streets could carry off the floods. Men slogged through knee-high floods. Horses slipped and sank to their bellies in the muck; floating logs hit them. August ended and September began; still the rains pelted the city. Finally, night fell on that fateful September 10, 1541.

In the black night, the volcano Fuego, three or four miles away, shook with the clogged lava within it, lava that could not come to the vent. Adobe walls in Ciudad Vieja, weakened by the constant rains, rumbled to the ground burying whole screaming families. Dona Beatriz and her ladies rushed to the rooftop chapel where the drapes with brocades were little comfort.

Fuego shook again in a final attempt to dislodge the lava from its throat. His sister volcano, Agua, even closer to the city, had a lake filling the crater top. A crack appeared on the edge of the lake; it widened; then the whole lip broke off. The entire lake thundered down the steep slope of Agua, gathering speed as it fell. As a giant street cleaner, the flood swept along trees, house rubble, monuments, bodies, dead and living animals. The rushing waters drowned people in the stone buildings and dashed their bodies against the inner walls.

Had Dona Beatriz and her twenty ladies stayed on the lower floor behind the blank walls, they might have survived. On the roof they did not have a chance. September 11 dawned on a city destroyed and depopulated.

We had been trailing through the mountains over country roads, getting ever closer to Fuego and Agua. Of a sudden we made a right turn and I found myself on Ciudad Vieja's only street, a rugged climb up the volcano's slope. Little shops, one-story homes and blank walls lined it. On one side, an old Spanish church was standing—old, but not of the original city. Across from it, we saw a cross erected, all that is left of the original church, bearing the date 1527 when Ciudad Vieja was a brand new capital shining with such hopes for the future. A small monument to Alvarado is further up the slope to the height from which queenly Agua reigns over the city she washed out. We were looking for any remains of Beatriz's palace.

Climbing up the steep slope, we found a schoolhouse. The children were outside sitting on stones and bent over papers. Ah! School examinations! Like death and taxes, they come to all men and all nations. Walking between the children absorbed in their task, we found a single wall, maybe twenty-five feet high with most of a great rounded arch still set in it. Fragments of other walls at either end showed that this was once part of a spacious hall. A plaque on it proved that we had found Beatriz's palace—the one spot in it that could have saved her from Agua's flood.

Looking over the pockmarked surface, I saw evidence that the last coat of paint on it had been black.

Dona Beatriz still bears the blame for the disaster. Even today, if you ask why the city was destroyed, people will tell you, "Because of Dona Beatriz."

Sister Kristin Marie and I stood at the foot of Agua and lifted our eyes up, up, up to its towering summit. Never again will she be able to flood the land. Never again can she contain a crater lake at her summit. The rent there at the very top is a permanent disfigurement. A cloud wafted over the broken crater lip, but I was glad that it was broken. The horror which roared down this street would never roar again.

To the west, the sun was setting over Acatenango volcano. We drove through the coffee fincas toward home, determined to carry on with the story of Guatemala's capitals the next day.

"This is like the old movie serials," Sister Kristin Marie said. "We leave the government sitting in the rubble of Ciudad Vieja, all washed out. We'll have to see what adventures it has in the next episode."

There are people who pay good money for tour conductors to see Antigua, Guatemala's third capital. I'm not saying their money is wasted, but certainly nobody can do the job that Guicho does. He was born and brought up in Antigua. He knows every broken archway and can call each cobblestone by name. We're fortunate that Guicho, medium in height and wiry in frame, is Monte Maria's driver, mechanic and multigraph operator. In his spare moments he drives a city bus. He has a way with machines; he respects them and they obey him. With Guicho behind the wheel en route to his native city, we knew we were in for a day. I have since been to Antigua many times, polishing up the information of that first visit.

Guicho did his good deed for the day en route. At the top of an incline, two traffic policemen on motorcycles stood slightly hidden, ready to sally out and catch the unwary speeder. As we continued, a bus approached on the other side of the road. Guicho executed a complicated wave to the driver and got one in return. He gave the same greeting to every truck he met for the next ten kilometers. It dawned on me that he was letting them know that police were waiting. Some did not get the warning—the frilly lady in the sports car, the Cadillac with uniformed chauffeur, the dark young man in a Ford who impatiently zipped around a truck and almost met us head on. Not only did Guicho let him go on unwarned, but he spat out his most horrible execration: "Stupid!" in English.

But all this was incidental. We caught up on the valiant attempts of the Spanish to set up a capital city in Guatemala.

After the dead had been buried, the remnants of the living at Ciudad Vieja began looking for a site for their capital. Three or four miles northeast in the fertile Panchoy Valley, they began again. This time they surpassed themselves. The city they raised well merited the title bestowed fifteen years later by Philip II of Spain—"La Muy Noble y Muy Leal Ciudad de Santiago de los Caballeros de Guatemala" (The very noble and very loyal city of St. James of the Knights of Guatemala).

It was the metropolis of Middle America. Tremendous buildings rose in just a few years. Church upon church, monasteries with hundreds of monks, convents with hundreds of nuns, oratories, hospitals, colleges and the Papal University of San Carlos were built. They were no flimsy constructions. The churches were towering edifices of stone with walls more than two yards thick. Dominicans, Franciscans, Mercedarians, Bethlehemites, Recollects, Capuchinas, Carmelites—all were here in droves. The Jesuits put up and staffed large schools. There were enough Poor Clares to fill a large monastery.

In the 1600's, Santiago with 40,000 inhabitants was second in importance on this hemisphere only to Peru's Lima. When New York was a Dutch village, Chicago had a few Indian huts and Buenos Aires was unknown, this was a center of culture and learning.

It had the first printing press in Middle America. Artists from Spain and other parts of Europe adorned its churches, made stained glass and engineered its great arches. By the end of the seventeenth century, some authorities say that 70,000 people lived there. It may be a much higher figure, for we do not know whether it includes the Indians who were slaves.

Things were quiet. Of course the volcanoes were always there, smoking and fuming a little, but the great disaster was 176 years back in history. You know how much we in 1966 would be affected by a disaster that happened in 1790! We have trouble remembering the Chicago fire of 1871, the Johnstown flood of '89, the blizzard of '88 and even the San Francisco earthquake of 1906.

When Fuego erupted a little, people said he was always shaking and rumbling, spitting out a little lava in a sort of chronic irritability. It was a good thing, they claimed, for it meant the suppressed power was coming out the vent rather than building up to a major earthquake. So when Fuego rumbled at the end of August, 1717, no one was too alarmed. For almost a month, the tremors came daily. Slowly, they loosened mortar, shook up stones, cracked foundations where the eye could not see. Then for three days—September 26, 27 and 28—not even a tremor occurred. Even timid souls relaxed.

September 29, Feast of St. Michael the Archangel, was celebrated fit for an archangel. At the big fiesta, some whispered about the strange stillness in the crystal-clear day. Some glanced at the strange clouds in the sky; the old folks said such clouds heralded earthquakes. Even today, the wise ones can read the clouds hours before the quake. On a Friday, one of my students, Maria Clara, told me that her grandmother predicted an earthquake. "She can see it in the clouds," Maria Clara said. Sure enough, on Saturday morning the chapel doors banged open and shut, my prie-Dieu rocked back and forth. Possibly the heat from the underground lava escapes to the surface and causes clouds to form in certain places. Guatemala could use somebody who had his "earthquake hunches" down to an exact science. It would have come in handy on that September 29, 1717.

At seven in the evening, the whole city was caught in a giant convulsion. Those tremendous buildings were too solidly built; they cracked and fell to the ground. Walls ripped open; huge hunks of rock fell from roofs to floors, crashed through the floors to rooms below and so on down. Hundreds of people were buried. Many monks and nuns were crushed as they knelt in their chapels; others ran screaming out into the night. The darkening streets re-echoed with horror.

1. A distant mound, seen from the Pan-American Highway near Huehuetenango, may mark a Mayan temple covered with the dust of centuries. Terraced wheat fields cover the mountain slopes in mid- and foreground.

3. Kaminaljuyu: A Mayan corbeled arch of modern workmanship connected the lower chambers of the temple.

2. ABOVE: *Kaminaljuyu: Lupe wanted me to photograph her beside a frog-shaped sacrificial bowl.* 4. BELOW: *Kaminaljuyu: Francisco and Jose leaned on the oil drum, awaiting our show of gratitude for the specimens on our laps.*

5. *Kaminaljuyu: Jaguar-priest sculpture was found here and moved to the Museum of History and Archaeology in Guatemala City.*

6. *Tiquisate: Sacrificial stone from the Pacific coastal region. The other side depicts a sad face.*

7. *Castanas: The women breathed deeply and feasted their eyes as the first water flowed in their pueblo.*

8. *Castanas: The fruit of her labor goes to market.*

9. Castanas: The village Headman turned the valve in the water system—a bare pipe.

10. Tikal: University of Pennsylvania archaeologists under Dr. Coe tunneled through northern areas of the Great Plaza to uncover occupational sequences.

11. Tikal: Temple II, Temple of the Masks, in the process of consolidation. 143 feet high.

12. *Tikal: Temple I, the Temple of the Giant Jaguar, rears its crest 155 feet above the foundation.*

DONACION DE LA SOCIEDAD SUIZA
'PRO-HELVETIA' AL MUSEO NACIONAL
DE ARQUEOLOGIA Y ETNOLOGIA DE
GUATEMALA

13. Tikal: Models of the carved wooden lintels which were taken to Basle, Switzerland, by Bernouilli hang in the Museum in Guatemala City in lieu of the originals.

14. *Tikal: Through the corbeled arch, the people could watch the sacrifice or the priests could watch the workers.*

15. *Tikal, Stela 22. Located in the center of Morley's "Group E" facing the single opening. Depicts a "corn-sowing" priest whose face seems to have been mutilated. Full profile, staff or bag on left arm, bag hangs from left wrist. Dedicatory date, 9.17.0.0.0. or 13 Ahau 18 Cumku.*

16. At Iximche, Mayan temples stood before the Spaniards attempted to establish their first capital.

17 The exquisite façade of La Merced escaped the earthquake devastation which felled most of Antigua, the third capital.

18. Antigua: Façade of Santa Clara Monastery.

19. Antigua: Las Capuchinas' convent patio has been cemented over with only a couple of bougainvillea in bloom.

20. *Antigua: La Recoleccion's great broken arch attests to the beauty of the monastery founded in 1708.*

21. *Chichicastenango: Pagan "costumbre" on the steps of Santo Tomas church.*

22. *Antigua: Ruins of the great church of Santa Clara, which was completed in 1734.*

23. Lake Atitlan, vacation paradise, lies at the base of towering volcanoes.

A second quake, as strong as the first, smashed even the sturdiest buildings. A third convulsion, far stronger, outdid the first two. Great stones from the cathedral arches crashed on the praying throngs below. Walls eight feet thick fell like a house of cards.

Even out in the fields, people could not stand upright. They lay on the heaving ground praying that it would not open up and swallow them. This they were spared.

The night had just begun. It was pandemonium; the trapped called for help, the dying moaned, the terror-stricken screamed, weakened walls toppled. By morning, the living could look around for wives, relatives, and children.

Shocks continued for ten days. Rescue work was dangerous for a minor tremor often put the finishing touch to a weakened wall. Many who could have been saved died, trapped in the ruins.

Strange to say, the great earthquake of 1717 did not discourage the people entirely. They pitched in—buried the dead and started to rebuild. Within fifty-six years, Santiago was again a large opulent city and again the earth shook.

Two quakes made a heap of rubble out of the proud city in approximately ten minutes on July 29, 1773. Nothing but a pile of rubbish remained of the great church of Santo Domingo and the entire area around it. Not only were people killed as before, but their will to rebuild died, too.

A few days later, the Captain General said the capital would move to the Valle de la Ermita, where the present Guatemala City is. The trek began early in September. Left behind were the ruins of eighty churches, seven colleges, a university, five hospitals and thousands of luxurious private homes. A few people remained, of course, to fix up living quarters in some part of the ruins. No completely new churches have been erected here since the devastation. The whole city is a national monument of Spanish colonial architecture and art. All churches now in use have been repaired according to the original plans. This makes Antigua, as the city is now called, a treasure trove of Spanish architecture.

Guicho got more and more expansive as we neared his home city, Antigua. He forgot the policemen waiting for the unwary speeders and the young driver he had execrated with his English "Stupid!" The mellowing process was complete as we came to a stop before the statue of Brother Pedro Betancourt. The good Brother is a legend of charity and kindness; he stands holding a crucifix over his head with his long skirts rippling behind him. A graceful statue alive with motion and benignity. An idealization, no doubt, for the Brother plodded along quite humbly on his works of mercy, but it does express the heavenward joyous yearning of the early friars who gave up all they had to teach the Indians.

Guicho took us first to the Church of San Francisco. "I never come to Antigua without praying at Brother Pedro's tomb," he said. Great doors, twelve feet high, lead into the church, but smaller ones are set into them to accommodate the twentieth-century congregation, most of whom don't go to Sunday Mass on horseback.

An Indian family sat on the steps of the main entrance to San Francisco. Papa faced me but mama and daughter had their backs to me. As I aimed the camera, papa gave a knowing nod to mama. Both women turned around, gave me a smile, smoothed down their dresses and rearranged their bare feet nicely. I shot them. They turned back to the family group and resumed their talking without comment. Women are women the world over!

Sister Kristin Marie and I were stopped in our tracks by several carved wood altars recently restored and covered with gold leaf as they had been in colonial times. The gleam of gold, the rich carvings, the colors placed here and there gave us some hint of Antigua when it dominated Middle America.

Guicho paid no heed. He made a bee-line to Brother Pedro's tomb, now a shrine. The poor Brother who in the seventeenth century tramped the city from morn to night on errands of mercy lies encased in a stone coffin set into the church walls. Even now he gets little rest, for the importunate knock on his tomb. The tradition is that if Brother Pedro intends to grant one's request, he will knock in return. We found Guicho praying but he did not knock.

"I haven't the courage to find out if Brother Pedro will grant it or not," he said with a smile. "I feel better when I can keep on hoping."

Originally, the church must have been as big as a cathedral. Only the central nave has been reconstructed for parish use. The Franciscan priests live in a section of the old monastery boarded-off by the church. This too is being rebuilt along the old lines. The inner courtyard once had a fountain and fish pool. Most of the rubble has been cleaned out; bags of cement and piles of sand are stacked under the arched cloister walk. The carved stones are neatly arrayed on the ground, ready to be replaced where they were nearly

200 years ago. Most of them are angel heads, big and little, hundreds of them, some with curly hair, some smiling, some looking up, some glancing sidewise. In another corner are gargoyles, stone filigrees and scroll designs. It is hard for us who live in an age of straight lines and sharp angles to imagine where so many decorations could be fitted in. There is even a mural painted on the old wall, showing St. Bonaventure, St. Thomas and possibly St. Dominic in reds and browns that have defied time and ruin.

Tourists walked around freely; workmen hoisted stone on stone; someone was planting flowers. Back in the church, people in the pews knelt in prayer and several men were hanging a red drape behind the main altar. San Francisco is a functioning parish church, even though a round gaping hole in the roof shows where the monumental dome above the sanctuary had once been. This too is being repaired; stone masons close the hole inch by inch as they set one stone upon another in a delicate balance. We found a number of square openings in the floor leading to a network of underground passages. Tombs for the religious? Escapes in case of Indian insurrection? Storage tunnels for defense needs? No one can be quite sure.

"Would you like to see the carpentry shop?" a pleasant voice said behind us.

We turned to see a broad figure in Franciscan brown. A cincture of white rope circled his waist; a pointed cowl fell over his shoulders; sandals shod his bare feet. He was a mediaeval vision but his broad, open face was infinitely alive. He introduced himself as Brother Pablo.

We followed the jolly Brother through a door and down a long corridor, emerging into a room redolent with fresh sawdust. Brother Pablo was in charge of workmen making benches for the church—exquisite carved stalls which in my opinion were as good as those in the Cloisters in New York City, brought over from old monasteries in Europe.

"It takes a long time to hand-make each bench," Brother Pablo said, "but it's rewarding."

I watched one workman polish the hardwood. He made a solution of shellac and alcohol so thin that I wondered if it would be effective. Then he wet a small piece of cotton in it and began to rub it over the wood. He rubbed and rubbed until it was really dry. I mean, really dry.

"Let me try it," I asked. I rubbed for some time and then handed my cotton to the workman for another dip. He refused. "Not dry yet," he said. "Keep on rubbing." This process takes days to achieve the right finish. One rubbed-in coat must dry before another can be applied. The result is a hard, resistant polish better than anything possible with varnish.

Out in the courtyard again, Brother Pablo gave us an idea of the size of the project to rebuild San Francisco. The church and monastery were begun in 1544 but not completed for twenty-one years. Eighteen years later, the school and the study hall attached to San Francisco were completed. The friars trained the Indians in all sorts of useful arts. With church, monastery and school built, all went well for more than a hundred years. The complex covered three city blocks; more than 400 Franciscans lived here. The dome dominated the city.

The earthquake of 1689 damaged San Francisco but it was rebuilt. It survived the 1717 quake but the 1773 disaster leveled it entirely except for one tower which tumbled in the quake of 1917. Since then, the friars have tried to repair it little by little.

Being a schoolmarm, I was interested in schools of that period. "Was San Francisco's the only school in the city in the 1500's?" I asked.

"Gracious, no!" Brother Pablo answered. "The Dominicans had a large, well-equipped school; their church and monastery was perhaps the greatest in the city. The Jesuits too opened splendid schools. Indeed, by 1600 almost every religious order in the Church had representatives here working for the Indians.

"It's too bad," he went on, "that the cruelty of colonial governors has tarnished the memory of these heroic men and women. They journeyed for months on small sailing vessels and many died en route. There were no jets or *Queen Elizabeth*s in those days."

"And no Dramamine or Bonine, either!" sighed Sister Kristin Marie who suffers on the high seas.

"The Caribbean had hurricanes then, just as it does now," I said. "Judging from the logs of old sailing vessels, the pattern of air currents hasn't changed in 400 years. So often we hear tales of shipwreck on the shores of Honduras, Guatemala and Quintana Roo. The Silver Virgin of Chiantla and the Cristo Yacente in Guatemala City were both salvaged from shipwrecks."

Once out in the patio again, we found Major-domo Halfpint

taking his car-minding duty very seriously. We gave him a double tip in hopes that it would help to fill his little tummy for a while.

Guicho drove us to the ruined Capuchinas' convent, not so far away in distance but a long, long way when one drives over huge cobblestones and maneuvers a path through a herd of goats as well. Small stores lined the streets, disdaining to display their wares in show windows, preferring rather to have a modest sign over the door to indicate that this was not a private home. With goats at our sides and cobblestones playing fiddlesticks with our spines, we might have been colonial dames ourselves on that street.

We fell into the hands of a professional guide at the famous Capuchinas' convent. We declined his services but he put up such a cry that it seemed best to go along with his party for a while, at least. He took us into the circular patio, complete with a fountain, but covered with cement. It gave me a twinge, even though two brilliant bougainvilleas had pushed up through the cement to cover the arches with glorious red. I can't imagine the gentle women, followers of St. Francis, content with a cemented patio. Surely, they had grass and flowers there as they had known them in Spain. A colonnaded walk runs around the patio. The rooms open off this; it serves as the only corridor between them. The climate in highland Guatemala is so invigorating, no one minded a bit of fresh air between rooms.

Reception rooms and general-purpose rooms are on the first floor. Up a flight of very uneven, worn steps are the nuns' sleeping quarters. They seem to have used large dormitories with thin partitions between the cubicles. Were we to put a modern bed into one, we would have to leave or enter by climbing over it. A small niche for a shrine was the only furnishing we saw.

"I wonder where they kept their clothes," Sister Kristin Marie said. "There isn't room even for a toothbrush here, but maybe they didn't bring one along."

Just off the dormitory is the choir loft overlooking the ruined church. One arch remains, a single soaring symbol of faith against the blue, blue sky. My eye followed the roofless, jagged walls to where they crumbled and went beyond them out into the rich landscape and distant mountains which the nuns never saw as they sang in that choir loft two hundred years ago.

A fragment of wall adjoining the loft holds an octagonal window, deep set into the thick masonry. A row of these high up would not admit much light. Filled with stained glass, there would be even less light but the tropical sun would have made them a display of glorious color to tell Bible stories.

Descending to the chapel floor, we walked in the hot sunshine among the voussoirs scattered on the floor where they had fallen in the earthquake of 1773. Would anyone ever attempt to fit these wedges together to make the arches soar again on high?

By this time we had left the guide and his group far behind. We stood alone in the church. Against the far wall, the altar had once stood. A little bump of stones was probably the raised platform upon which it stood. An iron grille set into the sanctuary wall shows where the cloistered nuns had heard Mass. Set in at the left is a door of smaller iron bars which opened so that they could receive Holy Communion.

We were glad to leave the Capuchinas' church. As Sister Kristin Marie expressed it, "It's so big, so empty and so ruined."

On to the more practical side of life! The laundry, pantry and kitchen are at the far end of the patio down a few steps. Guicho, who had been wandering around on his own, joined us as we went down the narrow stone steps to emerge into a charming little court-yard.

The laundry consists of four large stone tubs supplied by a foun-tain. They were set where the good tropical sunshine would serve as both bleach and disinfectant. Practical ladies, those Capuchinas! Under a low doorway, we entered the pantry. Food was passed into the dining-room through a "turn." This is standard equipment in a cloistered community—a hollow roller set into the wall so that when one side is open, the other side is closed. In this way those in the pan-try could serve the food without seeing the nuns.

And into the kitchen! We passed under an arch about ten feet high, and faced a magnificent barbecue fireplace. Black and sooty grease encrusted the air vent above it. I almost whistled in astonish-ment. There must have been some Texan parties prepared here!

A whole boar could have been spitted and roasted on that fire-place. I took out a tape measure to get the exact dimensions when, suddenly, the pantry and kitchen area was filled with military men, looking around here and there, poking into corners, conferring with one another. How come? Had we done something wrong? How serious a crime is it to measure a national treasure?

"Relax!" said Sister Kristin Marie. Her Spanish is better than mine. They were Mexican Army officers being given the grand tour by their brethren in the Guatemalan Army. Very friendly, too, once the ice was broken.

No doubt Indians had cooked here, chopping up the meat, pounding the bread dough, cleaning the vegetables. Hot, dirty work. Were they paid? Or were food and shelter their remuneration? On the other hand, in their times, did they expect hard cash? Would they know what to do with it? Would they prefer food and shelter as pay?

A round tower stands intact. It had weathered earthquakes and —still worse—the havoc of sheer time. The room below the ground level has no support other than a pillar in the center. "Some say it was for wine storage," Guicho commented. "Others think it was here the nuns dried their clothing in the rainy season." He shrugged. *"Quién sabe?* Who knows?"

A stairway leads to the floor above, level with the ground. In a side opening here, we saw two tubs built of stone, one large enough for baths, the other more of a size for sponge baths or a foot tub.

The real surprise was upstairs. We mounted to a central round foyer from which twenty wedge-shaped rooms open. Two of these have been restored completely with prie-Dieu, shelf, shrine and narrow bed. It startled us to see a brown-habited figure in each, one at her prie-Dieu, the other in a chair reading. They were so still that we soon realized they were manikins. Each room has, to the right of the entrance, a private toilet consisting of a stone seat and a hole which opens into running water beneath.

Guicho was ready with ideas. "Some say this was the novitiate; others hold it was for nuns making special days of prayer on retreat. But no one is really certain."

We went out into the garden which encircles the tower. There are indentations between the rooms where shrines must have been. Fourteen of them were probably used as the Stations of the Cross. They were lit at night, too, for bits of metal brackets which held lights still remain.

"A large building," was Sister Kristin Marie's summation of the Capuchinas' convent, "but the space for each nun seems to have been very meager. I for one would have claustrophobia if I had to live here."

I added "Me, too!"

Over more cobblestones to Santa Clara, a latecomer to the an-

cient city of Antigua, being constructed between 1700 and 1715 and
finished in 1734. The patio covers an entire city block enclosed by a
double tier of arches; the fountain in the center is still intact. Mountain water flows freely in Antigua, a real blessing.

From the topless bell tower at Santa Clara we looked out on the
city of ruins. Fuego in the distance surveyed his handiwork with
majestic disdain. Hulks of colonial churches, the Palace of the Governors, shattered walls and unexplained arches spread far out into
the landscape. Looking down, one saw the cobblestone streets lined
with those impressive blank Spanish walls. Here, no one sits on the
porch watching the neighbors go by. Rather, each family enjoys its
garden in privacy.

There is too much of colonial history, architecture, sociology,
engineering and art in Antigua to be described here. Others must
write of the exquisite fountain of La Merced Monastery, the plater-
esque façade of La Merced Church, the glorious, carefree arch of
La Recoleccion, the oil paintings and papal shields of San Carlos
University, the Arco de las Catarinas spanning the street so that the
nuns could pass from their property on one side to their house on the
other without being seen, the massive cathedral—these we must
omit.

We left the past to plunge into the present; we turned from
churches and convents to busy ourselves with the workaday world.
Guicho twisted and turned on the bumpy cobblestone streets to visit
a weaving family he knew.

We stepped off the street into a wide courtyard ablaze with
color. Near the entrance, a man sat winding cotton preparatory to
weaving it. Clotheslines hung the length of the yard, strung with
newly dyed thread in brilliant reds and oranges, tapering off into
delicate pastel shades. Made of cotton and maguey fibers, these textiles wear and keep their color. The industry accounts for the high
duty on imported textiles. Along the sides of the courtyard were
looms operated by hands and feet. The men were so intent on their
work they scarcely noticed us, but quickly answered any questions.
Each was weaving a different pattern; they rarely repeat a design.
An American woman was negotiating for a tablecloth. She wanted
it twelve feet long.

"We don't ordinarily weave a piece that big," the shop owner
said, "but we can do it for you."

"How much will it be?"

"Not more than ten quetzales [$10]."

"With napkins?"

"Oh, surely. Twelve napkins."

"Can I choose my own design?"

"Most certainly."

"Well, I want to use it at Christmas dinner. I want poinsettias."

"Bueno, Senora! Shall it be white on a red background or red on white?"

The woman looked at the red scarf one of the men was weaving at his loom. "I'd love white on a red background," she decided.

The shopkeeper bowed a little, his hands clasped in front of him. "It will be ready for the senora within three days."

The American woman was happy. She wandered off to the looms where bright-colored cloths with gold and silver borders were being woven.

"What are these?" she asked.

"Skirt and dress lengths," the shopman said. "Tourists like this sort of thing for themselves and for gifts."

As we left the town, Guicho grew reminiscent. "I was born and raised on a coffee finca near here. In fact, right on our way."

We stopped to take a long look at the coffee bushes, right then beautiful with red berries. I remembered the white waxy flowers, rather like orange blossoms, which had preceded the berries.

Coffee is generally planted near their "nurse trees," the grevillea, which we called the "silky oak" in Hawaii. They shade the young coffee and also provide nutriment in the soil for it.

Guicho knew his coffee. "In this area, the coffee is extremely good. There are larger fincas down near the Pacific coast but the lower altitude produces an inferior grade. Coffee grown at 5,000-feet elevation, as this is, commands a high price." He took a bunch of berries in hand, pinched them a little to test the moisture and grunted with satisfaction.

We drove into the finca through a large door, unchallenged by the guard. Rather, we got a wide smile and a wave. Guicho was surrounded by his relatives, big and little, and carried off. Sister and I faced a huge area, at least an acre, covered with cement. On it coffee lay drying. Men were pushing it here and there with tools that might have been rakes, but a flat wooden board had replaced the metal teeth. One of them explained:

"This helps it to dry. It takes three to five days for one batch of coffee to dry out here, depending on the weather. We try to dry it quickly so that we can lay down another batch."

"Is it bagged then?" I asked.

"No, indeed," he laughed. "Let us start at the beginning. When berries come from the bushes they are washed and some of the outer coats come off in that process. Then we dry it here. After that, we take more coats off by abrasion. Here at La Paloma finca (the "Farm of the Dove") we operate on a fairly small scale but—" he smiled "—we turn out a very high grade of coffee."

On the way back to Guatemala City, we ticked off Guatemala's calamities.

"We saw the very first capital that Pedro Alvarado set up at Iximche, near Tecpan, in 1524," Sister Kristin Marie started.

"And the Indians walked out on that one fine night four months later," I added.

"So in 1527 the Spanish moved to Ciudad Vieja when they could not induce the Indians to return, even after three years' blood and thunder."

"And Ciudad Vieja was flooded out completely when Fuego erupted and jarred the lip off Agua's crater lake in 1541."

"Remember Dona Beatriz? She was a calamity all in herself!"

"So the capital moved a few miles to the Very Noble and Loyal City of St. James of the Knights of Guatemala. Antigua, for short."

"What a city! Huge monuments, a glorious palace, many churches, convents, patios! It took a terrible beating from old Fuego in 1717 but rebuilt itself."

"Only to go down to defeat in the 'quake of '73."

"On to the fourth location!" she cried. "We're speeding to it right now. Our own Guatemala City!"

Yes. A week after the earthquake a mass meeting was held in the Plaza Real at Antigua; the governor and Captain General presided. Should they rebuild or not? Pros and cons held forth all afternoon. Then the decision was made: Move the capital thirty-seven kilometers, about twenty-five miles, almost due east to the Valle de la Ermita. A small village was there already and its 500 inhabitants were ecstatic about the climate and view. Of course, scouts from Antigua asked the villagers, "Do you have earthquakes?"

"Yes," they answered, "but not bad ones."

One would think that even a slight tremor would disqualify any location, but there was not much choice. Once the malarial swamps

on the coast were ruled out, only mountains—and volcanoes—
remained. Up north in Huehuetenango State the plateau is 10,000
feet above sea level; the Cuchumatanes Mountains there go up
higher, of course. The Sierra Madre range sweeps from Mexico into
San Marcos State on the west. The Sierra de Chuacus and Sierra de
las Minas keep the central part of the country pretty mountainous.
Peten, the northern state, is flat enough, but who wants a capital surrounded by bugs, beasts, jungle and chicle?

As for volcanoes, the place is full of them. If you tied a piece of
string twenty-five miles long to the top of Tacana volcano on the
border of Mexico, and swung it around in a half-circle, you would
include twenty volcanoes in the swing.

Not all twenty are active. But one, Santa Maria, is always ready
to pop off. With all these volcanoes up north, it is easy to see why
the councilmen hit on the Valle de la Ermita as ideal for the new
capital.

Guatemala is approximately 50,000 square miles, about half the
size of Oregon, a little larger than Ohio and New Jersey combined,
or about five eighths of Minnesota.

Once decided upon, the building began. Engineers laid out the
city with what they thought were wide avenues—for horses, that is.
They provided parks, the usual cathedral square and almost as many
churches as they had had in Antigua. Masonry conduits were built
to bring water from Pinula in the southeastern mountains and from
Mixco on the heights to the west. Arches of this aqueduct, reminiscent of the old Roman aqueducts, can be seen now on the road to
the airport. In one spot, a clear pool of water under an arch makes a
perfect picture.

The city grew as years passed. A restlessness filled the air. The
United States had wrested free from England; the Revolution had
done away with monarchy in France. From 1810 on, Mexico was in
constant revolt. Guatemala, too, chafed under colonial rule. On September 15, 1821, she won independence from Spain.

Now here a queer thing happened. In October that same year
Mexico sent a letter proposing that Guatemala be annexed to Mexico. Similar letters went to El Salvador, Honduras, Nicaragua and
Costa Rica. But these countries would have no truck with annexation. Guatemala, however, signed a treaty of annexation on Febru-
ary 21, 1822. She regretted it immediately and by July of the next
year had declared herself independent again. The "in and out" busi-

ness with Mexico cost her the States of Chiapas, Campeche, Tabasco and Yucatan. She was never able to pry them loose from Mexico.

She lost another state and most of her Caribbean coast. The State of Belice was promised to the English to pay for a bridge they had promised to build. When the promise was not fulfilled, Guatemala claimed Belice back, but it was British Honduras by then. This is still a sore point. Every fifteenth of September, posters appear proclaiming "Belice belongs to Guatemala!"

Politically, the country went up and down. However, as early as 1824, slavery was abolished, long before England, France, Spain or our own United States took the step. A strong man, General Justo Rufino Barrios, seized power after a revolution of less than a month. He organized the Liberal Party and began to change the face of the country. He was not an easy man to deal with. His reforms stepped on ecclesiastical toes as well as political, economical and social ones. He took huge chunks of property away from convents and monasteries which, perhaps, left the Church better off; it could do with much less than the old Spanish regime set apart for it.

Barrios now sallied out to get other Central American countries to join with him. Their "No, thank you" was met with an army led into El Salvador. There he was killed in the battle of Chalchuapa in April, 1885. Looking back now that the dust of irritation has settled, Guatemaltecans revere Barrios almost as the founder of their country. Many statues stand in town plazas dedicated to him. The statue near Guatemala City's railroad station shows him on a horse leaping into the air, balanced only on its hind legs. It is considered the most beautiful statue in Middle America.

After Barrios, history is a series of elections, assassinations, military coups and overthrows. However, buildings went up and the city took shape. Those far-distant days of earthquakes in Ciudad Vieja and Antigua faded from memory. A long, long time had passed without mishap. Life was good.

Shocks began November 17, 1917, and centered at Amatitlan, about fifteen miles from Guatemala City. Agua and Pacaya volcanoes are both nearby. It's impossible to say which is to blame, but Agua had been quiet for so long that probably it was Pacaya relieving pressure. These first convulsions pretty well leveled Amatitlan. In Guatemala City ten to thirty light quakes were counted daily. Some remembered stories of the light quakes which had preceded the Antigua blow. "Will it happen again?" they asked. It did.

Christmas night, 1917, at 10:20, a brisk shake did much damage but took few lives. People left homes to huddle in public squares. The night was clear, the season dry; a full moon shed what light she could on the anxious city. At 11:23, a really violent convulsion toppled buildings but no more than fifty people died. The hour's warning saved thousands.

Four days later, another shake toppled many buildings and strong walls. January 3, 1918, a long roll felled the cathedral and many of the sturdiest places. They had been built along colonial lines; they did not have the "give" needed to resist multi-directional shocks.

The worst quake of all came January 24, just as a full moon was rising. It centered right under the city and radiated out for thirty miles. Railroad rails were cut apart, cemeteries belched up their dead that had to be cremated later. Water mains were broken and all the city's water was contaminated. Once again, Guatemala government buildings, churches, office buildings—everything—was reduced to rubble. But warned so well in advance, the city lost not more than two hundred people.

Of course, reconstruction started immediately. There was no thought of moving the capital. For one thing, no other place seemed any better and, for another, the railroad station with its complex of tracks and bridges was too big an investment to move to another location.

More tremors in October and November of the next year made people wonder if it were really worthwhile to rebuild. But in the almost fifty years since then, only minor shakes—frightening enough to the newcomer—have been felt. None was severe enough to cause real damage.

Furthermore, architects take earthquakes into consideration in building plans. For instance, at Monte Maria each section is slightly apart from the next, so as to give leeway for sway. The beautiful new buildings in Guatemala City also "give." The light construction makes you think these structures could bend like a tree in a breeze and still remain intact.

It would be interesting to be around in the next earthquake just to see how the city holds its own. But I'm sure that Guatemaltecans have other ideas on that touchy subject.

CHICHICASTENANGO AND PAGAN COSTUMBRE

There's no accounting for national pastimes! The Spanish like to play hide-and-seek with a wild bull; the Samoans throw a flaming sword from hand to hand; the Chinese are addicted to skinning around a hairpin curve in a truck without brakes. In Formosa, a mother will give baby his first haircut by shaving his tender head with a cold steel chisel. In India, market entertainers play music for cobras to dance to; a Tanzanian child likes to keep a double-edged razor blade in his mouth and stick his tongue out the slot. Old ladies in the Philippines smoke their cigarettes backwards with the fire in their mouths.

People enjoy danger. Especially they like a seat where split-second timing means the difference between life and death. In the early days of the railroad, men had to walk along the top of box cars, leaping lightly from one to another even when the train was hurtling around a curve. Just before a tunnel or low bridge, a fringe of leather straps was hung over the tracks to warn a man who might be on top of a boxcar, lest he be swept off. It got to be a game among railroad men to see if they could cut off one of those leather straps and duck in time to avoid the low bridge or tunnel.

The men of Chichicastenango celebrate St. Thomas the Apostle's feast day, December 21, with a game far more spectacular. It's not unlike spinning a platter on a stick, only there are men spinning around on the platter and the stick is as high as a six-story building. It is a hazardous game to watch; one might get a heart attack. He is certain to suffer from a crick in his neck for days afterwards.

I got both when I stood in the plaza in front of St. Thomas

Church in Chichicastenango (called "Chichi" by those who love the town). I was watching two men climb higher and higher up a homemade rope ladder wound around a sixty-foot pole set rather loosely in a hole in the ground. For all its height, the pole was thin. "Possibly a white pine trunk," I thought.

The two small figures high up continued to mount on one crude crosspiece of rope after another. Then the pole swayed a bit and they stopped to damp the vibration. Again they mounted step by step. What if one of those rungs should give way? It looked as if one strand alone kept each rope crosspiece attached. What if the bottom should shift ever so slightly in the loose, dry dirt?

At the top of the pole was a crude square cap consisting of four triangles joined at the apex. This cap was not attached to the pole-top; the whole contraption could slip to the ground if it unbalanced. Ropes usually hang from the four corners, but on this they hung only from two diagonal corners. The whole upper part of the pole had been wound with rope. As they swung around and around, the rope would unwind.

As I watched, the two Indians had reached the top. The top man was a little above the loop of rope prepared for him; the second could stretch up to get his. The crowd of onlookers grew; this game is a prime attraction for the fiesta of St. Thomas. But they were cagey enough to stand far enough back to be out of the way should the men or the pole come toppling down. They have seen it year after year but they fear disaster just the same.

The two men rested up there—a tense, alert rest. Then with perfect timing they leaped into space. Slowly at first and then faster the rope on the pole unwound, dropping them inch by inch as they circled above us. The circle got wider and wider, faster and faster. The gyrating riders swung their bodies upward and through their loops so that they could "sit down" for the rest of their wild ride.

"This is a new type of space travel!" I said.

"It's as close as we can come to being cosmonauts," laughed Alejandro. One of the employees at Monte Maria, he had taken Sister Anne Regina and me up the long trail to Chichicastenango. Like all Guatemaltecans he had a wide knowledge of Indian lore.

"This Flying Pole game," he said, "is really a commemoration of the deluge."

"Do you mean the same deluge we read about in our Bible?" I asked.

In the Maya-Quiche bible, the Popol-Vuh, there are so many stories similar to our own that some think it may have originally been founded on the books handed down by the Jewish tribes. According to the Popol-Vuh, when the gods sent the deluge, people climbed trees to escape. The trees swelled with the rising waters and it was difficult to hang on. Many people fell to the ground and drowned. The few who managed to hang on sprouted tails and turned into monkeys.

This was a different twist to the evolution theory! Many scientists take as gospel truth the idea that man descended from a monkey; the Indians believed that men climbed trees to become monkeys. Not bad!

Sister Anne Regina nodded sagely. "Most likely the Quiches are right. Some men make monkeys of themselves, but no monkeys are making men of themselves."

By this time, the two space travelers had landed on the ground and walked off into the crowd, with the same plodding Indian pace everybody else had. The crowd was thinning and I could survey that great pole from top to bottom.

"It must take a great deal of searching to find a tree so straight and tall," I said.

"Not only searching but many pagan rites and prayers as well," Alejandro answered.

It seems that each year, when the fiesta of St. Thomas comes close, the oldest and most influential men of the soothsayer class select a propitious day to get the "palo volador"—that is, the flying or spinning pole. On this day, they go to Mount Pocohil, two miles away, and pray to the stone idol who holds court there. They pray that it may not break when it falls, that no one will be hurt in getting it. Then they go, some forty or fifty men, into the forests to get their tree. They take food and drink, for the task requires several days.

Felling the giant is not easy, for where can you find a nice sixty-foot open space for it to fall into? Then, carrying it from the forest is another job. Anyone who has tried to carry skis lengthwise through a crowd can sympathize. Once in town, the bark is removed and the trunk smoothed. A rope ladder is wound around it. Then it is raised into place with the base resting in a hole in the town plaza. Workmen climb to the top, put on the gyratory cap and wind the rope for descent around the pole.

By this time, the flying pole was ready for two more riders. A pair of Indians set foot to the ladder and began climbing up. We turned away, however, and started looking around the town for other sights. It is easier to witness three orbits around the world on television than to see this precarious travel above us.

Chichicastenango, high in the mountains, has a flavor all its own. It is off the usual track of tourist traffic which flows along the main roads. That morning, Alejandro, Sister Anne Regina and I had started from Monte Maria at 7:30 and followed the main road east for two hours. Patzicia, Patzun, Panajachel with its breathtaking view of Lake Atitlan, Solola and finally a little town called Encuentros, or "Traffic Circle," where the road to Chichi goes off. It's a narrow dirt road with all the world's ruts, dust, jumps and waves concentrated on its twenty-mile length.

We traveled at fifteen miles an hour to avoid burying the Indians in our dust as they walked along the road, as well as to preserve our bones intact. Often we stopped completely as cows or horses crossed in front of us. Even at such a slow pace, it was a wild ride. At every foot of it, I admired the plodding Indians.

They carried on their backs four-legged wooden racks piled high with cargo—pottery, cloth, firewood, whatever—which were supported by a broad tump-line of leather over the forehead. The "cacaxte," as the rack is called, is packed ingeniously; usually it is the kernel of a pack three times its size. Occasionally, during the trek of a hundred miles or more, the Indian has to rest. As he squats on the ground the legs on the cacaxte balance the weight behind him and he can remove the tump-line from his head, revealing a bald spot worn shiny by constant rubbing as he jogs along.

Besides their packs of salable cargo, Indians on the road are strung with their itinerant housekeeping needs. A roll to sleep on, tin cans to cook with, a few onions or garlic and—always!—a piece of plastic which he whips out and spreads over himself and cargo when the first drop of rain falls on him.

All the towns' names ending in "tenango" mean "the place of." Chichicastenango is "the place of the chichicaste plant," a prickly plant with broad leaves found everywhere in the area. The town of 35,000 people centers around the great church of Santo Tomas. Turning a corner of that mountain road, we saw the towering white façade. Built in the second half of the sixteenth century, it is another monument—one of many throughout Latin America—to the tireless energy of the Spanish conquest. Just as we pulled into the plaza, we found the Flying Pole ritual, which I described above, going on.

We saw one pair up and safely back on earth. Then we turned to other things. I set up my tripod and movie camera some fifteen feet from the church steps. Chichi is so colorful at fiesta time that many tourists jolt their way up the mountains to view it all. The Indians are wise to this; they demand a fee if they find they have been snapped. To avoid this posing, I set the camera quietly and tripped the shutter at ordinary things as they happened. The crowd of brightly dressed Indians forgot about me; they went about their fiesta doings as if I did not exist.

The costumbre on the church steps was my primary interest. Alejandro had an encyclopedic knowledge of pagan rites. A woman sat at the bottom of the steps near a blackened half of an oil drum which had a fire in it. She was selling copal, Alejandro said, and letting people light it from the fire. Copal is a resin exuded from a tree known here as the copal tree. I watched the Indians as they carefully placed the smoking pieces into their incense pots.

"Is this the same copal found in Zanzibar which is highly prized to make varnishes?" I asked.

"I think it is," he said. "At least it's a member of the *Senna* sub-family."

"Trachylobium verrucosum," I supplied.

Alejandro laughed. "You have me on the technical name. All I know is that the tree has white flowers and oval seed-pods which are closed up tight until the seeds are ready to be dispersed. When they open, they show an orange decoration around the edge."

The copal resin is also dug out of the ground in a sort of fossilized state, like amber. Impurities in it may color it yellow, red, brown or brownish black. Commercial uses put it into lacquers, linoleum and plastics, as well as varnish. There is no solvent for it unless it has first been heated.

The Indians at Chichi burn it on the lowest step of the church as incense, or "pom" as they sometimes call it, in a pagan ceremony dating back centuries. They believe the rising smoke takes their prayers more surely to the gods in heaven. The wood and bark of the copal tree are burned for incense, when it is difficult to obtain the pure resin.

Copal is burned at the church on "good" days. The Indians go to great pains to find what might be good days for petitioning the gods. If they cannot figure it out themselves, they consult a sooth-sayer. On good days they pray for blessings on their families, their crops, their animals.

The man of the family slowly goes up the steps of the church, incensing all the time, while he prays a veritable litany of requests for all he holds dear. On the top step he sways back and forth, back and forth for hours, praying over and over again for each person and each intention. Then his wife joins him with candles and flower petals. These are visual aids to let the gods see exactly what are the intentions. White petals are for the dead, colored petals for the living. The woman sprinkles some petals on the top step and the whole family enters the church. With his wife and children clustered around him, the man takes a candle, addresses it as the spirit of an ancestor. He tells the little candle what to pray for; then he lights it and places it on a space on the floor he has set aside as his family's altar. Thus he treats each candle, speaking to each as a person representing one of his ancestors who is to be his emissary to the gods. When the candles are all lighted and set in place, the flower petals are sprinkled among them. Often an alcoholic drink is poured over the petals. Even the Indians are not certain what this means, but in pre-Columbian pagan rites drinking was part of the ceremony.

If it happens that market day falls on a day that is not good, the church will be practically empty. Evil days are set apart for prayers for revenge and the Indian feels that the Christian God in the church will not help him. So, he takes himself up Mount Pascual Abaj, about a third of a mile south of the town. There, in front of the black stone, leering idol Tur-Ka, he incenses, lights his candles and scatters petals asking his ancestors to help him get revenge on his enemies.

"What a gift of prayer these Indians have!" I thought as I picked my way up the church steps between the incense-swinging people. They scarcely noticed me. For them, prayer was the work of the moment and all their bodily powers were absorbed in it.

I passed from the bright sunlight into the church and paused breathless. Hundreds of candles on the floor burned between me and the altar, dimly perceived through the smoke. The church was paved with flames. Gradually, the kneeling, praying people came into view, all intensely absorbed in prayer. The murmur of voices, the occasional sharp rise as some petition got special stress, the women stretching to sprinkle petals into the smoky air, told me that these simple, forthright people were praying to their ancestors, confident of being heard and, eventually, helped. I watched one family group as they finished the session around their candles on the floor, and moved together up toward the various shrines of the saints. Finally, they knelt before the altar. Their Catholicism and ancient paganism are so confused that I am sure they did not understand Who was there in the tabernacle before them. Yet their devotion was complete. I yearned to begin at the beginning and to show them, as St. Paul says, that what their ancestors saw as through a dark glass, they now can worship as shining Truth. What mystics these people are!

Outside once more, we wandered through the market. Alejandro knew everything on display. He pointed out blankets from Momostenango; skirt lengths, belts and ceremonial bands from Totonicapan; pottery from Chiantla; garlic and onions from Solola; luscious apples from Nabaj. Little stands were piled high with oranges, tomatoes, squash, gourds, sapote, manzanitas, papaya and pineapples. Black beans were weighed out on antique hand-scales. Maize, wheat, limestone, dyed sawdust were sold by the measure. Piled up in the sun were cloths in lengths suitable for a "huipile" (blouse), a skirt or a "tzute" (a scarf for holding a baby or, folded, to cover the head). Shirts of bright hand-woven materials, made up for the tourist trade, hung on racks overhead; none cost more than $1.25. Some stalls had old glass counters displaying cheap toys, baubles, glittery bracelets and plastic sheets. This was fiesta time when everyone must have a bit of luxury even if it set his finances back for another year. So there were delicious apples and grapes from California, lovely Christmas crèche sets from Spain, delicately carved bone-handled knives and wooden and plaster dolls from mountain carvers. Every shopkeeper was confident that sundown would find his shelves empty and his money pouch full.

Besides the merchants who kept to one place, many others, mostly children, threaded their way through the crowds with trays of wares hanging around their necks. A girl came up to us with the air of one who had never sold things at the fiesta before. She had leather sheaths for knives, nicely decorated and put together. We admired them.

"Who makes these things?" we asked.

She flushed with pleasure. "I do. And my sisters and brothers. We like to make each one different and each one nice."

Others had rattles made, I think, from small gourds, and painted black and red by some secret process. I tried to get the ingredients from the vendor. "I do not know how we do it," he said, "just that we have always colored the gourds so."

One enterprising youngster had knives with odd, lumpy handles. I could not imagine what they were made of. Alejandro, however, talked in Quiche and found out that the boy had melted the handles of many toothbrushes and moulded the mass into the knife handles.

I got behind my movie camera again and filmed the scene. A persistent tug at my arm came simultaneously with a small voice speaking perfect English, "Lady, want to buy a machete?"

I looked down to see the high-powered salesman. He was no more than two and a half feet tall; his blue denim pants and red checked shirt had been mended often. Roguish dark eyes twinkled up at me as he held out for inspection a wicked-looking, eighteen-inch machete.

"What is your name, little man?" I asked.

"John," he said.

"It can't be John. You are either Spanish or Indian."

"I am Indian, lady, and my name is John. I speak English; I do not speak Spanish at all."

"Where did you learn English?" I asked.

"In school. They teach us English so we can talk to people like you. Then we can sell you what we make."

"Smart lad!" I commented. "And smart teachers. You are aiming for the tourist trade, I see."

But John was not to be turned aside from his main purpose.

"You want to buy this machete?" he asked again.

"Now what in the world would I do with a machete?" I countered.

"You could use it to open letters."

I burst out laughing. "Open letters? What kind of envelopes do you think my friends use?"

"Well, you could tell them you want to open their letters with a machete, so they had better send big ones!" He was elated with this solution. Another tike, seeing us friendly, came up too.

"Want to buy a dagger, lady?" was his pitch.

"Do you think I need a dagger?"

"Sure, everybody needs a dagger."

"What would I use it for?" I asked, beleaguered.

"Kill your enemies."

"I don't have any enemies I want killed," I said.

Dropping his voice, he muttered in conspiratorial tones, "Daggers are very good for killing all the fleas you see."

I had him there. "But the fleas that bite me run before I see them, so I can't use your dagger."

That brought another laugh from my young friend John and the second boy, Pete. And friends they were. They were with me for several hours as I ground away at the camera. They ran out in front to get into the picture; they calculated the distances accurately. Now and then, they disappeared to run after a tourist who might be a customer, but they came back to me as homing pigeons. They could have been pesky but I enjoyed them immensely.

The bright sunshine, colorful market wares, majestic white church, quaint Indian dress and customs—we were so absorbed by it all that time passed unobserved. Then the crowds thinned. Fiesta merchants began to pack up their wares ready to move on to whatever town held market tomorrow. The more stable shops started putting the baubles and toys inside and pulling the doors shut. The fruit vendors pleaded with the passersby to buy fruit lest they have to eat it themselves if not sold.

Obviously, the fiesta was shifting gears. John and Pete watched the plaza cleared of stalls and produce. "The Conquistador dance!" they told us. "They are making space for the dancers."

Only in the week preceding December 21, feast of St. Thomas the Apostle, can one see both the flying pole and the Conquistador dance.

"This dance commemorates the Spanish conquest," Alejandro told us. "For days, the Indians have been making masks and getting their costumes together. I think that by now they have forgotten what the dance stands for. It's just an interesting, fun-filled event."

Two groups of dancers ran whooping into the plaza—one represented the Indians, the other the Spaniards. Masks for the Indians were dark and had the typical Mayan nose. Those for the Spanish were reddish complexioned, with fabulous yellow hair and mustaches. Of course the costumes are not authentic. The Spanish headdress, basically the tri-corner hat with braid and fringes, also is festooned with feathers and beads which are very Indian. The rest of the outfit was such that any Spanish grandee would envy. Fantastic epaulets, embroidered kneepads, elaborate chest decorations and sleeves so encrusted with sequins and gold that the elbows won't bend made the dancers glitter in the sun.

The dance itself had little form and no precise steps. The crowds filled in around dancing areas in which the twisting, turning "Spanish" and "Indians" fought in dance rhythm. The bloody, cruel dance of death which wove back and forth all over these mountains in the sixteenth century had been all horror. It was now all fiesta celebration. What amazing changes four hundred years can make!

As the dances died down, Alejandro cried, "Look at the belfry!"

As we did, a small toy horse and rider came sliding down from the church tower on a wire stretched diagonally to the ground.

"Nobody really knows whom he represents," Alejandro said. "Some say Santiago (St. James Compostela). The Spanish were always praying to him so the Indians surmised that he must be in the inner circle of gods. Others think it is the first Spaniard who brought fireworks to Guatemala. They call him Zicolaj. Or, he might represent a messenger who brings messages between the gods and man."

No matter who he was supposed to be, the little rider and his horse were welcomed by the crowds. He was seized by several men, elevated to their shoulders and carried about with joy while fireworks burst all around the plaza.

It was almost 3 P.M. We turned our steps and our thoughts to the Maya Inn, about the only restaurant in town. The outer courtyard was filled with extravagant baskets of pink orchids similar to the Monja Blanca ("White Nun") orchid, national flower of Guatemala. Alamanda vines with large, golden, trumpet-like flowers climbed the stone stairway to an upper floor. Stone idols taken from some unknown ruins punctuated the beds of nasturtiums, geraniums, roses and the little red impatiens. Bougainvillea—red, violet and rust-colored—arched over doorways in glorious prodigality. We washed up in a country-club-type lounge and were ushered to the dining-room, a wood-paneled luxury room. I looked at Sister Anne Regina uneasily.

"I hope we have enough money between us!"

"I was just wondering the same thing," she smiled.

We need not have worried. The listing of Guatemaltecan and American foods showed reasonable prices. Furthermore, we were served by a prince of the Blood Royal of Ancient Maya-land, if one could judge from the costume he wore. Surely in old Mayan times, no mere waiter wore such a gorgeous outfit. Some of the glamor evaporated, however, when we saw our waiter step into a back room, shed his ceremonial robes and go "off duty" in more comfortable white shirt and blue denim pants.

The incident, small as it was, sharpened a question that had been germinating. Just how much of the Indian activity at Chichicastenango is really old custom and how much is affected for the tourist trade? What inroads has commercialism made?

"What do you think, Alejandro?" I asked. "How much of the pagan worship is play-acting and how much is real?"

"Most of it is real, I think," he said. "People are not pretending when they pray as we saw those people pray in church. Some costumes may be just for show but, again, these people take pride in the dress which shows their rank. The Aj-Kijo wants to show he is an astronomer, so he wears a white suit. The nobles have to have their black, palm-leaf hats with black ribbons to prove they are not of the common herd."

I wondered how long visitors will see what we saw at Chichicastenango. The flying pole, pagan rites with candles and petals, the dances which tell history in rhythmic form—they are passing from the heartfelt to the picturesque and into the theatrical. I have seen how Waikiki has gone into Coney Island with fake grass huts and debased hula dancing. Here at Chichi youngsters learning English in school so that they can sell stuff to tourists get the "fast-buck" mentality. They will grow up men of an entirely different outlook from their fathers.

One cannot hope to push back the advance of the new civilization. It is climbing up to these mountain recesses bringing many gifts with it. One can only pray that the English-speaking lads will combine the best of the new and the old.

EXPORT BASKET

A beach? It looked more like a Pennsylvania coal dump. Only the white-capped waves pounding on the shore, surging up to my feet in foaming eddies and sweeping back into the Pacific, made it real. This really was a beach, this seashore at San Jose; the sand was black but it was a beach.

Further evidence was a pier, probing like a long finger out into the ocean for the next ship. Several freighters stood at anchor some miles out, waiting to leave their cargo and be on their way. Passenger ships stopped here, too, and swung their people to the dock in a basket. A perilous way to land cargo as well as people. More than one crate has come to grief. Once my students brought me bags of plastic cubes they had scooped off the beach.

Other beaches came to my mind's eye: the white sand near the lighthouse at Watch Hill, Rhode Island; the cream-colored stretches at Lanikai in Hawaii going out into the blue Pacific; Indiana's dunes of white sand with coarse grass growing from them; the luscious, sun-lit beaches at Caribbean ports. This black beach at San Jose in southern Guatemala did not fit into the picture at all.

At Monte Maria, when I had asked for iron filings for my physics classes, the Sisters said, "Take a magnet to San Jose and get all you want for nothing." So now, as I stood on the black beach, I pulled out a magnet and stuck it down into the sand. Up it came almost buried in pure iron. No wonder rumor had it that the Japanese were trying to buy a beach! They need iron badly.

A walk on the squooshy black sand was rewarded by other finds. There were lovely pink shells, *Tellina rubescens;* the bivalves, *Chama* and *Donax;* the heavy white *Arca;* and strange little *Fis-*

surella which we often call the keyhole limpet. On the dark sand, their shapes and colors stood out like gems displayed on black velvet. I picked up a number of sea urchins and sting-ray spines. There were dried morro fruits, too. They must have come down the rivers into the sea and, floating lightly on the waves, were tossed on this beach. Someone would find them, I thought, cut the thin shells in half and paint on them bright scenes of Guatemala. In the markets these pretty little souvenirs sell for a few centavos.

This black beach at San Jose was no recent development; the sand was lava, twisted and turned by the sea and ground to small particles. There is another such beach, Kalapana, on the island of Hawaii, called the "Big Island" of the Hawaiian group. I never saw it in daylight, but once while photographing a volcanic eruption at night I passed close to it.

Walking around at San Jose, pushing the magnet into the sand and scraping off particles of iron, I wondered how the ancient Mayas had ever missed it. This beach was here when they built their temples and traveled all over this area in dugout canoes. Why did they never learn to use iron? After all, they knew how to heat limestone and to make cement. With a little more heat, they could have melted iron and moved themselves into another stage of civilization.

Besides the beautiful shells, uglier things lurk in these coastal towns. Malaria, typhoid, typhus, a hundred and one parasitic diseases thrive in the hot, humid climate. Less than two hours' drive from Guatemala City, where at 5,000-feet elevation one can forget that the equator lies fourteen degrees south, these sea-level areas never let you forget it.

The first hour's drive, with Sister Maria Carmen at the wheel, had brought us to Escuintla, a mere 1,000-feet elevation. There's a great overlook here. Forty miles of fertile land, called the "Export Basket of Guatemala," stretched out toward the Pacific Ocean. On a rock beside the road someone had painted a large "quetzal," complete with red and green plumage. The quetzal is Guatemala's national bird, adopted by the nation because it cannot live in captivity. Seeing it painted so vividly on the rock gave us the same thrill that a painting of the American eagle on a rocky prominence near a highway would give in the States. Farther off, to the right, Acatenango and Fuego stood side by side; behind us, sitting astride the road, was

Agua. The last of the volcanic foursome, Pacaya, was over to the east somewhere but lost to view.

Then we plunged down a steep descent. Hot air parched our throats and cut our faces. At sea level for the last long stretch, we stopped to photograph two pools of water hyacinths on either side of the road. These fascinating "blue" flowers, called "quiapo" in the Philippines where they regularly clog the Pasig River, made a field of beauty out of ugly swamp country. I know they are a nuisance to transportation in Florida and throughout our southern states, but I felt no remorse in admiring the lovely mass of lavender here.

Fields of cotton were ready for picking. Hundreds of workers bent over, stuffing the fluffy white balls into big bags. Trucks picked up the bags and took them to cleaning and baling machines in long buildings near the road. Rows of bales piled up to form a wall of cotton, stood ready to be hauled to ships in San Jose or across the country to Puerto Barrios on the Caribbean side.

We passed acres and acres of banana plants. Some were in flower; on others, the banana stalk was growing as the reddish-purple petals turned back and fell, revealing a tiny hand of bananas developing under each petal. Each plant produces but one stalk before it dies down.

A few enterprising farmers used the bananas as "nurse" trees for young coffee bushes. Most of its life, coffee must be shielded from the sun. The *Grevillea robusta* (Hawaii's "silky oak") is best for this; it furnishes not only shade above ground but also nutriment to the soil. This coffee grown under bananas would not be good—no coffee grown at sea level is good—but it would bring in a little money and the land was not being wasted.

We passed a field bare except for clumps of grass about two feet wide and perhaps eighteen inches high.

"That is citronella," Sister Maria Carmen said. Sister was born and brought up in Guatemala. "Extracting oil of citronella is big business here. Lemon extract is made from a similar grass."

Of course I jumped out of the car to secure some of the long, coarse grass. Crushed in the hand, it smells very like the bottled extract that has scared many a mosquito away.

"Inviting, isn't it!" Sister said, pointing to a rickety stand in the shade of a large ceiba tree. A row of green coconuts, prepared for drinking, stood waiting for customers. The process is simple; unripe coconuts, in which the nut meat has not yet solidified, are taken from the tree and rid of their outer husks. Then the top is sliced off, a straw inserted, and a cooling drink is ready for the next customer. Most of the coconuts are used this way. In Guatemala, I was never able to get a ripe one to enjoy the hard nut meat as we do in the States.

Busy looking at plants by the road, I had not noticed how few people we passed going on foot from one place to another. Usually in Guatemala there is constant long-distance foot traffic. Here in the lowlands, we passed people on horseback. Several children would pile on one horse, men cantered along and, more than once, a woman with a baby in her arms went by at full gallop.

"This is a plantation area," Sister Maria Carmen explained. "Being workers and even overseers at the fincas, the people have use of the animals. You will rarely find anyone plodding along the road here, as they do up in the mountains. The Indians with the long hills to climb have to walk; down here, where everything's flat, the people can ride!"

They deserved a ride in the stifling heat. Even the ocean breeze did little to lift the blanket of humidity. Up to then, it had seemed impossible that Guatemala, as I knew it in delightful Guatemala City, lay in the Torrid Zone. But after a night gasping in this coastal town, there was no doubt of it.

Heat, however, is important for what we wanted to see—the Firestone experimental rubber plantation at Retalhuleu, two hours on a good road up the coast from San Jose. Mr. Mike Vonesh of Chicago lives here and directs the experiments. His brother, Msgr. Raymond Vonesh, teaches at Mundelein Seminary in Chicago. His daughters attend Monte Maria, so we felt quite at home with this tall American, his wife who has lived most of her life in Latin America and their younger children playing around the comfortable colonial house which is the center of this huge plantation. Indeed, we had lunch out on the lawn under a mango tree. Mrs. Vonesh makes her own butter from the fruit of the oil palm. For dessert all one had to do was to reach up and pluck a mango. All the more enjoyable when one knows that such a fruit costs a dollar or more in New York!

Then we saw the fantastic care industry goes to to produce high-quality rubber. The finished rubber tree is a citizen of many parts of the world and native to none. To begin with, the seed stock is raised in Africa and airmailed to this plantation in Guatemala. Mr. Vonesh had worked with it in Liberia before coming to Guatemala. As the young trees grow they are tested for latex content and resistance to disease. So far as my eye could reach, these young trees were planted. Some were only two or three feet high; others reached perhaps fifteen or twenty feet. Don't for a minute think of the potted rubber trees one sees in greenhouses or in hotel lobbies. A mention of that plant of the genus *Ficus* brings a snort from any knowledgeable rubber man.

"That rubber tree doesn't have enough latex to make a rubber band!" said Mr. Vonesh.

Hevea brasiliensis (a native of India really!) is a plant with medium-sized leaves and white flowers. This is used at Retalhuleu. As the hardy stock plants grow in the field, they are bud-grafted from proved high-yield trees. Mr. Vonesh pointed out his very best tree for latex yield. It was about fifteen-feet high and the trunk was perhaps ten inches in diameter. This particular tree is kept for bud-grafting. It was fascinating to see the workers slit the bark of the young tree, insert the buds, making sure that the cambium layer of the bud contacted the cambium layer of the stock tree.

Then they grow in an open field; a goodly number contract tropical blight. The broad, flat leaves lose their meat, develop holes, become dull and brittle. Those that resist the blight are tapped at regular intervals and the latex content determined.

Trees that pass all tests are airmailed to Florida. There they grow for a year to make certain they have no disease. From Florida, they fly back to Africa where they grow in large plantations in a climate perfect for rubber cultivation. All this goes into the making of a rubber tire!

We went around with the men gathering latex. The process is simple enough—the worker makes a diagonal cut on one side of the tree trunk. White, milky sap runs down the cut and into a small, round cup where it forms a resilient, tough, little pancake. Later, after being tested for latex, these are run through two presses, to flatten them out into roundish sheets. Dried in large ovens, they are baled for shipment. Not much rubber is collected this way, but none of it is lost.

The Voneshes took us to a cacao finca next to the Firestone experimental plant. First we went to the propagation sheds, a long wooden shelter with latticed sides. Here we watched workers graft branches from high-bearing cacao trees in the field onto young plants. The temperature was controlled; every few minutes a sprinkler system turned on, keeping the humidity high. With tender care, a worker's calloused hands took a tender branch and inserted it skillfully into the bark of a bush. Then he wrapped it round with violet plastic bandage and let nature take its course.

I had seen pictures of large cacao seed-pods hanging from a tree, but it was a real thrill to open a pod and suck the white, jelly-like acid covering of each seed. Mr. Vonesh had men collect eight different varieties of cacao pods so I could photograph them. He opened a couple to show the seeds growing on a central stem.

In the same shed, cacao seeds were fermenting in a tank; we smelled them before we saw them! From the tank, they go out in the sun to dry. The inner pulp loses its violet color and turns to real chocolate brown. They are then ready to be ground up for cocoa and chocolate.

Cacao is native to the Americas. It was used for money by the ancient Mayan peoples. The name comes from a Nahautl word, cacahuatl, meaning "cacao seed."

Later, I went back to the propagation shed on my own and found a young, black pepper plant. Bending down to photograph it, I was a prime target for the automatic sprayers which took that moment to turn on. Drenched and sodden, still I got the black pepper on film!

Coming back to the Voneshes' comfortable house, we passed acres of small trees with red flowers. Something like the "tiger claw" in Hawaii. "We use these for vanilla extract," Mrs. Vonesh told me. "The vanilla orchid is not cultivated extensively here. We use this bush instead. The fruit is a bean." She put into my hand a small, semicircular bean containing eight red seeds.

Rubber, cacao, vanilla. There was one more plant grown in Guatemala's lowlands I wanted to see—quinine. In a nearby plantation we examined the rough reddish bark of the tree which produces this old-time remedy. In my childhood, quinine was a component of cold pills and fever mixtures. Memory of the faith I had in it then and still have made me stroke that rough bark tenderly and smooth the large, ovate leaves between my hands. How many scientists, architects, explorers, researchers, engineers and soldiers would have died in the tropics, if quinine had not been discovered by the Indians? Without cinchona bark, our world would now be a sorrier place.

We started to head toward Guatemala City. Along the road, truck after truck roared by, loaded with sugar cane for the refineries. Cane grows abundantly in this coastal region. Several times I thought I was back in Hawaii as the road wound through acres of tall cane with grassy leaves and thick stalks. At one of the processing plants, we were shown around by the foreman, a German. Individual farmers deliver the cane raised on their small patches of land. They are paid by weight. When the cane goes through the great rolling crushers, the sap runs off to be channeled into boilers and driers. At one spot, the molasses is drawn off; at another, brown sugar drops into bags. At the end of the line, white sugar, a little greyer than we are used to, is bagged ready for the local markets. That destined for the United States is bleached further when it gets to the States. This takes added chemicals, of course. I was just as glad to get the not-so-white sugar without the bleaching.

The last product we saw in Guatemala's Export Basket was coffee drying. Escuintla is a sort of midway station between lowlands and highlands. The sugar cane is brought up from the coastal area; the coffee comes down from the highlands. Ripe coffee, beautiful red berries, were going through some nine washings to remove the outer coats. On huge cement plazas, they were spread out to dry, a definitely larger project than at La Paloma. Two small tractors equipped with snowplows whizzed back and forth, pushing the berries hither and yon to hasten the drying. The process takes three to five days and only a few thousand pounds can be spread out at once. Naturally, the main idea is to speed the process, for tons of berries ripen at the same season.

When dry, the beans are rubbed together in large tanks to wear off the inner coat. Then into the bags they go, graded according to size. Germany is willing to pay the highest price; the first-grade beans in brightly painted bags go to German markets. The hausfrau buys her coffee directly from this bag.

The second-grade goes to the United States. Before it is bagged, workers go over the beans, carefully picking out any that do not look the pink of perfection. Lopsided beans make just as good coffee as the beautiful oval ones but Americans are finicky about the looks of things. Then it is put into plain bags; no housewife ever sees it in the original bag. Mixed with other coffees, roasted, ground and packaged under a brand name, Guatemala coffee loses its identity as one of the most delicious coffees in the world.

The third-grade stays home for the Guatemaltecans. This is a country of roasting-coffee aromas floating vaguely through the air. Often at Monte Maria as I tried valiantly to finish a class before lunch time, the odor of roasting coffee floated in through the classroom windows from the Incasa Company just down the street. How can one teach when tantalized so?

We left the combination sugar refinery and coffee-drying plant at Escuintla and started up the rugged mountainside to the highlands. Gaining altitude, we breathed more easily. Heat has its uses, I know, and we all love bananas, cotton, coffee, sugar, rubber, coconut, vanilla, chocolate and even citronella. Still, the clear, invigorating air of Guatemala City came like a blessing to our lungs. I was glad to leave the Export Basket behind.

HOLY WEEK

The glitter and clank of shields and helmets; the blast of a trumpet; the soft swirl of hundreds of long, purple robes; the blinding white of Palestinian headdresses bound around the forehead with coils of brown.

Roman soldiers in helmets and body-armor, with red and gold straps hanging down their thighs, advanced in a solid phalanx. People pressed back against the iron-grilled windows set in the walls lining the street. At a corner, they stopped. With his bright red cape catching the tropical sunshine, the trumpeter put his instrument to his lips and let out a long, clear call for attention.

Then a soldier bearing a placard on a standard advanced and the centurian read in a stentorian voice the decree of Pontius Pilate, governor of Judea, condemning one Jesus, a Nazarene, to death. It was in perfect Spanish.

Up to this point, I might have been in the Jerusalem of 2,000 years ago. Certainly, when the Spanish set out to teach religion with visual aids, their motto was: THINK BIG. All over Latin America, the story of the Passion is told as vividly as actors, scenery, symbolism, statues can make it. But I should not say "actors"; those taking part in Holy Week processions are deeply involved in the action. There is no levity, no cynicism. Men and women are engaged in a solemn religious act.

I was on the balcony of the Ximenes' house. Senora de Ximenes beside me watched the red and gold phalanx come slowly toward us. One of each group carried a banner with a picture of one of the fourteen episodes on the Via Dolorosa, known as the Stations of the

Cross. At the street corners, the trumpet flourished and Pilate's proc-
lamation was read.

"Each man owns his own costume," Senora explained. "They
have probably been in the family for years and are passed down.
Taking part in these processions is matter for prestige and family
custom."

As she spoke, I saw one of the Roman soldiers with his son beside him, attired likewise in brilliant red and gold armor. The child
matched his steps to his father's solemn tread. In years to come, this
boy too will break any appointment, rise from sickness, disappoint
any meeting, rather than miss his chance to represent his family in
Guatemala's Palm Sunday procession. He will wear his father's
Roman helmet, shield and armor; perhaps his own small son will be
stretching his short legs to keep the measured pace beside him.

Walking in a continuous line near the curb were men in long
purple robes belted loosely at the waist. They wore black capes and
purple caps, shaped something like the caps surgeons wear in the
operating room. Each carried a staff with a U-shaped top of strong
metal.

"These men will take turns carrying one of the andas," Andrea
Ximenes, the daughter of the house, said. The "anda" is the heavy
wooden platform on which a statue rests. Often the statue occupies
only a small part of the area; the rest of the anda is covered with
flowers, carpets, thrones, symbols worked out in many ways. The
idea of a float in a parade is similar, but a float is something you
stand by passively and watch. A better example might be enthusiastic devotees of a concert singer who, in the old romantic days, took
the horses from her carriage and insisted on pulling it themselves.
Only, in Latin America, they would lift her, carriage, horses and all,
on their shoulders and carry it with shouts and songs down the
street. An even better simile would be a congregation so swayed by a
preacher that they took not only the preacher but the pulpit, and
much of the church floor as well, out to walk around town. The
Latin American is not content to sit still when he hears the word of
God; he would not be content either with a wave of applause. His
religious enthusiasm makes him put his physical strength into real
contact with the holy object.

Some of the andas are so heavy that the carriers cannot go more
than a block without relief. During this, they rest the anda on the U-
shaped staffs until ready to go on. At each corner, a new group of

carriers takes over; even with this changing, some andas are so heavy that there must be a stop within the block.

One such came majestically down the street. Fully sixty feet long and so wide that it took up most of a two-lane thoroughfare, it filled the work-a-day street with brilliant color.

"Eighty men are carrying that anda," Andrea said. "Thirty are on each side and the rest are underneath. One man in front and one in back guide it."

The great anda, like a great, full-dress stage, advanced slowly, swaying slightly back and forth in beat with the rhythm of the bearers. The weight rested on the men's shoulders. Obviously eighty men were none too many. The bearers strained under their burden; every muscle tensed for the effort. But, while the muscles in their throats stood out with the strain, their faces were calm and prayerful.

They were fascinating faces. Full-blooded Indians with the high-bridged Mayan nose and the long upper lip. Pure Spanish faces, some faces with light skin and, often, auburn hair. All the shades between, as well. Some of these bearers had been among the Indians who came down from the mountains for Holy Week; groups of them had straggled along the roads for almost a week before. Others were professional men, merchants, teachers, clerks—the high, low and in-between people in any city.

I was struck with the reverence of the marchers and of the people lining the street. This was a real meditation, a miracle play. They were caught up in the action as if they had lined the streets of Jerusalem long ago.

Andrea Ximenes pointed out one of the bearers who carried the anda on one shoulder and, on the other, his three-year-old son. "He is Senor Cabrera, a friend of ours," she said. "The child is quite ill. In fact, the doctor has told our friend that there is no cure possible. Senor Cabrera told me that he would take upon himself the added pain of carrying both the anda and his son, as a petition for the boy's cure."

How many others among these men of all stations in life were making a humble prayer as they struggled along under the anda? Critics of this form of devotion say that the anda carriers believe that, just by taking a place in the line-up of bearers, all the sins of the past year are completely wiped out. Senora de Ximenes recognized many faces as the city's leaders. They would know better.

How much superstition was there among the poor Indians, the ignorant workmen, the uninstructed of the middle class?

I thought, "What would happen if this great religious platform, with its straining bearers beneath, were to advance up Fifth Avenue, or Sunset Boulevard, or Michigan Avenue? How would Washington, D.C. react to this anda swaying along Pennsylvania Avenue? Would the scurrying millions stop, stand alongside and ponder the beginning of Holy Week? Would the Palm Sunday spring fashion parade get a jolt?"

By now, the anda was close to our balcony. The sixty-foot length was covered with white cloth and a red carpet ran down the middle of it. Three steps had been built up at the front; a throne of white and gold with high canopy terminated the red carpet. Spaced irregularly on either side of the red carpet were various symbols of incidents in the Passion story—a cock for St. Peter's denial, a chalice to represent the Last Supper, palm branches for the triumphal entry into Jerusalem, a pitcher and basin for Pilate to wash his hands and an angel to comfort Our Lord in the Garden of Olives.

Slightly behind mid-point on the anda was the statue of Christ, bearing His cross. Like many others, it had been carved in Spain in the fifteenth century by artists who had thought deep thoughts on the sufferings of God-made-man and knew how to express them in wood. The Spaniard is so intense—so factual—that he is not content with a placid Christ flecked a bit with blood but serene amid His sufferings. The Christ he carves is in human agony, exhausted, spent, abandoned by His friends, rejected by His nation, His flesh gouged by the whips of sneering Romans, His mind so befuddled with pain He is barely able to hold His purpose clearly in sight.

"My God, My God!" He cried. "Why have you forsaken Me?"

All this on the face of Christ, even though He wore a robe of pine-green fit for a king, and the cross He carried was encrusted with pure gold. These were added to Him by repentant people, heaped upon Him, but His face was that of a king in royal robes with pain running riot through body and heart.

Many smaller andas followed—Mary Magdalen, St. John, Peter, the Blessed Mother. They were beautiful, but I had seen their like before. The huge anda of Christ under His cross with symbols of perfidy, worldly ambition, fickle praise lying on the ground near Him, had set the tone for Holy Week. The old Spanish missioners had intended it should. They knew what they were about when they taught religion to unlettered people.

Five days later, on Good Friday, Antigua held its famous procession of the sawdust carpets. Along the line of march, colored sawdust is laid out two or three inches thick in intricate designs. Some small efforts of this are made in Guatemala City on both Palm Sunday and Good Friday—perhaps a street intersection is transformed into a bright rug—but these are nothing to the Antigua carpets. Here is curb-to-curb carpeting for blocks, meandering through the city.

All Holy Thursday night, certain families are out making the sawdust carpets. Weeks of dyeing the sawdust, planning the design, allotting each man and woman, boy and girl, his share in the project, precede this night's work. Fathers have taught their sons the exacting task of making each chip of sawdust stay where it is needed. The women soak it with native mineral or vegetable dyes to vivid hues. Patterns are studied and miniatures made to scale. There is no time for experimentation on Holy Thursday night. Each man or boy must know exactly what he is to do and work ahead with precision and speed. Sometimes, if a design is repeated often, a metal stencil is used, but on the whole, the decorators work free hand. There are few or no street lights in old Antigua; flashlights of all types stab the darkness and play over the bright sawdust colors. When the carpets are completed, broad pathways of green pine needles are laid along both sides. Lesser characters in the procession—the soldiers, the banner carriers, even St. John and Mary Magdalen—will walk on the pine needles. Only the bearers of the andas of Christ and the Blessed Mother may walk through the sawdust.

Early-morning sun brings dazzle to the streets. Inside the church, the andas are ready. They have been stored in the sacristy and in the recesses of the huge church. Draped and cleaned, the statues are dressed anew. Outside, the Roman soldiers are restive; in Antigua they are mounted on horses.

At 7:30 A.M., the procession starts with measured tread down the two side-paths of green pine needles. Out they come—mounted Roman soldiers, a band playing a funeral march, purple-clad "penitentes," women bearing pictures of Our Lady's Sorrows.

We saw them start and then skipped over several blocks so as to watch them coming toward us down the sawdust-carpeted streets as they returned to La Merced. The carpet nearest us stretched for nearly 200 feet. The background of tawny yellow was probably twenty feet wide. Down the center were blocks of stylized roses in red; white and red strips ran down either side and, finally, a row of green scrolls melded into the green pine needles at the sides. It sounds horrible; but the result was a bold, vigorous use of color as flamboyant as a wild flower created to bloom in one night and be trampled by a marching army the next morning.

Beyond this tawny yellow stretch were smaller carpets, separate but all enclosed within a red border, to make a solid paving of sawdust. The designs included everything that God had ever made, it seemed. A butterfly was outlined in black; the body was green, the wings red spotted with yellow. Four fleur-de-lis grew in the next carpet, formed something like a Maltese cross. Another had green squares crossed with yellow lines on a rose background. Still another was emerald green. Beyond that was a brown carpet with white designs. Nature ran riot on them. A black double-headed eagle on emerald green. Pure white swans on a grey lake between cattails and water lilies. Large white birds in blue sky above a golden sun. On some, lace-like borders extended on both sides for the entire length. A black and gold inner border would have been suitable for a Persian carpet. Red and green designs could have come from the Orient. A lush Axminster would have done well with a black and red border I saw.

It was hard to believe that this intricate creation would have an existence as fleeting as a sunbeam. Already, the first of the procession had rounded the corner far down the dazzling street. The preliminary marchers were advancing along the pine needle side-paths. The mournful music grew louder. In just a few minutes, the Christ-bearing anda would turn the corner, too, walking along that brilliant center. It would take only seconds for feet to crush these lovely patterns into a confusion of colored blobs of sawdust. But why bemoan this? It was made and was saved as a tribute to Him.

Hundreds of men in loose purple gowns and white headdresses came by. Each bore a spear or a banner proclaiming a prophecy of Christ's death. They marched with intent faces, aware that they were dramatizing the moment in history when heaven and earth met on a cross. Rich men, poor men, Indians from hundreds of miles away, business men from the nearby office, all marched together on the pine needles beside the sawdust carpets. Occasionally they broke ranks to allow a Roman soldier on his beautiful mount to prance down the street.

Smaller andas, carried by twelve to eighteen men, followed. Statues of Christ in the Garden of Olives, Christ crowned with thorns, Christ scourged, Christ prone on the ground beneath His cross—the carved wood caught the manhood of His body weighted with agony. Multitudes watched silently on the sidelines; their lips moved voicelessly. The rustle of pine needles as the barefooted marchers went by scarcely muted the unhallowed whirring of my movie camera. Silence, prayer, meditation, loving sacrifice. What else could these people give their suffering God on Good Friday!

There was a lull in the passing marchers. A man standing near me whispered, "The main anda is coming. It will be all right for you to go right into the center to photograph it if you wish."

I smiled my thanks to him and walked carefully to the very center of the end of the sawdust carpet. In a cloud of billowing smoke, a single line of purple-clad men walked backward on the pine needles on each side, swinging large censers toward the anda. Down the carpet it came, guided in front by Jose Garcia Bauer, a prominent layman. The purple-clad bearers with white gloves, white head-veils and white sashes strained and prayed silently as they scattered the sawdust with bare or sandal-shod feet.

The anda, as big as that tremendous float I had seen in Guatemala City on Palm Sunday, swayed to the rhythm of shuffling feet. The black Christ, dark enough to be ebony, surmounted it. Crowned with thorns and dressed in brilliant scarlet, He carried a wooden cross, a tree trunk from which only part of the bark had been removed. Tradition says that the monks used ebony so that the dark-skinned Indians would feel more at home with Him. At His feet rested the most beautiful and exotic flowers that could be gathered in Antigua's gardens.

It was the face of Christ as He bent under His cross that fascinated me. He seemed to be looking from His high anda at the sawdust carpet laid to do Him honor, at His bearers struggling forward, at the back of Jose Garcia Bauer guiding the conveyance, at me standing there in the middle of the street. I was carried away with the meaning of this ceremony. I barely stepped to the side in time. Whoever carved that face knew the mercy and compassion of Christ.

Minor characters in the Passion story followed. St. John in a dark-blue robe carried a chalice; Mary Magdalen, draped in green silk, held her alabaster vase; Veronica showed forth her towel bearing the image of Christ on it. Men carried the men saints; women bore the feminine ones. They walked on the pine paths beside the now sadly mangled sawdust carpet.

Our Lady brought up the rear. Her anda was decked with Bird-of-Paradise flowers; she wore a lavender gown and a large, cream-colored cape. In spite of the jewelry on her neck, the large silver halo, the splendid veil and earrings—she was the picture of human sorrow. A golden sword was thrust through her heart.

The procession was to pause in front of a prison before ending at La Merced. I turned quickly to hurry down a side street to see this, and, as I stepped back a bit, almost bumped into a movie camera grinding away at me, of all people. It was the National Broadcasting Company filming *International Highway*. Months later, it was shown on TV, but by that time the footage on me was left on the cutting-room floor.

The procession stopped before the large colonial prison, which might have been lifted from mediaeval Spain intact. The prisoners were grouped on the upper balcony, singing a chant, "Lord, have mercy," over and over again. It is a custom here that, in memory of Barabbas, a prisoner is released on Good Friday. A guard touched one of the convicts, a mere boy, and motioned him to follow him from the balcony. A few moments later, he emerged from the prison door to the street. Jose Garcia Bauer led him over to join the procession. A rope chain was put around his neck so that all could see he had obtained his freedom. In a way he was a symbol of us all, freed from Satan by Christ's redemptive act.

Rejoicing in his reprieve, the lad walked with the rest of us back to La Merced. As the last of the andas—Blessed Mother herself—disappeared in the huge church doorway, I turned to walk down once again the street of the sawdust carpets. Hundreds had ploughed through them, hurrying home on the work-a-day business of getting dinner for the family. The crowds had dispersed. I kicked through the sawdust myself, delighting in the colors. But it was dreary enough; an hour ago, it had been so bright and new.

It was a quiet drive back to Guatemala City. The deep fervor of these people, the stark agony in the wooden figures, the rich clothing and gleaming silver and gold, the sawdust carpets constructed with such care to be a royal pathway utterly destroyed—they were fresh and deep impressions we all wanted to mull over.

From noon to three o'clock on Good Friday—the *tres horas* during which Christ hung on the cross—is a silent time for all devout Christians. Guatemala City, it seemed, held its breath.

Mass of the Pre-Sanctified was at three. Many went to the churches at noon, sitting quietly in the pews until the services would begin. After the short service they still stayed, some of them, and then slowly drifted out into the street. I, too, rested a while before the empty tabernacle.

Then, once more, the slow beat of drums, the wailing of reeds, wood and brass instruments started up. The dead Christ would be carried through the city, for all to see and mourn. In fact, two of them; one funeral procession comes out of Santo Domingo Church and another comes out of the Cathedral. Both follow the same route but space themselves about an hour apart.

There was no color here. The robes were somber with only a white badge to identify the anda bearers. The statues, too, wore black and the priests who walked behind the main andas were vested in black copes. Many of the people standing on the streets as the processions passed were dressed in mourning, women in black with black mantillas, men with black arm-bands. Christ's death was real for them.

The Cathedral procession came first. At the very beginning came the great anda bearing the dead Christ. The carved figure retold the agony of the past hours. The chest was pulled and taut, the knees and legs bent, the head bent down on the breast. A pure-white platform, bearing eight large pillars and a seven-step approach to the raised section where the body lay, was decorated with blood-red roses. Beside it, eighty pall-bearers walked in close formation.

The woman who owned the house was beside me on the balcony. She was a society woman, able to handle the world, one who had traveled and could hold her own in any society. As the dead Christ was borne past her house, she dropped to her knees and was lost in prayer.

Sixty women carried Our Lady behind the dead Christ. Dressed in black velvet with a long, trailing, black and silver cape, she stood in a huge silver chalice, surrounded by angels. Behind her was a large silver cross draped with white linen.

Scarcely had Our Lady gone, when the Santo Domingo funeral march was heard. However, a good forty minutes passed before the greatest statue of all in Guatemala City, the Cristo Yacente ("Christ Lying Down"), was visible in the gathering twilight. Tradition says that this statue was in England but, when Henry VIII declared himself head of the Church of England, it was spirited out of the country. The vessel on which it traveled, like so many others in the Caribbean, was wrecked off the coast of Honduras. Guatemaltecans sent a delegation to claim it. It is not clear just what right they had to it, but claim it they did and brought it to Guatemala City where it landed in Santo Domingo Church. Just how long it took to travel from England, what by-stops it made and for how long, who put it on the ill-fated vessel and where the ship was going when it was wrecked, nobody seems to know.

No doubt about it, the Guatemaltecans got a beauty. To protect the exquisite carving of the face and body, the Dominicans encased the whole statue in a large glass shrine about the size and shape of a crate enclosing a coffin. Except for this procession on Good Friday, the Cristo Yacente reposes on top of a high altar in an alcove at the right of the main altar. One can see through the glass but the shrine is so high it is difficult to get a good view.

But now, from my perch on the balcony, I could see the figure clearly. No hint of the Passion agony remained on the corpus. It lay relaxed and quiet in death. A long white tunic edged in gold covered the figure to ankles and wrists. The long black hair was neatly arranged on the silk pillow. Again, the anda was white, but at both front and end were "gardens" of flowers.

Dusk was deepening; lights glowed behind window shades. Some of us hurried to Santo Domingo Church and saw the procession coming back to its year-long home. Floodlights on the andas silhouetted the majestic figures against the darkening sky. One by one, they moved in stately procession through the great doors. There they would be placed again above the altars. The empty andas would be covered with cloths or plastic and stored away. Bearers, both men and women, would turn in their badges and slip away.

Good Friday had ended.

HIGHLAND LAKES

Honking as though on the way to a seven-alarm fire, our little Volkswagen took the corners of this mountain road at a precarious ten miles an hour. The road had all the disabilities possible to any road. It was single lane; it made hairpin turns; there was mush on one shoulder and a hundred-foot drop on the other. At any spot where we could see ahead for more than ten feet, we took bearings and quickly decided whether we could make it to the next corner before opposing traffic hove in sight. It was a game of musical chairs played on wheels.

Sister Marilyn Jean laughed at my tremors. "Wait until you ride on the San Miguel Acatan road. You'll think this is the North Shore Drive then!" You see, she comes from Chicago, too.

It was a good thing we were not in a Cadillac; the rear wheels would have been over the abyss when the front ones edged around the curves. Nevertheless, Cadillacs do come up that road, for we were en route to Lake Atitlan, summer home for many wealthy people. With Raoul at the wheel of our humble Volkswagen, we bounced cheerfully up the road toward a friend's house.

Some three hours and fifty-six tortuous miles from Guatemala City, we stopped to draw our breath and feast our eyes at a "mirador," or lookout, some 7,000 feet above sea level near Panajachel. Before us lay the blue waters of Lake Atitlan, 2,600 feet below. Four volcanoes across the lake served as backdrop. Toliman, 10,347 feet, sloped right down to the southern shore and behind it Atitlan rose 11,562 feet. In the deepening west, San Pedro and Santa Clara stood stark against the sky, each of them well over 9,000 feet high. The sun was sending golden rays through the clouds to touch the lake with diamonds. It was fun to forget meteorology for a moment and think the display was put on just for us.

Below, so close one was tempted to jump right off the cliff and land in the town, was the village of Santa Catarina Palopo. There are twelve villages around the lake which guidebooks like to refer to as "the twelve apostles," forgetting that some are named after women saints. Names of Guatemalan villages are long and, at first, confusing to the stranger. The first part is the Spanish designation, usually the name of the parish church; the second is the Indian name or something to indicate location. For instance, five sizable towns are named Santiago for St. James. They need some last name to tell them apart. San Jose is even more popular; eighteen towns claim him. It's like Springfields in the United States. Cities of that name are in Illinois, Kentucky, Massachusetts, Minnesota, Missouri, New Jersey, Ohio, Oregon, Tennessee and Vermont. Take your choice!

The towns ringing Lake Atitlan are like a litany: San Marcos La Laguna, San Juan La Laguna, San Pedro La Laguna, Santa Clara La Laguna, San Pablo La Laguna and Santa Cruz La Laguna—brothers and sister of the Lake family—Saints Mark, John, Peter, Clara, Paul and, finally, Holy Cross. Santiago Atitlan, St. James of Atitlan, sits on the shore where Atitlan slopes into the water. San Lucas Toliman, St. Luke of Toliman, does the same on his volcano. Santa Catarina Palopo and San Antonio Palopo, Saint Catherine and Saint Anthony of Palopo, are close together on the eastern shore.

Before we ventured on the steep descent to the lake, we paused a while at Panajachel. It's a delightful pueblo, boasting a colonial church which has been completely renovated. An enterprising priest found the shell of a façade and has restored the whole church on the old foundations. A beautiful thing. The usual civic center on the plaza, consisting of police station, post office and city hall all in one building, and the church, were freshly painted and clean. Men in this town wore short, red-and-white-striped trousers, white shirts with red stripes and red sleeves and a black-and-white-checked piece of cloth around the trousers, like a short, wrap-around skirt. They seemed very informal, chatting to one another on the street, or sitting together on the church steps, resting their burdens beside them. Women in Panajachel wear red huipiles, striped in brown. Red sashes held their dark-blue skirts in place, and red tzutes covered their hair. As they walked across the plaza bearing water jars on their heads, I thought that charm schools could well take up this business of balancing a jar on the head, to develop poise and dignity in carriage.

On the main street, just ten minutes from the lake, was the Hotel Xocomil, a lush resort place with green lawns, bright flower gardens, cool drinks and famous moonlight. The name, pronounced Cho-co-mil, is Indian; and thereby hangs a tale.

For all its sparkling blue, Lake Atitlan is treacherous. Wind currents hit the lake in the middle of each day; the waves get so wild that no boat, even a modern speedboat, is safe. This disturbance is "the Xocomil," stirred up by an unfriendly deity. Raoul explained:

"Tourists here just cannot understand why the boat owners will not take them across the lake whenever they want to go. 'Why start at 8:00 in the morning?' they ask. 'Why not just before lunch?' But the skippers are adamant; they know their lake. Tourists scoff at this talk of the Xocomil.

"But they learn. Just last week, six tourists could not get anyone to take them across the lake when they were ready to go, so they hired a boat. Believe me, the owner charged them every penny the boat was worth; he knew he would never see it again. They were in the middle of the lake when the Xocomil struck. Within minutes, waves filled the boat and sank it. The tourists were a sorry sight when they reached shore, wet, bedraggled and frightened. They were lucky to get off with their lives; cameras, purses, extra clothes are all on the bottom with the boat.

"And a couple of months ago, a boat capsized out there and everyone in it was drowned. It's best to let the Xocomil have the lake to himself in the afternoons."

The boat schedules, I noticed, provided for boats to return at 1:00 P.M. Was it safe then?

"For speedboats, yes. The Xocomil reaches full fury after two o'clock. By five o'clock, waves lash the shore like a first-rate typhoon, but the lake is like glass by seven."

He smiled with a bit of pride. "You can set your watch by the Xocomil."

It was pretty late now, and Raoul was getting strangely nervous.

He introduced us to another Indian spirit as our Volkswagen negotiated down a steep curve toward the water's edge. We were passing
the entrance to a small farm when Raoul said,

"Here it happened."

"What happened?"

"She wore red. Bright red. Red like the fluorescent markings
policemen wear at night. She—it—she stood right here."

We waited for him to make sense of his story.

"It happened last week. I had had supper in the village and, in
the early darkness, started up this road. Right here, standing at the
side but very close to the road, was what looked like a young girl
dressed in fluorescent red. She glowed, I tell you."

"Did she wave or call out to you?" I asked.

"No, she just stood there, waiting for me to come by."

Sister Marilyn Jean scoffed. "Maybe it was just some sort of
slow-down sign."

"No," said Raoul firmly.

"Well, what did you do? Did you ask if she needed help?"

"I did not! I stepped on the gas and went past as fast as I could
go. If someone had been with me, I would have stopped. Alone, I
could not. A man's not safe alone on the roads at night. Everyone
knows that."

I did not ask why. I knew. Stories of weird creatures abound
with the old people in Guatemala. One of the favorites is of the
Tzecha. An old man had told me about her.

"We were walking along, my fieldman and I. The air moved
gently through the trees; it was a lovely evening. Then we heard the
sound of a horse galloping.

" 'He's coming our way,' I said.

"The fieldman listened. 'No, he's not,' he said. 'He has
stopped.'

"Again the hoofbeats started up. They got faster and faster,
wilder and wilder. Just as the rider should have come into view, he
must have turned down a side-road. We heard the wild hoofbeats
die away in the distance.

"The fieldman blanched. 'That man has met the Tzecha,' he
said in hollow tones. 'But we need not be afraid, for there are two of
us.' "

The legend is that the Tzecha stands in the middle of the road in a long white dress. She has black eyes and a beautiful mouth, but God help the man who rides alone and meets her. She asks for a ride. She must go to her mother who is ill. Her mother is always in whatever town is near, so the victim cannot refuse through lack of time.

If the man offers her the front part of his saddle, she turns around to look at him. If he has her sit behind him, she talks so that he turns around and looks at her. She is transformed as she rides: her face looks like a horse's face; her eyes throw out fire; a stench comes from her open mouth. Some men who have ridden with the Tzecha are found dead beside the road with eyes open, staring with fright. Others live but are deformed. No one is ever the same after seeing the Tzecha on his horse. However, the fieldman was right when he said there was safety in numbers; the spectre never troubles two men together, just one alone.

I wondered if the girl Raoul saw was the Tzecha gone modern in fluorescent red, hitch-hiking on cars, not horses.

We reached our friend's cottage not twenty feet from the water, and Raoul left for the village. By candlelight, we fixed a supper over the oil-burning stove and turned our weary bones in for the night.

I was up with the dawn and quietly took the movie camera with me. For I had a rendezvous with Lake Atitlan. I would film her from the first streaks of light touching Toliman and Atitlan until full sunlight burst forth. And that I did.

At first, the two volcanoes were barely tinged with blue light, so faint as to be scarcely distinguished from the blackness of night. Gradually, the blue intensified; the lake lightened. A fisherman in a small canoe was trailing his line behind him. He whistled a bit, but most of the time he sat silent, quietly dipping his oar into the satiny water.

Golden rays tipped the volcano peaks. The sun shot out above the shadowy mountains. Another silent fisherman glided near shore. Suddenly there was a plop on the water's surface, somewhere to the left. Probably a zambullidor, a sort of hell-diver (*Polilymbus gigas*), an almost flightless relative of the pied-billed grebe. I would have given anything to have seen him for this zambullidor is found no-where else in the world. His cousin lives at Lake Izabal far to the west, but Lake Atitlan's zambullidor stays right here. A truly flight-less relative claims Lake Titicaca as home.

Each moment, sunlight tipped the ripples, the trees, the swinging Spanish moss, the sharp-pointed maguey, the tall red geraniums, the brilliant cerise bougainvilleas, the dainty, waving bamboo.

A bluebird "dearied" me as he winged past. Swallows dipped dangerously near the calm water, now an intense blue. A large boat-tailed grackle sang a liquid song he never uses further north. Blue jays, magpies, larks and even a noisy mockingbird saluted the morning.

The sun was too high to be gold, now. The light was so clear I could pick out individual trees on the volcano peaks against a sky of rich, Hawaiian blue. Children trudging along the beach in their bare feet called to one another and thus broke the silent spell. Another day was under way.

After Mass in the village church, we set out in the Volkswagen to visit the pueblos that encircle the lake. Lake Atitlan is large—eleven by eighteen miles with a winding circumference of sixty-seven miles. Possibly it is a crater lake. If it is, it must have been formed by a huge volcanic disturbance. In Hawaii, a good-sized crater is only three miles in diameter.

In each of these ringside villages beside Atitlan, the people wear distinctive dress. For instance, if a woman wears her head-covering rolled and twisted into a sort of red halo, she is from Santiago Atitlan and nowhere else.

However, this custom is breaking down. I had expected to see the Indians in local costume. But conventional clothes are cheaper and, now, more available. Men with the long pajama-like pants or knee-length trousers of their tribal costume often wore States-side shirts. The women were more traditional, but even they did not adhere to the original color scheme because much of the material was no longer handwoven. It comes on bolts from Japan, England or the United States to be made into huipiles, skirts and sashes. Most of the tzutes, however, were handwoven because they must be extra strong. The long scarf-like piece of cloth must serve as head covering, baby carriage on mother's back, or a carry-all shawl. I did see, too, wrap-around skirts of lovely blue material, rich in delicate designs. One tiny miss in such a skirt wore a huipile gay in reds and balanced a water jug on her small head. She daintily set her bare feet down between the boulders near the water.

San Lucas Toliman is large (3,385 inhabitants) and busy. A crossroads of trade between the highlands and lowlands, it nestles on a bay at the base of Toliman volcano. The waters of deep blue are a perfect foil for the women washing along the water's edge and the gleaming white colonial church. It was a travel poster come to life. The road into the town is steep and narrow; Indians walk along it, both in the middle and at the sides.

As we left the shore, climbing the slope of Toliman, we ran into a luxurious growth of coffee. The bushes sprang up between boulders in the shade of the large grevillea trees. Waxy white flowers, like small orange blossoms, had faded and the green berries had ripened to a deep red. Indians with baskets were picking the berries by hand—only the ripe berries. They would make trip after trip through this coffee finca, picking pulpy berries as they ripened.

Guardian of the finca was Jorge. He and Maria lived in a home with bamboo siding and thatched roof. The sound of an industrious hammer led us to where Jorge was working on the rear of his house.

"I'm building an addition to our home," he explained. "Now we have one child but there will be more, we hope, and we will need the room."

He had erected the side walls and was completing the crossed beams for the roof. Layer upon layer of palm leaves would make the roof rainproof. He hoped to finish it before the rainy season.

"We have three months before the rains start," he said. "So every day, I do a little bit as my other work allows."

Maria was weaving on a small loom, a most simple and yet ingenious device. She sat on the ground; one end of the frame with the half-done tzute she was weaving was tied to the house wall, the other wrapped around her waist to hold it taut. Thus she could conveniently slip the shuttle through the threads right in front of her. As the tzute grew longer, she could either move farther from the house or tie up more to the house wall. She had to work outside, for there is no light in the house at all. Maria smiled at us pleasantly, but she spoke no English and only a pitifully small amount of Spanish.

Santiago, on a deep, narrow inlet of the lake, clings to the sides of Atitlan volcano. Here, the ancient Tzutohil tribe built its capital city and held its greatest religious ceremonies. Here, four of Alvarado's messengers were killed. Here, the conquistador himself led his army in revenge and seized not only the capital but all the villages which, even then, dotted the lake shore. Here, too, is the ruin

of a church, one of those great buildings the Spanish left everywhere. It had been built in 1541, just about twenty years after Magel-
lan rounded Cape Horn and twenty-two years after Cortez set foot
in Mexico.

To get a picture of the tremendous energy of the conquistadors,
we might take a look at the rest of the New World in 1541. Only
eight years before, Cartier had gone up the St. Lawrence and discovered Canada. That same year, De Soto was finding out that there
was a Mississippi River. The Pilgrims weren't due in Massachusetts
for eighty years. It would be sixty-eight years before Hendrik Hudson found the Hudson River and one hundred and thirty before
Marquette and Joliet would prowl around the upper Mississippi. Yet
here in this hinterland town on Lake Atitlan, a colonial church was
erected.

The whole pueblo of Santiago is built on a giant-size dump of
lava fragments. Houses, fences, roads and gardens are made of, or
decorated with, black lava lumps some four feet high. Red pre-
dominates in both men's and women's clothes; when they gather
each day to display their wares at the market, it's a gay affair. The
women, with halo-encircled heads, take over as they sit on the
ground beside baskets of oranges, materials, painted gourds and
henequen mats. Indians from other villages show their wares at the
Santiago market, too, for this is a big city here. So big, indeed, that
merchants set up stalls selling plastics, cheap toys, buttons, combs,
pins, what-you-will.

Market day for the Indians is what the old-fashioned wake was
for the Irish—a time to renew acquaintances, exchange bits of news
and gossip, discuss crops and weather. Children play around the
stalls perfectly at home in the sun or under a shady tree. When
mealtime comes, mama makes tortillas right on the spot. When
baby is hungry, she swings the lump on her back forward, uncovers
the little head and guides the wee lips to her breast. Not willing to
take time out from business even then, she unconcernedly sells
onions or handicrafts while her free hand supports the baby.

For the market hours the mat on which their wares are displayed is home to each Indian family. When buyers go away late in
the evening the family packs up what is left and either totes it to the
next market site many miles away, or takes it home. The more important cities, such as Guatemala City, Coban, and this Santiago
Atitlan, hold market every day. Most pueblos hold market only two

or three times a week. The Spanish tried to stagger market days for the villages; although not strictly followed, the law accounts for the present custom.

We went on to San Jorge La Laguna, more difficult to reach than the other lake villages. One climbs up to it by a footpath which is called a road and after this stiff ascent drops down to a lovely gorge which cradles the village and borders on the lake. Because of its inaccessibility, the San Jorge Indians wear their colorful native costumes. Men are in red-and-white-striped shirts with white sleeves ornamented with red stripes. Women reverse the color scheme: their huipiles are white with red stripes, the sleeves are red with white stripes. Red and brown tzutes are worn folded on their heads when not used as baby carriages, market baskets or for other purposes. There was a Spanish note about the men's pleated collars and cuffs of stiff white material. But the Spanish would never have worn knee-length trousers striped in red, nor a white-checked woolen apron as they chatted at the local fruit stand. Much less a red tzute rolled roguishly around their heads.

We found we had visited these villages the hard way. Launches from the hotel hedge-hop across the lake; they don't have to fight the undergrowth along the shores. Sister Marilyn Jean assured me that a boat in ten minutes could equal a three-hour hike overland, and she let me understand that she knew this from experience. Nevertheless, I felt that slugging it out with the weeds and undergrowth, I got closer to Lake Atitlan, considered to be one of the most beautiful lakes in the world.

There is another lake with a name almost the same, Amatitlan, located at 4,000 feet above sea level, south of Guatemala City. People call it the "little lake" for it is just three miles wide and eight miles long. Vacationists love it.

Sister Rose Angela and I arrived there one day a little before noon. Already the tortillas were cooking; colorful candy was selling in booths; boatmen stood ready to take passengers on a tour of the deep-blue lake, 150 feet in average depth. Many men here wore flowers in their hats. This was an indication, Sister said, that they had just returned from the Shrine of the Black Christ at Esquipulas.

"Any way you make it," she said, "it's a long trip and dangerous. You can go the 160 miles by auto, bus or plane but all are perilous. Last week, a plane coming in for a landing on the field leveled out of the mountains, crashed and all the pilgrims were killed. An old woman I know once made the trip in a bus. A bridge had been washed out and no warning was posted. Only the driver's quick thinking saved the whole busload. One often hears of disasters on the way to Esquipulas."

"And yet many people do make the long pilgrimage," I countered. Crowds of people show their devotion there. The story is that the ancient Mayas worshiped a "black lord" called Ek-Ahau. So this statue of Christ was made to resemble the Indians' complexion to wean them away from their Mayan idol.

"I guess God has helped, too, for I hear of many miracles wrought by the Black Christ of Esquipulas. You know, I'm sure, the copy of the statue in the cathedral at Guatemala City."

"Indeed, I do!" I laughed. "I tried to take a picture and could not get a moment when someone was not kissing or embracing it! Is this all Christian? Isn't there some paganism in such devotion to a statue?"

"That's what we all wonder," Sister said. "It's the religious puzzle of this country and all of Latin America. So much pagan worship is mixed in with true Christianity.

"As an example: A young man was recently put in jail, unjustly. His wife brought him food and clothing but he would not take them. Nothing is served in the jails here, so this refusal meant he did not eat nor have anything to protect him from the cold. A priest we know managed to get him out of jail in three days. 'Why did you refuse the food and clothes?' he asked.

" 'No one brought Christ food or clothing when He was in jail,' the young man replied. This certainly shows a deep personal love of Christ, a desire for mystical one-ness with Him. This is one side of the coin here. On the other side are the people who will kiss a statue over and over again, and yet will ignore the basic concepts of social justice. If Christ were living today, He would be a miserable worker on their plantations."

As she spoke, she looked down the lake where the waters lapped against the terraces of luxurious summer homes. Others perched on the steep banks rising up to the surrounding mountains. Amatitlan is a famous vacation spot, but I had other reasons for visiting it.

Sometime in the distant past, the Indians threw idols, statues, bowls, utensils and treasures into the depths of this lake. Sister Rose Angela had a special knack for locating these things with her feet in shallow water. As a consequence, Monte Maria had quite a collection of things she had brought to the surface.

"I'll take you to the place I found most productive," she offered. It was under a pier built out into the water for a launch.

We found that tourists had discovered the same source of Indian archaeological artifacts. A number of them were diving off the pier and coming up with greyish bowls, some smooth, others with points all over the sides.

"Any luck?" I asked them.

"Plenty of luck," one replied, "but some of the best things down there we never could bring up."

"For instance?" I inquired.

"Jim, over there, dived into the deep water. He says he saw a large idol down there. Must weigh tons."

Jim, a tall, athletic man, equipped with an aqua-lung, was getting ready for another plunge. He volunteered information.

"Besides the stone idol, there are other heavy things down there. Many large pieces are at least a hundred feet down. It would take a derrick to get them up. I can't stay down long enough to investigate as I want to, because we have no equipment here, in case I get the bends."

The gleam of a real archaeologist shone in his eyes. "Boy! I'd like to organize an expedition to explore this lake!"

Remembering how eager Senor Espinoza had been to share his archaeological knowledge with me at Kaminaljuyu, I said, "I'm sure the Guatemala authorities would be glad to help you and would be grateful for any help you give them. Why don't you work with them? Have you seen the collection of things brought up from Lake Amatitlan in the Archaeological Museum?"

"I looked at every piece on display," the young man said. "But I saw nothing from here."

"They are in a special room in the basement," I answered. "Next time you are there, ask Senor Espinoza to show them to you. His official title is Inspector General of Monuments but you might say he is really Guardian of Everything Mayan."

"Few people have seen them, I guess," Sister Rose Angela said. "Is the collection large?"

"One whole room is filled with Amatitlan things. If I remember correctly, there are a dozen four-foot statues, ornamented with elaborate headdresses, earplugs and all. Also some smaller pieces and, of course, bowls of various sizes and decorations. I wonder why, when and where these things were thrown into the lake."

"One story is," Sister said, "that the Indians wanted to save them from the Spanish."

"But if there is a large idol sunk at the bottom of this lake, and I saw it with my own eyes," Jim put in, "how did the Indians get it there? Were they able to float it out on a raft?"

"Maybe there was a settlement here which was later covered by water," suggested Sister Rose Angela. "Yet there is no evidence that this was ever anything except a lake."

Jim left us to swim a hundred feet or more offshore for his next dive. We kicked around in the sand for a little while and looked at the things the tourists had found. The question Jim raised was a puzzler. Indeed, it was possible that a village was down there at the bottom. Amatitlan is close to Pacaya. The rumblings are heard distinctly along the shore. Could it have been that, centuries ago when Pacaya was young and more active, it exploded molten rock which had collected under the earth's surface? Then, might not the earth have settled down into the space left by the lava, carrying a village with it? Underground water would then have flowed into the depression, formed the lake and covered the pueblo. When I saw the volcano erupting in Hawaii, the land near Kapoho village dropped five feet in that single night. And the Great Lakes chiseled out by glaciers were filled with water. So were the Finger Lakes in New York State. Any depression is a ready spot in which water can collect.

As I handled the bowls, bits of stone and artifacts tourists had taken from the lake, something else struck me. Once again, the skin of my hands began to itch. It had been the same when I examined the bowls that Sister Rose Angela had found. The idols taken from Amatitlan and stored in the Archaeological Museum had had the same effect. I have practically no allergies; this was most unusual. Was it caused by something in the original pottery? Or by a sulfur deposit left in the water itself? I can swim in the lake without any prickles; it doesn't seem to be that strong in the water. But I have learned to wash thoroughly immediately after handling Amatitlan articles.

Driving back to Monte Maria, the questions came up again and again. Was this once a flourishing city? If so, when? Are there remnants of it on the land, or are they all submerged? When the fine homes along the shores and mountainsides were built, was pottery found? Old pottery? I would have liked to go from house to house and ask.

So I left Amatitlan, as I had left every archaeological site, with myriads of unanswered questions buzzing in my head. Sometime, maybe Jim will organize an expedition. Possibly, a hundred feet below the water's surface, he will find answers.

HUEHUETENANGO, MOUNTAIN STATE

To Guatemaltecans, the town of Huehuetenango goes by the nickname of Huehue, pronounced Way-way. That's enough, they infer, for the kind of likeable, small pueblo it is, even though it is listed as capital of the Huehuetenango State, that sparsely inhabited northwestern section up in the high Cuchumatanes Mountains. The state has the highest elevations in Central America.

Huehue is a nice little town of about 6,000 people. The streets are paved and the paving lasts a long, long time; there are not enough Jeeps in town to wear it out. A few local skyscrapers soar to a full two stories high, but because of earthquakes most of the buildings are low adobe structures painted in pleasing pastel shades. Huehue is a town you feel at home in, because everyone in the town knows who you are and why you came and is glad you did so. Huehuetenango really means "the Place of the Old People." Before I left I knew why people managed to live long enough to have given it the name.

As a town it spans the centuries. On the outskirts is the famous reconstruction of Zaculeu, a joint project of the United Fruit Company and the Guatemalan government's Institute of Anthropology and History. Zaculeu is one of the few fully restored Mayan cities. There are Spanish reminders, too, not only in the church and plaza of Huehue but in the national taste for bullfighting, as I'll show you later. The nineteenth century is there in the adobe houses, the Indian costumes, the travel by horseback from one mountain village to another. And the twentieth century has come rushing in with Jeeps and planes. Just about the only quick way one can get to Huehue is by plane.

The airport boasts of a soggy grass strip and a shack with telegraph and radio communication facilities. The flight takes only twenty minutes but there are long waits for weather to clear at both ends. The overcast in Guatemala City and the cloudbursts in Huehue have to lift before the planes take off. The pilots are cautious. "If it rains any more tonight," our pilot said as we sloshed over the airfield from the plane to the shack, "I won't try to fly back tomorrow." Not long before, a plane had sunk so low into the wet field that a slight tilt had ripped off a wing.

Sister Albert showed me around town. Sister is one of those fabulous missioners who can be all things to all men, as St. Paul was. As a teacher in Clarence County, New York State, she got a good training for mission life. She was in up-country China for nineteen years until communists took over the country. Since then, she has spent fourteen years in Bolivia, Panama and now Guatemala.

We walked through town, savoring the sights and smells and sounds. We spent much time in the cemetery looking at the inscriptions, designs and decorations on the burial spots. Some monuments were almost as big as a fair-sized church; others were just a name on a cement slab in the four-foot-thick wall.

Then we started down the main street. The Maryknoll Fathers who have spiritual care of this mountainous state maintain a center house in town. One of the big difficulties is the inaccessibility of towns hidden in the jumble of mountains. Jeeps can go only to where the road ends; horses carry on from there. To go to Jacaltenango, for instance, required four hours by Jeep and then five hours on horseback. The center house at Huehue keeps in touch with many missions only by ham radio.

I was shooting at a lovely statue just within the garden gates when Brother Felix caught me. "Another photographer!" he exclaimed. "Come in and see what I'm doing." Just what he was doing was not quite clear. It involved taking the whole camera apart and putting it together again.

"I hope it comes out right," he commented cheerfully. "It better had! I don't know much, but I know more about cameras than anyone else in town."

Brother Carl drove in in a Jeep. He was elated that he had won second prize at the agricultural fair just then going on in the city. Brother has been introducing new crops; his experimental farm has raised the nourishment level of the area to a new high.

We continued down Main Street, past the long, grey city hospital, now under the direction of the Incarnate Word Sisters. "You cannot imagine what they have done with that hospital," Sister Albert said. "It used to be dreadful. The dirt and grime were beyond words. Nobody seemed to take an interest in it. Now the Sisters have made it a really efficient hospital and the city cooperates with everything they do."

A vision out of an old World War I poster strode toward us; a tall, good-looking Indian in red striped pants and short blue jacket. "We call them Uncle Sam Boys," Sister Albert laughed. "They are the Indians from Todos Santos, miles and miles away from Huehue. But they bring their products here to be sold." The living replica of Uncle Sam saw my camera and obligingly posed. I watched him swing down Main Street and thought, "Too bad he hasn't a goatee and a top hat!"

Sister Albert was thinking of him, too. "The Maryknoll Fathers who work in Todos Santos admire these Indians. We Sisters have gone to the village a few times on mission trips but it is so difficult to reach that even a horse finds the footpath strenuous in the rainy season. I do wish we could set up a school in Todos Santos. They learn so readily."

I missed nothing along the street. The houses, nearly all one-story adobe, were red, green, violet, blue or any color that happened to suit the owner. Many Indians passed us. Sister identified each from his costume.

"He's from San Rafael. That one's from San Sebastian. There's an Indian from La Democracia."

A hullabaloo across the street made me turn as red-headed James Reed, a Peace Corp worker, descended upon me. Stopping just before he ran me down, he waited to catch his breath and then introduced a short, dark man, muscular and quick.

"My friend, Alfonso Paez from Colombia," Jim said. "He's a matador, here for the bullfights next Sunday."

I raised my eyes to an ad posted on the wall which I had just read. Yes, it said B U L L F I G H T—saturday, 2 p.m.

"Sunday?" I questioned.

"Sunday," Alfonso said.

"The ad says Saturday," I objected.

"No. I will fight on Sunday. Ad or no ad."

"Why?" asked matter-of-fact Sister Albert.

Alfonso shrugged his shoulders. "Why? Well, it just is." And that was that.

Once he had been a seminarian, Alfonso said, but "I am much better at fighting bulls than at praying."

Well, there was once a novice in England, I remembered, who had left the convent to go on to lion-taming.

"Have you a piece of paper?" he continued. "I will write you something with my name."

We hadn't, and didn't look too hard to find one. I'm not an autograph collector—not even of matadors' autographs.

There was desultory talk and we parted.

That evening two of the muddiest and merriest Maryknoll Sisters I ever saw came in. They were Sister Rose Cordis and Sister Bernice Marie, doctor and nurse stationed at Jacaltenango at a small hospital there—a hospital which is a miracle in itself. They had left Jacaltenango twelve hours earlier and came down the muddy trail on horseback.

"It was so slippery," Sister Bernice Marie told us, "that I began to think the horses had learned to ski on their bellies. When they went down on their knees, our riding boots got full of mud. That was bad enough, but when all four feet went out in opposite directions and they came down *kerplop,* knocking their chins on the ground, that's when mud splashed over our faces." They washed and dressed and sat down to a late supper. Of course, they were in town on business—and pleasure, too. At the fair, they hoped to pick up native woolen blankets for the hospital. Also medical supplies, pans, equipment of some sort. The two of them sat around our table, chatting, figuring out how many of each thing they could buy, estimating the cost, wondering how they would stow the materials on their horses or on pack animals, and I marveled at what they were doing out there in their small hospital in Jacaltenango.

Sister Rose Cordis and Sister Bernice Marie are the doctor-nurse team which worked all through a night to rejoin a child's foot to her leg. It was hanging by three-eighths of an inch of skin when the mother rushed the eighteen-month-old baby from a village nearby to Jacaltenango. A similar case, involving a boy's arm, had occurred in Boston not long before. But there, a team of doctors and nurses had worked with all the modern facilities of a large hospital. In Jacaltenango, the lone doctor and nurse worked with a kerosene lamp and limited supply of instruments. This was a real miracle. The child runs and plays now like any other youngster.

Saturday, we plunged into the past. A twenty-minute ride through peaceful grazing land, surrounded by rugged peaks of the Cuchumatanes, took us back 1,500 years.

"Look at that," Sister Maria Esperanza, who drove the Jeep, said. We stood on a mountain curve with a wide, verdant plateau spread below us. Lifting their heads above the large trees were snow-white temples, not as high as Tikal, but trim and dignified with classic lines.

"Zaculeu, isn't it?" I asked.

This was the city the United Fruit Company restored, hiring the famous archaeologist, John M. Dimick, to direct the work.

Going on, the road turned and dipped down to the plateau level. As we entered the ancient city, not a soul was in sight. It seemed strange to be alone here—almost as if we had wandered out of the forest of the fretful present into the calm of the past. The Mayas, we thought, might come back at any moment to welcome us to their empty stronghold. The restoration is complete; each stone is in place. Even the original workmen could not have done a more perfect work.

"According to the investigations carried on by the United Fruit Company," Sister said, "Zaculeu was originally founded by an aboriginal race. They had fully established themselves in this area by the fourth century A.D. and, of course, it could have been earlier. They were still here in the seventh century.

"We do not know what the city's first name was. Quicab, a Quiche chieftain, invaded this city and conquered it in the thirteenth century A.D. It was he who named it Zaculeu.

"The Quiches in turn surrendered to the Mam Indians, a tribe which still inhabits the State of Huehuetenango. The Mam were living here at Zaculeu when the Spanish arrived."

A neo-classical pyramid temple dominates the plaza. It is made up of nine receding layers and crowned by a severely plain temple, almost early Grecian in proportions. A flight of some forty to fifty steep, narrow steps climbed up one side. There is none of the ornate carving so common to other Mayan restorations. But, most severe in its lines, it yet conveys an impression of lightness.

A large ball court is at the left—two long, sloping walls with ample space on the top for spectator seats. Stairways at the ends make it easy to climb up to the viewing stands. However, the usual large stone rings through which the ball had to pass are missing.

Beyond this is a dainty building something like a low pyramid. Again, as in the larger temple, the summit is crowned by a temple which relied on its proportion for beauty, rather than on ornamentation. Slender, but plain columns form doorways for it.

"I always call that the Greek Temple," said Sister Maria Esperanza. "Last month I brought the Girl Scouts here on an outing and when the rain burst upon us, we took refuge up there in the shelter. It was a thrill to look out at the cloudburst through those lovely openings."

The city is naturally fortified, completely surrounded by water. Rivers and streams and, in some places, trenches and moats made a natural fortification. So many of the early Mayan cities protected themselves thus.

The Zaculeu architecture is much different than any other ruin I had seen. There are no ornate roof-crests as at Tikal, no Toltec decoration such as Chichen Itza boasts, no Chenes over-all, carved façades like the temple atop the Pyramid of the Magician at Uxmal.

A small museum houses a number of ceramics—bowls, pots, pitchers and what-not—found there at Zaculeu. The most startling is a large bowl containing a skeleton hunched up to fit the round shape. Interred with him in the bowl were several pieces of pottery. I stood before the glass case where this old Maya and his last resting place have been so blatantly displayed to public view—and greeted him.

"Thanks for letting us see your city," I told him. "You called it Zaculeu, meaning 'White Earth.' If you gave me the privilege of re-naming it I'd call it 'Sunlit Temples.'"

Out of the classic past, we rode straight into the all-too-turbulent present. Sister Albert met us at the convent door with news. We would go to the county fair that afternoon, even though it was raining. Also, she held a large white envelope in her hand addressed to her and to me. In it was a nice bevel-edged card with very fancy lettering to the effect that the two of us and three other Sisters were invited to attend the bullfight, as guests of Alfonso Paez, matador from Colombia, Sunday, at two P.M., at the football stadium.

"It's the chance of a lifetime!" Sister Maria Esperanza exulted. She is a native of Ecuador; it had been a long time since she had seen a bullfight. The other Sisters had their reservations.

"Must be terribly bloody."

"My parents saw one in Mexico City. They were jittery for days afterwards."

"Sisters don't go to bullfights. Just as they don't go to prize fights in the States."

The Ecuadorian had some good arguments. "In the big cities, no, we do not go. But this exhibition of courage and skill is part of Latin American culture, part of the background of our people. Besides, this is the first bullfight Huehue ever had. It will be very tame. Held in the football stadium, no doubt it will turn into a game of tag—the matadors chasing the bull and then the bull going after the matadors. Blood? I don't think you'll see a drop of it!"

How right she was!

"Let the idea simmer until tomorrow," said the wisest among us. "We'll see how the fair goes, first."

Two o'clock, and pouring rain. But thousands of people were milling around the booths, looking and, now and then, buying. Grass baskets of all sizes hung from the racks or were stacked on the ground. Hats made from the local maguey (called sisal in other parts of the world) were stacked up until they reached above our heads. Some were plain; some had a band and a feather. Newer models for the young blades were shaped roguishly and had a strap to go under the chin. Booths displayed flowers for very low prices; others had fruit or green coconuts with a straw stuck through a hole in the husk, inviting the thirsty. Native candies were gay in color and spun sugar of dainty pink quickly melted in the rain.

Competitive exhibits brought drifting fair-goers to examine the awards pinned to them. Father William Woods stood proudly beside his collection of native woods. He had arranged small pieces of wood in an attractive design which had won first prize. The whole collection of beautiful woods seemed to shout, "This is one of your resources. Let's use it!"

Brother Carl's exhibit of corn, maize, vegetables, coffee, was not only a winner, but also an education to the Indians passing by. Many people from other areas of Huehuetenango State remarked, "Do you suppose we could get Brother to help us a bit?"

We neared the sideshow area. A loudspeaker was blaring again and again, "When I was a little girl, I was not obedient to my mother and this is what happened to me."

"That must be the snake-lady's booth!" Sister Rose Anna exclaimed.

It was. We went into the dirty, tattered, canvas tent and looked at something that quite definitely seemed to be a snake with a woman's head. Sister Rose Cordis as a doctor looked long and hard. We agreed that certainly there apparently was not room for a woman's body in the snake figure and it moved with more joints than most women have. It must have been an optical illusion but extremely clever. A convincing fake, certainly.

At the race track we saw the end of the donkey races and the first of the bicycle races. In spite of the rain, three of the Sisters missed nothing; they stood near the judges' stand and got, not the main downpour, but a lot of the drips. As for me, I sat in the car right beside the race track. A good-ish crowd stood alongside, most of them encased in plastic. Whole families held a piece of blue or red plastic over their collective heads and went en masse from spot to spot as the races changed. The plastic sort of floated along with legs and feet under it.

"Looks like a movable breakfast nook," Sister Bernice Marie commented.

Plastic is certainly God's gift to Guatemala. Everywhere sheets of it protect vegetables, fabrics, people. Market stalls move the plastic from side to side, from overhead to underfoot, as the need arises. When papa pulls a cartload of furniture to market and rain threatens, plastic goes over his cart and more of it over papa. Cheap and effective, it serves mama to wrap herself and the baby strapped to her shoulders as she operates a tortilla stand in the street, cooking them to order—not unlike the old popcorn stands that popped a bag for you as you waited. Rainy days in Guatemala are even more colorful than sunny ones. Brilliant, naked reds, yellows, blues, greens brighten the grey streets. No halfway colors for the Indian; he likes his colors definite.

After bicycle races came horses. The same three jockeys rode all the horses. One was in blue, another yellow and a third red. Only two or three horses raced at a time; usually two.

How could such a poor little place as Huehue produce such horses? A young boy led a beautiful white stallion into the center of the track, prancing, tossing its head, dancing like a ballet performer. The boy wanted to race him, but this magnificent beast had too much spirit and not enough control.

At least ten races showed us handsome animals, descendants of those mounts the conquistadors brought over. The jockeys rode bareback, with their long capes streaming behind them; a picture of primitive beauty. Such racing, such riding! I wondered if the Aqueduct, Churchill Downs, Pimlico, Hialeah could have equaled this rustic exhibit of horsemanship.

Just to get background for the bullfight decision, we went around to the football stadium. Built of strong wire fencing, it was open to view. The only solid parts were, first, a huge door of heavy wood which opened to the center of the field, and then two side doors flanked by ticket windows. It looked as though no one had opened the center doors for years; the wood was warped and the hinges rusted. It was probably made for trucks while people would use the side doors to reach the spectator areas.

"This is it," said Sister Rose Anna.

Looking at the center field, I envisioned a brave matador and ferocious bull. "Where could he hide? It's a long way to any fence or door."

Sister Esperanza pooh-poohed the idea. "These bulls are brought in from the mountains destined for the dinner table. They would have to be tantalized or injured to really get mad."

Sunday morning, we made up our collective mind. We would go as the guests of Alfonso Paez, and try to absorb a little more of Guatemala's culture.

Sister Maria Esperanza was doing some calculation. "Let's see. It's advertised to start at 2:00. It won't, of course. But this is Huehue's first bullfight, so a lot of people will be going. To get good seats we ought to be very early. Yes, we should get there by 2:15."

We did—and we were first in line by a long, long shot. Through the wire fence, we could see a few men inside, leisurely nailing boards together to make a sort of chicken coop.

"Probably an enclosure for the bulls," Sister Maria Esperanza said, "although that thing is too flimsy even for dogs."

We walked around the corner and found the bulls in a pen, packed like sardines, but very patient about it all. There were seven, two for each of the three matadors and one extra. It gave me the creeps to look at these inoffensive animals who, in a few hours, would all be dead. And, in dying, might gore a matador, disembowel him, drag him through the bloody sand, trample his broken corpse to unrecognizable jelly. Ah! Little did I know.

2:45. Back we went to the ticket office. No claimers for first place yet. We settled down to wait it out. Soon others came and formed a line.

"Where are the tickets?" I asked.

"Probably in the matadors' pockets," our Ecuadorian Sister said. "Usually neither the city officials nor the matadors trust one another."

Enter the mystery woman. A tall brunette, dressed in black, escorted by two male editions of the same, came by. The three of them walked here and there, passing back and forth, eying us and yet trying desperately to ignore us.

"Who's she?" I asked.

"Not local," said Sister Albert. "All three are outsiders." And Sister would know. "Hmmm! Call in Agatha Christie," I muttered. "This is going to be good."

The crowd behind us was growing fast. They were always pushing, so one more shove didn't matter much. Then we saw Alfonso Paez beside us. He greeted us warmly; we thanked him for the passes.

Sister Albert, with the carnage of the bullfight drawing closer, murmured, "And we'll pray for your safety."

"Thank you, Sister," he replied with a far-off look directed at the wire fence, "I will need it today."

He introduced his friend, a tall, lean matador known as El Seville directly from Spain. Both wore rose-colored outfits, lavishly embroidered in gold, tight as their skins and far too gorgeous to wear to a bloody old bullfight.

Alfonso pounded on the door beside the ticket booth. Eventually, a man with a key wobbled over the field to open it. Plainly he had fortified himself for the afternoon's ordeal so much that he found it difficult to find the keyhole. As the two matadors entered the arena Alfonso turned to let me take a picture of him.

"I hope that won't be the last picture he ever has taken," Sister Albert moaned.

The two matadors did have the tickets with them. They went to the ticket windows to instruct the sellers. But still no one would sell tickets.

3:30. The crowd surged forward again—a greater surge than

ever before. Now people were jammed into a pushing, shoving mass a half-block back to the road. The cause of this surge was the third matador. A short, thin fellow from Guatemala, he was dressed in blue satin bedight with gold embroidery. He strode up to the gate before us and pounded again and again. No result. He threw his arms out, struck his breast and shouted, "I am a matador! I am here to fight the bulls. Let me at those bulls!"

"Take it easy, Blueboy," I muttered. "You're not missing anything. The bulls are still calmly in their pen."

But Blueboy flailed his arms and beat the door. He got the worst of his fight with the door. Sister Maria Esperanza looked through the crowd behind us, saw one of her Boy Scouts, and motioned him to squeeze his way to us. We locked our hands together and hoisted him over the eight-foot fencing.

"Find the gatekeeper. If he is still ambulatory tell him to open the door and let this matador in to his bull," she said.

The lad scrambled down the other side of the fence and ran for the gatekeeper. In ten minutes he was back.

"He's out cold," he reported.

"Then go tell Alfonso and the other matador," Sister said, "or we'll be battered black and blue by this wild man. Tell them to put the gatekeeper on his feet and propel him to the door. They can hold his hand if need be until the gate is opened."

Which is just what they did.

4:00. Blueboy slipped through the gate and so did the woman in black and her two guards. They all went straight to the ticket booth.

"Now the tickets will be sold." The man at my left breathed out his relief.

"Why, now?" I asked.

"Ah, you do not know. The matadors brought the tickets. The town officials do not trust the matadors. The matadors do not trust the town officials. All want their share of the money. And that lady in black—nobody trusts her. Now they are all together. Business will begin."

He was right. The ticket-booth windows flew up. The gates opened and we entered. In the mad rush for the roofed-bleacher sections on either side of the center field, we managed to use elbows to good advantage and secure places on the fourth bench up. It was soon jammed tight. The man behind me thrust his toes into the small of my back and wiggled them from time to time. Two mothers with babies in front of me carried on the necessities of baby-feeding without a worry in the world.

5:00. The crowd overflowed the seats and stood in a solid mass behind the wire which separated the center field from the spectator areas on either side. Every tree, window and wall overlooking the stadium was jammed with free-loaders. The woman in black and the two men crossed the field from one side to the other, bent on some inscrutable purpose. No one greeted them; they spoke to no one.

5:15. By now, the crowd was so jammed up against the small doors, it was impossible to bring the bulls into the stadium. So the management decided to open the large double door in the center. Rusted and boarded up for years, it would not open. With hammer and machete they pried off the boards. Even then the door, large enough to admit a house trailer, would not swing. Ah, a crowbar! Pushing mightily on the door and using the crowbar as a lever, they strained and panted. At last! The rusted hinges broke and the whole half-door fell with a crash.

This posed a problem. The bull could now get in, but how to keep him in? It was solved easily. Seven men on horseback had gone out with a flourish and brought in one bewildered bull. As he wandered in, two men stood at either side of the gaping door-hole and held a plank across it. This would keep the ferocious bull inside the arena.

The inoffensive animal patiently permitted himself to be tied to a slat in the enclosure they had batted together that afternoon. The matadors started practicing passes at the tied-up bull. El Seville got a little close. The bull lunged and El Seville sprinted up a fence.

Then Blueboy made a few passes with his "capa." The bull twisted his head and captured the capa on one horn. Blueboy took to his heels.

Sister Albert put her hands over her eyes. "I'm not going to look if it gets too bad. Don't tell me what's happening, either. I only want to know when it's all over."

Alfonso was waiting for the bull to be free. For what seemed an age—probably five minutes—they eyed each other. The spectators eyed them. The guards at the broken door eyed the situation and noted means of exit, should trouble come their way. It was a scene of frozen waiting.

There came a mighty roar, a violent lunge. The large white bull yanked off the plank he was tied to and trotted into the arena with a blue capa draped roguishly on one horn and a plank tied round his neck. All three matadors pushed back as far as they could go. The men at the broken door stood on one foot ready to sprint elsewhere. The horsemen edged away with their horses. The audience held its collective breath.

The bull strolled to the center of the field, looked over the spectators and leisurely walked toward the door, flipping the capa jauntily and dragging his plank.

The men at the door dropped their board and ran in opposite directions. The horsemen fidgeted. The matadors ran to intercept their adversary, but he had a head start. As he neared the exit, he tossed the capa off and the plank slid out of the rope, so he picked up speed. After him a furious parade poured out the broken door— horsemen, matadors, guards and hundreds of spectators. In all the commotion a woman and her four offspring slipped in the gate free!

Rumors started to pass among the spectators left inside.

"The bull knocked a woman down. Badly injured. Now in the hospital."

"He ran into a group of children. My Jose! I hope he's safe!"

The matadors returned and leaned against a fence. They were as bored as the rest of us. I improved the shining hours taking pictures of the women on the bench in front of us. One baby was so small, his mother had to open his blanket every once in a while to see if he was all right. The other held a little girl in her arms. Both fed the children to while away the time.

6:30. We started for home. The bullfight would fizzle out into a lynching perhaps? Muttered threats boded ill for the matadors.

Just outside the gate, we found a pretty situation. A horseman had lassoed the bull and was pulling him up to a tree. Suddenly violent protests came down from the leafy branches. Five men had scrambled up there in mortal fear of the bull and here he was tied to the very tree they had sought refuge in! Their safety spot turned out to be a hot spot.

Amid yells from below and yells from above, the bull's head was tied tightly to one side of the trunk while the five refugees slid nervously down the other side of it. Laughing and clapping, we spectators thought it was the best part of the show.

The three matadors walked around to the pen to choose another bull. El Seville would fight this one. Which one did he want? That one away back in the rear. The attendants looked annoyed. How to get one bull out of a pen crowded with six, however, was their problem, not his. They solved it brilliantly. How about letting the first five out and then catching the last one? A first-rate idea. The only flaw was that, once the gate was open, all six made a prison break at high speed. In a matter of seconds, only the horsemen and the three matadors were left in the bull pen.

A howl went up from the spectators. The howl re-echoed round the field; it went from bleachers to bleachers; it grew to an angry roar. The crowd surged onto the field.

"What's the idea?"

"Beat them up!"

"The gyps!"

"Hanging's too good."

The police surrounded the matadors on the field and they crawled off into the darkening streets to the local jail until the crowd dispersed. Then they went to the local hotel for the night.

By that time, the crowd had something else to ponder. All the ticket money was stolen. The finger of suspicion rested on the lady in black and her two escorts. The town officials thought she was employed by the matadors; and the matadors thought she was working for the officials. In the end, both came to the conclusion that she was a city slicker working for herself.

The other matadors left town the next morning, but Alfonso tried on Tuesday to stage a bullfight to give the people what they had paid for. He came around to the convent and told us the result.

"I selected a big, brutal-looking animal and egged him on to do something.

"But what did he do? He looked me in the eye for a minute and then bent down to munch all the grass he could hold.

"I heard him say—heard him distinctly, Sisters. 'Caramba! Go fight your city bulls! Up here we're happy without you!'"

SAN MIGUEL ACATAN

Not too often, two or three times a year at most, Maryknoll Sisters in the mountains of Guatemala can sit around a table to talk of people and places we all know. Usually two or three are living in some mountain fastness conducting a school and a clinic and it's a long, long way by Jeep and/or horseback to the next Maryknoll convent.

But at Huehue I was lucky enough to sit with six who happened to come in from the distant missions to get supplies just before the big rains would isolate them for months.

We were a jolly group. I had known all these hardy Sisters at Maryknoll; I had guided their steps through college botany, biology, astronomy. I had seen them dissect frogs, construct miniature solar systems, collect and identify butterflies and plants. I had taken them on expeditions to study rocks which show the geological ages, to marvel at fossil trilobite remains, to bring home in triumph garnet, quartz, galena, iron-ore from mine dumps. Some had gone on for further studies; others were teaching Indian children in these mountains. It was a joy to look around at these seasoned missioners, only a few of the hundreds in many a far-flung corner of the world, whom I had had the privilege of helping to train for this work.

They were—of course!—talking of roads and weather and distances.

"Come to San Antonio Huista!" invited Sister Thomas Marie, as if her school at the end of nowhere were right next door.

"No, no, Jacaltenango first," said Sister Rose Cordis, who has a clinic and small hospital away off in the mountains.

But I was cautious. These hardy perennials don't realize how frail a science teacher can be. "How far to your houses?"

"No more than eight or nine hours to reach Jacaltenango, if the going is good," Sister Rose Cordis boasted. "Usually, four hours by Jeep to Rosario and five hours from there by horse or mule. But," she admitted, "it could take twelve hours if the trail is bad. It took us twelve hours the other day."

"San Antonio Huista is much easier," Sister Thomas Marie said. "The Jeep makes it to Providencia in three hours and we're only two hours by horse from there. And if you wanted to go on to Jacaltenango from our place, it's only over a mountain range—about three hours on horseback."

"Sounds wonderful!" I said. "But I'm a city girl from Chicago. I've never ridden a horse in my life. I'd like to try, but the first lesson shouldn't be on a narrow mountain trail where one stirrup scrapes the mountain wall and the other hangs over a sheer drop. Also, I remember what you looked like when you came in a few nights ago. Getting muddy in a good cause is fine, but I don't want to roll over a cliff and become extinct."

"Come now!" Sister Rose Cordis cajoled. "You can ride my pet mule, steady as a rock, and Jose will lead him all the way."

"And Jose would walk the whole distance?"

"He often does it. Our men are used to walking; it's the ordinary means of transportation for them. Why, just the other day, they took turns in groups carrying our new, 600-pound generator up mountains and down mountains to the hospital. This is normal."

Even so. Having Jose fall over the cliff with me would make it not such a lonely end, but it wouldn't be quite fair to him.

Sister Thomas Marie was more sensible. "If you haven't ridden a horse, you're right not to want to go. San Antonio Huista is a cinch in the dry season, but the roads are really bad now. I've been going in and out for years, and this last trip was no picnic. Besides, we have landslides now. You have to dismount and climb gingerly over the rocks and mud to the other side. When a rock you have been counting on slips out from under your feet and crashes down the slope, it scares you. The horses not encumbered with riders usually make it."

"Usually?"

"Oh, we've had some go over the side."

"What do you do then?"

"We walk until help comes. Word spreads and someone sends us a mount."

"How about those two Sisters who walked so far they wore out their riding boots and had blisters all over their feet?"

"They got over it well enough. God takes care of us. We'll start back tomorrow morning because we have to reach home before the rains get too bad. But you had better not try it now."

Sister Francis Christine took the cue to come forward.

"How about my place, San Miguel Acatan? You can go all the way by Jeep. It might take ten years off your life and put grey hairs where you never had them before, but you will get there. Our driver is very, very dependable. And, if we do have to transfer to a horse, it will be for less than an hour."

"That sounds within my capabilities," I sighed. "You can count me in."

Sister Francis Christine began laying her plans.

"Tonight, I'll wire Father Daniel Jensen at San Miguel asking about the weather and the roads. He'll be able to get an answer back here early."

"Wire? About weather? Why not phone?"

"Mercy, no! The whole State of Huehuetenango has no phones other than privately installed intercoms. Telegrams are cheap and reliable. The one Father will send in the morning will cost thirty centavos (thirty cents) and will get here in an hour. And that would be a rush telegram; others would be fifteen cents."

We would start at 8:15 A.M. If all went well, we should arrive at 1:15 P.M. We could pray it wouldn't be later, for the daily rains up there at San Miguel usually start around 2:30 and that end of the road would be dangerous then.

I went to bed, fortified with road maps showing the mountain ranges, all-weather roads and even footpaths in the state of Huehuetenango. Outside of the capital city, there wasn't a paved road in the whole state. However, the all-weather roads are passable except in extremely heavy rain. The big danger is from landslides. Even the Pan-American Highway is unpaved in Huehuetenango.

We would probably follow 9N north to San Juan Ixcoy, then branch off west across the mountains to San Rafael and on to San Miguel Acatan. Tracing the road, my eye slipped over to Aguacatan on the east. Aguacatan! One of the most fascinating geological places.

Aguacatan gets its name from the fact that the Rio Blanca bursts out of the mountains there. It's really the San Juan in disguise. Up at San Juan Ixcoy, the San Juan River flows a few miles above ground and then disappears into the mountainside. Some observant soul at Aguacatan, twenty-five miles southeast, noted that when the Rio Blanca bursts out of the mountain, it carries apples which grow only in San Juan Ixcoy. He deduced logically that the San Juan dips into the blackness, changes name and costume, and emerges as the Blanca.

What a cave system there must be in the mountains! What fun it would be to float on the river through those twenty-five miles! These are dreams any geologist recognizes; we all go through them. Memories of the famous Lanquin Caves, 100 or so miles northeast of Guatemala City, came to deter my proposing that we rent a boat and follow the San Juan through the mountain channel.

The Lanquin Caves could be the most beautiful in the world. The formations at Meramec, Luray and even Carlsbad are not as interesting. But in those places, one can really see the stalactites and stalagmites because lights have been installed. At Lanquin, we had ocote, flaming slivers of white pine, as torches. Even at that, we saw room after room with high, vaulted ceilings, cascades of organ-pipe stalactites, huge stalagmites known to the Indians as altars, gods and goddesses.

One of these lime formations growing up from the cavern floor was an altar used for human sacrifices. The bodies were thrown down into the black abyss which yawned at the side of the room. I threw a stone down and could count seconds before the splash came back to us. The Rio Lanquin flows through the caves. Indeed, it probably was the force which hollowed them out. Some fourteen days' trek into the caves, the guides told us, it widens into a large lake, all underground. But fourteen days' trek into that place would be a fourteen years' march for me!

There were four-foot boulders to be crawled over, narrow passages to squeeze through, walls to skirt on an almost non-existent ledge and through it all you knew that a misstep would plunge you into the inky depths below.

"If I were at the head of the tourist bureau of Guatemala," I had told the Sisters, "I'd hire a fleet of trucks, take a few million loads of junk out of the caves, put in electricity that could not be removed by a needy soul, grade the walks and ring them with handrails. For

American tourists, it probably would be necessary to get an exterminator to eliminate the livestock."

Sister Thomas Marie had laughed. "More fleas?"

"Worse than that. There were five-inch tarantulas on the walls and ants on every stalactite. At one stage, Sister Maria Carmen and I decided we had had enough and thought we would sit on a flat stalagmite until the rest of the group returned. Luckily, we inspected the area with the feeble light from our ocote and found big, hairy tarantulas in possession, so we stayed in a small, clear spot. The two hours I spent in those caves were like a nightmare. Nevertheless, I'm glad I saw what caverns are like before they are cleared out."

After the Lanquin experience, I decided not to investigate what the San Juan River was doing under the mountain. We could bypass Aguacatan and go on to Chiantla to see the Silver Virgin. Then go north over a 10,000-foot plateau between parallel ranges of the Cuchumatanes Mountains on a road constructed for a galena (zinc sulphide) mine at Villa Linda. After that, the last stage of the journey would be anybody's guess. It was here that our Mother General got bogged down as she visited the missions. She wasn't the first, nor was she the last to sink to the hub caps in mud.

Sister Francis Christine had said we could "pick up horses" at A Chi if needed. A Chi wasn't marked on any map I had—maps that plainly showed hamlets like Chiantla and Chemal and Ixcoy and blared in large type about Huehuetenango. A Chi must be very, very small, I concluded, falling to sleep. Probably one man and three horses. At least, I hoped there were three.

Vigorous ringing of the doorbell woke us at dawn the next day. The telegraph boy was on his bicycle outside, waving an envelope. The message was brief and encouraging. The word "Bueno" said it all. Roads not washed out during the night, weather fair, no troubles brewing.

Mateo and the Fathers' four-wheel-drive Jeep stood at the front door at eight o'clock sharp. A young man with flashing eyes and dark curly hair, with ready smile and quick repartee, Mateo makes the round trip to San Miguel in a day. Often he has to do it three or four times a week. The nerve-racking trip might give a lesser man the jitters but Mateo takes it in stride. His thin, agile frame belies the strength he commands in moments of crisis; his mind comes to quick decisions when confronted by danger.

This morning, as he loaded the Jeep with the Sisters' purchases in Huehuetenango, he chuckled.

"It looks as though you won't be coming out very soon again!"

"You're so right, Mateo!" Sister Francis Christine said. "We won't budge out of San Miguel until the rainy season lets up. If these provisions don't last five months—well, we'll live as best we can on what we can get up in our neck of the woods."

"What if you break your glasses, or need shoes repaired, or want something from the grocery store?" I asked.

"The glasses, shoes or such things can go out on the local Jeep which makes a trip now and then as a sort of substitute bus. For the rest, we wait until the dry season. Soggy roads are dangerous here."

"Is it that bad?" I asked.

"Come now, don't be scared," laughed Sister Jacinta Marie, the other half of the San Miguel Acatan team. "We've been making this trip several times a year for years, safe and sound. But, of course, there's always a first time."

"We remember that the Sisters at the Motherhouse are before the altar praying for travelers every half-hour. That should keep us on the road," added Sister Francis Christine.

All loaded up, the Jeep with Mateo and me in front and Sisters Francis Christine and Jacinta Marie behind took off on 9N. Within no time we were seeing the pueblo of Chiantla as we rounded a mountain peak. I was used, by now, to seeing a large, white colonial church surrounded by small adobe dwellings. The Spanish left their mark on every town and village of Latin America. We drove through town and into the plaza. Father Albert Reymann, the Maryknoll pastor, waved from the church steps.

"Want a good guide?" he called. "I've some free moments and will be glad to show you our Silver Virgin. We just had a real electric light put in near the statue." He glanced at my camera. "You can take a picture now."

Stepping into the great old church, once again the word "bulk" flashed to my mind as it always does in Spanish churches. They are bulky constructions with massive walls five or more feet thick. Except for the belfry, each one has the same squarishness in front and longishness on the sides. They could have been molded in the same great, out-size apple box. But the belfries are distinctive. Local workmen, tired of the sameness, let their ingenuity run riot in the belfries.

Daintily arched with open spaces, they hang one, three or five bells.

Inside the church, scaffolding had been erected. "Wait till you see how we're restoring the shrine." Father laughed like a boy. "It's good, if I say so myself."

The ceiling caught my eye. Carved pieces hung from above, painted red on one side, blue on the other, so that when one stood at the entrance and looked forward, the ceiling was red. Standing at the altar and looking back, the ceiling was blue.

"We just touched up the original colors," Father said.

Sister Jacinta Marie drew my attention to a balcony over the main altar. "The Silver Virgin stands there."

Father Reymann took us up a narrow stairway to the balcony. With a dramatic gesture, he flipped on the light.

"That's how you turn on a light you have had only twenty-four hours," he announced.

The Silver Virgin holding the Child Jesus took my breath away. In flash pictures she seems hard, dour, with staring eyes and a tight little mouth. But the Virgin I saw had large, luminous eyes and a serious mouth set in a long face. Something in the way she held the Child made me think she knew what was in store for Him. The head and hands are carved wood. Our Lady wears two silver garments—an inner straight dress and an outer cape. The Child is covered with a fitted silver dress.

The Virgin's origin is variously told. Some say she was carved by Quirio Catano right here in Guatemala; they say that the robes were made from silver mined in these mountains. Others contend that she was brought from Europe and, like so many others, was shipwrecked on these shores.

"How long has she been here in Chiantla?" I asked.

"At least 350 years," Father answered. "As early as 1619, Chiantla was a flourishing parish under the Dominican Fathers. Even then, large pilgrimages came to see the Silver Virgin here."

"And the Pilgrims had not yet landed at Plymouth!" I exclaimed.

I examined the silver robes carefully. "My guess is that the designs on these robes were made either in Europe or by someone here who had learned the technique there," I commented.

"How so?" the others asked.

"Look at these scrolls and birds and flowers. They are the very same designs on the tapestries in the Cloisters in New York City.

The same technique for shading with curved lines occurs in both the tapestries and here in the Chiantla Virgin's cloak."

"It may have been done in a monastery in Spain or France," Sister Jacinta Marie said, "or by someone who had once lived in a European monastery."

Father spoke up. "I don't know who did the robes," he said, "but I do know that the Indians in this area can duplicate the designs. In recovering the altar in this church, I have had to use aluminum instead of silver; it serves the purpose even better because it does not tarnish. The local people have no difficulty at all in duplicating these same designs on aluminum."

Just then, an Indian and his wife approached the statue and burst out into loud prayers. The woman rubbed her husband's head and looked to Our Lady. Their dialect was unintelligible to me but plainly she told Our Lady where her husband's head hurt, and asked for a cure.

Descending the narrow stairway, Father pointed to decorations in the sanctuary. "That's the aluminum," he said.

"And the front of the main altar?" I asked.

"That too. In fact, everything that looks like silver is aluminum. The only silver is in the robes of the statue. Much of the silver has disappeared from the church. There was enough left to finance our restoration. Just enough."

Chiantla is 6,000 feet above sea level. Leaving it, we noticed a gentle but continuous rise in elevation. Before long, we were on a lookout at 10,000-feet altitude. Cold? It was below 40° and a high wind tore at our clothes.

The view was tremendous. Our eyes ranged over almost the whole western part of Guatemala, much of it blanketed in clouds just then. But far to the south, I could see my old friends above the rolling mists. Left to right, I ticked them off. "Pacaya, Agua, Fuego, Acatenango, Santa Maria and, just on the border of Mexico, Tacana. Some of those are a hundred miles from here!"

"Doesn't Santa Maria look innocent?" said Sister Jacinta Marie. "She seems no more dangerous than a blue cone pasted on the horizon. Yet Santa Maria is the most unpredictable volcano in Guatemala."

"How high are those volcanoes?" I asked, scarcely expecting a complete answer.

"That's easy!" Sister laughed. "The children have to learn it in the fourth grade. Tacana is 13,411 feet above sea level; Santa Maria, 12,434; Acatenango, 14,190; Fuego, 13,695; Agua, 12,382; and Pacaya, 8,415."

"What a memory you have!"

"Drilling the children every year is very good memory-training for the teacher!"

A group of ragged, freezing children had surrounded us, shivering in union with us. A boy's tummy, a small girl's thin shoulder, various parts here and there showed through the holes. The children pulled their tatters close around them; their dark eyes looked to us.

"Have we anything to give them?" I asked.

"Not money," Sister Francis Christine said. "It would probably go into drink for the first man who saw them with it. These children don't know what money is. Better that we share our lunch with them."

We gave them sandwiches and cookies. I thought they would wolf it all down, but they covered the food with a corner of their tatters and started down the hill.

"Where are they going?" I asked.

"Probably home to share it with mother, father or other children." She paused, reading my thoughts. "That's how we all feel. We want to clothe all the naked, feed all the hungry, teach all the ignorant, and do it all today. We come to know that one person can do only a little bit of the job; it will take generations to do it all. Frustrating? Yes, but it's also a great happiness to be able to play even a small part to help our brothers and sisters wherever we find them."

How right she was! This is the missioner's ache in the heart, that he can't accomplish everything before the children grow up.

We drove off on the 10,000-foot plateau I had noted on the map the night before. It was hard to believe the road was so high, for parallel rows of Cuchumatanes peaks reared their grey, jagged crests on either side. I had to twist my neck through the Jeep window to see the tops. It was worth a twisted neck. Fantastic shapes blossomed from the peaks; wide-open fan structures seemed to have been unfolded by some giant hand on the other side of the crags. There they were, tilted, ready for use should a warm day hit this chilling atmosphere. Boulders littered the mountainsides, pushed through the thin layer of soil, formed rock gardens with the red, violet, yellow and white alpine flowers that blanketed the slopes.

"What does it remind you of?" Sister Jacinta Marie asked.

Almost unconsciously, my lips formed, "Vermont!"

"Me, too," she agreed.

Of a sudden I called out. "Mateo! Stop a moment!"

He jerked the Jeep to a halt. I climbed out and walked over to a group of rocks. Yes, it was what I thought it was—glacier striation on the rock.

The other two had followed me. They had been students at Maryknoll and knew my fascination with rocks.

"Glacier?" one asked.

"I think so," I said slowly. "In fact, I'm positive. But here? Sixteen degrees north of the equator? Well, yes, it could be. Remember that geologic period, the Permian, some 200 to 300 million years ago, when glaciers formed south of the equator and moved south—away from the equator? I never read about glaciers forming north of the equator and moving north, but why couldn't they have done so? If, as some scientists think, the poles were once at the equator, so that the earth spun around with a polar ice cap over what are now equatorial countries, then certainly the glaciers melted and flowed both north and south. One of the indications that the world as we know it now really was topsy-turvy in bygone geologic eras is that breadfruit fossils have been found in Greenland. If there was tropical fruit in Greenland, probably there were glaciers in Guatemala."

"Sounds logical to me," said Sister Jacinta Marie. "Nothing but glaciers can make glacial striations over such a wide area."

"Other factors played a part, too."

"A transgression of the sea?" suggested Sister Francis Christine.

"Definitely," I said. "What else could have worn the surfaces so smooth? There is also a good deposit of limestone here which indicates that sea water was once over it all. Probably mines are in this area, too."

Yes, indeed, the Sisters assured me. Antimony, galena, copper and silver are mined, but due to the difficulty in getting heavy equipment up here, most of the diggings have been worked sporadically. However, children at school had said that nine mines were to be reopened. Their fathers hoped for steady work.

Ah! What about that half-fabled mercury mine which the Todos Santos Indians were said to have? Wasn't it right in this area? The fascinating tale was translated by Carlos Samayoa Chinchilla in *The Emerald Lizard*.

A son of a politician was up here in these mountains trying to find the Indians' mercury mine. "It is guarded by a sorcerer," he was told. Finally, he persuaded an Indian to guide him in, although the poor fellow was scared stiff. They found the sorcerer but he refused to give any leads as to where the mercury mine might be.

The young man decided to stay around anyway, and camped in the mountains. The first night, his guide was bitten on the arm—something that looked like a mountain lion bite although he saw no such animal. They moved camp, but the second night the Indian was nipped on the leg. On the third night, the poor man's face was badly mauled. That morning, the young man looked out from his camp and saw a large mountain lion maul a small badger. So he pulled out his gun and put a well-placed bullet between the mountain lion's shoulders. The animal leaped up and ran off, badly wounded.

Later that day, the man and his guide returned to the village. The Indians were standing around the sorcerer's hut in consternation because the old magic-man had been found that morning, killed by a shot in his back. It was the same caliber bullet which the young man had fired into the mountain lion. No one else in the area had a gun like his. He concluded that the sorcerer had turned into a mountain lion, had wreaked his vengeance on the poor guide and got his just desserts. Certainly the Indian suffered no more mysterious assaults. He concludes that the Todos Santos Indians certainly have a mercury mine and that they know how to refine the precious mineral, because they pay their bills, he says, "with a reed full of mercury."

Voodoo spells are believable up in these mountains where boulders of fantastic shapes conjure up weird images.

"Anyone could believe a sorcerer lives around the corner, up here," I shuddered.

"It's moon country, yes?" Sister Jacinta Marie agreed. "Look at those rocks over there. Makes me think of bears at Brookfield Zoo near Chicago."

"And the apes in a huddle beyond. They must have belonged to the local soccer team, yes?" I parried.

"Well, look who is joining us!" said Sister Francis Christine. "An Uncle Sam Boy, himself!"

Sure enough, there he was with two small editions of himself, all three dressed in red-and-white pants and blue jackets. Over all, they wore black "capixais" (wide jackets like ponchos) made of pure wool. The boys were encouraging a herd of sheep to get going but stopped when they saw us. Noting the camera, the elder Todos Santero stopped and posed for me. The two boys were shy; they hid behind their father, one behind each leg.

Back in the Jeep, Sister Francis Christine said, "Did you notice the make-up of that herd?"

"Many black sheep in it," I said.

"Farther up in the mountains, you will see black sheep only. In this area, part of the wool is made into blankets; up farther, all of it is woven into capixais. These are black, so it saves time and dye to raise black wool."

"Smart people, these Indians!" Mateo commented.

We could feel the pull of the Jeep as the altitude climbed steadily. Spreading trees twisted by winds into grotesque shapes dotted the rock-strewn slopes on either side of the road. Grey lichens on grey rocks rested on grey debris. Everywhere the rock-shapes were made only a little less unbelievable by the reds, yellows and violets of the tiny flowers at their base. Seemingly for no special reason, Mateo stopped.

"Here we are at the 12,000-foot place," he announced. "This is the highest spot on any public road in Central America."

No sign marked it, but I jumped out, camera in hand.

"Take it easy," called Sister Francis Christine. "You are not used to this altitude."

In less than a minute the wisdom of her words struck me. My head began to swim. By breathing deep I got enough oxygen to focus the camera and snap the shutter. That done, I stooped to pick up a sample of "reindeer moss" near the road. Then sky and mountains, people and trees began going around and around. I grabbed the Jeep and swung myself aboard, glad to get seated. Breathing deep and being quiet was the remedy.

Mateo drove on. The talk turned to sports. No deer that anyone had heard of, but hunting wild boar is popular. People from the lowlands soon become accustomed to the altitude if they take it gradually.

Maybe it was the altitude. Maybe it was the good company. Maybe delusions of grandeur set in. At any rate, a hunting lodge of vainglorious proportions began to rise in my imagination.

"Right on the top of a ledge in these mountains! A perfect replica of a Mayan hunting lodge. Large fireplaces, deep chairs, fascinating food. I can see the ad in the Sunday travel section of *The New York Times:* 'Forget the crowds. Lose yourself (and how!) in the amazing Cuchumatanes. No wait, no worry. Helicopter service daily to the top of our ledge.' That's a good name—'the Lodge on the Ledge.' We would organize trips to hunt wild boar. We'd give them a chance to see Goblins' Parlor, Devil's Ledge, Lovers' Cliff, Moon Sala and the Sorcerer's Mercury Mine."

Mateo brought me to earth. "Sounds fine!" he laughed. "You build it and keep it serviced and I'll run it for you."

A few minutes later we left the high plateau and wound around the mountains. Mateo was reassuring. "Don't worry as we turn these corners," he said. "Even though you cannot see a road ahead, nevertheless it will be there when we need it."

It was plain what he meant when we made a 270-degree turn on an ascending road. The Jeep seemed headed for a daredevil leap into space. "We just keep on turning as long as the road holds out," Mateo said.

On one of these climbs we saw ahead two huge black rocks, pointed and surely fifty feet tall, standing on either side of the road. Could they be the cores of eroded volcanic peaks?

"Maybe they are," Sister Jacinta Marie said. "There's a local legend about them.

"They are known as the Captsin Rocks. It seems that Cap was a prince and Tsin was a princess, royal lovers. They had no permission to marry and so ran away into the deep wilderness up here in the mountains. They thought the king's soldiers could not find them. As they stood here clasped in each other's arms, hoofbeats sounded. The soldiers were coming fast. They looked around for an escape. Below was the deep valley, that was all. So, together, they hurled themselves down.

"When the soldiers came up they dismounted and searched the underbrush inch by inch. They found neither Cap nor Tsin. They found only these two tall, dark rocks on either side of the narrow road."

A nice story, but not too logical. "But then, the rocks should be in the valley if Cap and Tsin threw themselves over the ledge."

"That's a scientist for you!" laughed Sister Francis Christine. "Don't be so logical."

"And this idea of taking up stations on either side of the road. I thought they wanted to stay together."

"Come, come!" she urged. "It *is* a good story, isn't it?"

"Yes," I agreed. "The names are interesting. Certainly not Indian. Tsin sounds more like the Chinese Tsien. Any connection?"

"Who knows?" We left it at that.

Certainly, it seems to me these two rocks are the cores of two volcanoes or it is the single core of one which had two lava ducts. They are almost identical with one I investigated in Hawaii. But why is only the hard core left? In Hawaii, the sea had eroded and washed away the softer outer parts. While water-worn rocks had indicated an inundation of the ocean some miles back on the plateau, there was no evidence of it here. Perhaps earthquakes had shaken off the volcano's outer shell. Perhaps . . . perhaps . . . another unanswered question!

The road began to describe a large horseshoe curve at least three miles in diameter. Down in the valley some 5,000 feet below, a silver river ribboned its way between fertile green fields. On a single-lane road, we could not stop, as we could not see far enough ahead to be warned of an oncoming car. Across the wide valley on the far side of the horseshoe was a waterfall—a tremendous thing, quite wide and with a great length of fall. It was impressive even seeing it three miles away.

"Called 'Magdalen's Hair,'" said Sister Jacinta Marie. A good name, for it looked like a wealth of silver tresses laid along the slope to dry.

Somehow it seemed a bit familiar. Oh, yes, it looked like the locale of a movie the Maryknoll Fathers had made about a Guatemaltecan boy. Sister Jacinta Marie assured me, they had filmed the movie on this very road. There wasn't room to set up a tripod on this road, it seemed to me. Why did they not set up their outdoor studio nearer Huehuetenango?

"It would have been more practical," Sister Francis Christine agreed, "but not so authentic. This is just the locale that Juan Mateo, the Indian lad, called home. It has Spanish moss and everything."

Few people seeing the movie will realize what the Maryknoll priests went through to make their film authentic. Just then, for me too, the methods of filming movies in mountainous areas were secondary in interest.

Mateo was honking his horn continuously, as he always did when rounding a curve on a single-lane road. I suppose he could see the road ahead, since he was in the driver's seat; nothing but empty space stretched ahead of me, sitting beside him. For once in my life, I did not want a clear view of the scenery. "Let me see road, just two feet or so of it, ahead of the car!" was my prayer.

"Don't worry," comforted Sister Francis Christine. "We'll make it. We always do."

And we did.

Four more hairpin curves brought us within sight of San Juan's colonial church. The town is built in a valley enclosed within towering mountains, covered with verdure. We stood on a height overlooking the town.

"What are those white, ghost-like figures floating around on the streets?" I asked.

Laughing with delight, Sister Jacinta Marie told me, "Those are the local ladies dressed in their long white huipiles. Most Indian women wear huipiles like blouses, but here in San Juan and in San Miguel, the huipiles reach to the ankles. And they wear white veils, also to the ankles."

In the town's main plaza, we walked over to the church. It is in the care of a Maryknoll pastor but he was away at the time substituting for the pastor of a much larger church in Soloma. On the church steps and inside the great doors, many Indians were burning incense and lighting candles on the floor.

The smell of burning wax, the flames of cheap candles, the murmur of prayers, the smoke-blackened walls were a blur until my eyes grew accustomed to it all.

"This is all pagan costumbre," whispered Sister Jacinta Marie.

"Don't miss the statues," Sister Francis Christine said.

Twenty-four statues poked out from the walls, all of them of carved wood, worth a great deal of money to an art collector perhaps, but a bugbear here in the church. To begin with, the Sisters said, no fewer than eighty statues greeted the Maryknoll pastor when he took over the parish. They left no room for the congregation. But the people are so attached to statues that all the energetic young pastor could do was to move most of them out to a room near the door. Idolatry has so twined its roots around the proper veneration of statues that the Indians become violent when anything happens to them. The parish priest cannot sell the images nor dismantle them. Gradually, at San Juan Ixcoy, Father is getting the statues out of the church, one at a time. It takes patience, and it can be dangerous.

In 1960, the pastor took action against a tall wooden cross on the other side of the plaza. Pagan ceremonies and superstitions kept a continual crowd there in a mockery of what should be a Christian symbol. The impetuous priest had the cross cut down. The Indians almost killed him, ran him out of the parish, rebuilt the cross and dated it 1960.

"Sometimes, one feels that Christianity isn't even skin deep here," Sister Francis Christine said, "but then one meets deeply religious people, too, and that upsets all our generalizations. For instance, Bernardo. Here he comes!"

A slight man, dressed in Western clothes that fitted him poorly, Bernardo was sacristan of the church. In Father's absence he played host. "We're making repairs. Let me show them to you," he offered. Picking our way through the mud to the rectory, Bernardo showed us the carpenter's shop he had set up. He was making doors, sawing and planing by hand, to be fitted into the new addition he hoped to put onto the rectory.

The ghosts I had seen afar off in San Juan's streets, I found out, preferred to remain ghosts. One of "the ladies in white" came walking down the street, billowing along like a ship under full sail. I grabbed my camera. Seeing this, she shifted into high gear and all I was able to shoot was her disappearing back. Word must have passed through town that a bad lady near the Jeep carried a loaded camera; nary a white-clad figure came near us. I saw them deliberately go around the far side of the plaza, and then double back to keep out of range.

"They fear you will take some of their personality away when you photograph them," Mateo explained. "San Juan Ixcoy is pretty far away from modern civilization; the people are still held fast in their superstitions. It must be hard for American priests in these isolated parishes."

The San Juan River was some 500 yards further on. This was the split-personality stream. It flowed quietly through an apple orchard in San Juan Ixcoy and disappeared into the mountains, only to roar out as a raging torrent twenty-five miles later at Aguacatan. What happened to it in the dark caves of the underground passage? Just another unanswered question!

Off in the Jeep again! Winding between green fields of maize, the road was pretty good. I became hopeful.

"Have we left the bad part of the road behind?" I asked.

Mateo looked at me with a pitying grin. "We haven't even come to the bad part of the road. It begins after we leave Villa Linda."

Sister Jacinta Marie interrupted. "Watch the left side for mounds," she directed. "I think there's a buried Mayan city here. I've found pottery and the mounds are most peculiar in shape."

A dust cloud coming along the road toward us slowed and re-solved into the form of another Jeep loaded with people. Both Jeeps stopped and everyone in the other one spilled out to tell Sister Fran-cis Christine the news. At the time, there was no nurse in San Mi-guel Acatan, for Sister Agnes Miriam had been called to Guatemala City on urgent business. Senor and Senora, their many children and the Jeep driver all spoke at once. Out of the babble, Sister learned that little Marta, a toddler, had been getting sicker and sicker the last few days. Large, angry, open sores broke out on her face, sides and back. Marta herself, wrapped in dirty cloths, confirmed their story with a loud squall. They would all go to Huehuetenango to find a doctor.

Under his breath, Mateo diagnosed the case. "Bad food. No cleanliness." Sister Francis Christine directed the family to the In-carnate Word Sisters' hospital, knowing they would get adequate care there.

The family piled back into the Jeep and drove off.

"It's a relief to know we won't meet a car on the bad road ahead," Sister Francis Christine sighed.

"How come?" I asked.

"There are only two cars on this road beyond Villa Linda. That one and Father Jensen's Jeep. Since Father is not coming out today, we will have the road to ourselves."

Nice to be able to tie up a traffic problem that easily!

We were upon the mounds in no time. Even with maize grow-ing on them, anyone could see they were not natural hills. "Let's dig up some pottery!" said Sister Jacinta Marie who has a streak of ar-chaeology in her.

"What about the maize?" I asked.

"Long ago, the farmer said we could dig all we liked in be-tween the rows and on the shady side where he has not planted. He trusts us not to damage his precious plants."

She ran to the top of the small mound; I pulled out pottery near the bottom of the heap on the supposition that it would be older.

"I think this is just the top of the mound," Sister said as I joined her. "There must be much more of it buried completely. Look over there. The mounds stretch along the river for nearly a mile. Beginning at the river's edge, terraces rise step by step until they meet in a mound. Throughout this whole area, we have found flat cut stones, the kind the Mayas used for temple walls. I think this was probably a large Mayan city."

"A city no one has as yet investigated!" I gasped.

"I'm pretty certain it is. Sister and I dig here sporadically as a hobby, so we haven't unearthed much. The terraces intrigue me. They may not be land terraces at all, but the levels of temples overgrown with vegetation. The maize plantings have kept the growth low enough to let us see the step structure. When we get to San Miguel, I'll show you the bowls we dug out of the ground here. I found only small pieces but they fit together like pieces of a jigsaw puzzle. Two bowls are decorated with a polychrome domino design, the like of which I have not seen in any museum."

What a place, this Guatemala! An archaeologist's paradise! Kaminaljuyu just started, Tikal almost half restored, Zaculeu finished and standing in its original beauty, and here, deep in the mountains, cities unknown except for a few terraces, some mounds and bits of pottery.

"I wonder how these mounds rank in age with the other sites?" I asked.

"Father Jensen has a friend who does carbon dating. Father sent him a piece of pottery and he dated it around 500 A.D. I don't know how he was able to do this with pottery but that is what he told me."

"And that piece must have been from the very top layer of what is here; you have not dug down under the surface. These mounds could have been begun before Christ, well before Christ."

"There are not many missioners in the world," laughed Sister Jacinta Marie, "complete with their own private archaeological site for recreation."

I wanted to start on the mounds immediately. What fun to map the surface, hire a crew to carefully take off the growing layer, label every piece of pottery and catalogue it as it was unearthed, possibly find a tomb. . . . My dreams gave way to reality. I was not in

Guatemala as an archaeologist but as a substitute teacher. I had no money, no crew, no supplies. All I could do was taste what the thrill might be and then pass on.

"Better start if you want to avoid the rains!" announced Mateo. So the three of us piled back into the Jeep.

The road twisted and turned between, above, over and around mountains all the way to Villa Linda. A Canadian mining company had operated a galena mine here and at San Rafael, not far away. The company had chiseled out of the mountains the road we had ridden from Huehuetenango, so that their trucks could transport the ore. Did all the trucks make it? How many rolled over the mountainside?

At any rate, the mine had been closed down. The Indians still live in both villages, but they have no work. Villa Linda, the once "pretty village," now stood paintless, roofless, windowless and tottering on its foundations. A crowd of children in tatters ran out to the Jeep to greet the two Sisters. Every week they make the dangerous trip from San Miguel to teach these youngsters.

Villa Linda is one of the fourteen "aldeas," or out-stations, of the San Miguel parish. Each morning, one of the two priests stationed at San Miguel says Mass at one of these aldeas; one of them also says an evening Mass at San Miguel each day. It is exhausting travel for the priests, as all the roads and footpaths are dangerous.

Both priests and Sisters usually travel by horse. Part of the year a Jeep can be used but the horse is more reliable, Sister Francis Christine explained.

I picked up a piece of pure crystalline galena from the roadside. "This ore is rich," I noted. "It resembles the ore mined at Galena, Illinois. No wonder it was worth while building that road! Is this one of the mines to be reopened?"

"I'm not certain," Sister said. "I think the children mean nine mines closer to Huehue. If they pan out . . . maybe! If not, Villa Linda will remain a ghost town."

We hurried back into the Jeep, still anxious to beat those afternoon rains. The galena company's road was no more. In fact, every semblance of a road was gone. We were bumping over a grassy meadow toward a shed.

"This is A Chi," Sister Francis Christine said. "We pick up horses when needed for San Miguel. The road to the left goes to Rosario where we get horses for Jacaltenango."

"Rosario? I couldn't find it on the map."

"Oh, it's not a town! We named it Rosario because we say the rosary while we make connections."

No wonder I could not find it on any map! We continued bumping along in the Jeep.

"Is this a road?" I asked.

"Believe it or not," said Sister, "it's the start of the worst road in these bad parts. Just now, field and road are blended, but that will not last long."

"No, it will be all road," grinned Mateo.

Sure enough, the field fell away and we began to climb a red, muddy strip a few inches wider than the Jeep. We hugged the mountainside as we jolted along. "Just in case the outer side gives way," Mateo explained.

He held the wheel tightly; every muscle tensed to the task at hand—to deliver himself and us safely.

At every foot of the road, it seemed, men were working on repairs. They dragged stones from the overhang to fill in ruts left by yesterday's rain. They braced the sides and dug little trenches to drain the soggy clay. Mateo honked incessantly as we rounded ascending curves and the road crews flattened themselves against the mountainside to give us room.

Occasionally, we met a train of pack mules on its way to market in Huehue. The mules stood on the very edge of the cliff looking out into the distance while their drivers held the reins tightly lest they panic. Our Jeep almost tunneled into the mountain to pass the beasts. Every shift of gears, every application of the brakes was achieved with slow precision. We must not skid here. There was no room. The two Sisters behind were quiet. Praying, I thought. I, too, found myself repeating over and over, "Our Lady of the Highway, protect us!" Highway! The incongruity of it made me chuckle.

At the bottom of a slight decline, we stopped as a work crew stepped aside. Mateo refused to go on until some of the stones recently put into the rut ahead were removed. The boulders were too big; they could rip the gas tank off. Before we could start, another pack train approached. Mateo then waited while the mules squeezed past us on the mountainside. The driver smiled and called a clear "Gracias!" It was one less hazard for him.

"We're coming to those no-road-ahead turns," Mateo announced. Going at the risky speed of six miles an hour, keeping our wheels in the deep ruts for balance, we went up and over and around the right curves. I, on the mountainside, watched the high cliffs go by, and tried not to think of Mateo's side and the deep drop. "Dear Lord," I prayed. "Please, no skids." A skid on that wet clay could send us only one place—over the side.

Then, passing over a tottering bridge, just forty awesome minutes after we had left Villa Linda, we hit cobblestone streets.

"Welcome to San Miguel!" said Sister Francis Christine.

As we bounced and jolted along, faces appeared at every window, hands waved, children ran to the road and formed a joyous escort for the two returning Madres. They eyed me over from head to toe but, so long as I came with them, they accepted me on the spot. At exactly 1:30, we turned in at the school gate. Five hours to travel fifty miles!

I was amazed at the size of the school and the bustling activity around us. Classes would take them in at 2:00; the children spent their noon recess milling around in welcome.

"The two-story building ahead of us contains classrooms," Sister Francis Christine pointed out. "This building to the left has classrooms on the first floor and the convent on the second. The church and rectory are on the right; they have entrances on the street."

At the convent door, Maria met us. "She's a very good cook," Sister Francis Christine said. "She comes from a hut with a dirt floor and, of course, knew no English or Spanish but only her Indian dialect. I had to use an interpreter to tell her how to prepare our meals. Now she sets up the table, serves and cooks like a pro."

Maria, like the rest of the people in this area, does not have a surname. Her mother did not take her husband's name at marriage for he also had no surname. Maria Jose, the girl, remained Maria Jose as a married woman.

A few names are used over and over again with the same family. Two or more children may have the same name. In the long run, it doesn't matter very much, because on an average not more than two out of ten children survive to adulthood. Sister Jacinta Marie gave me an idea of how names are given.

"Suppose Juan Pablo marries Maria Jose. Their first boy reverses his father's name; he is Pablo Juan. The first girl combines her parents' first names; she is Maria Juan. The second boy repeats his father's name, Juan Pablo. The second girl will double up on her father's name, making it Juana Juan. There is no common surname throughout the family."

"What do you do on school records for the Ministerio of Education?" I asked, having puzzled over names like Ann Kelly and Anne Kelley in my time.

"It's very difficult, of course. We are expected to list the children alphabetically, but we have so many Maria Juans and Maria Joses and Juan Pablos that such a listing means nothing. We have tried to introduce different names, just to pry them loose from the dozen they use over and over again. Recently, the governor was here," Sister went on. "He made a good suggestion. Why not combine the last names of both parents into a two-word surname? Thus in the family I spoke of the children would be:

Pablo Pablo Jose
Maria Pablo Jose
Juan Pablo Jose
Juana Pablo Jose

"In time, these surnames will not be any stranger than English ones like Howard or James or Williams or the hyphenated British ones like Armstrong-Jones."

"Right!" I agreed. "After all, Lopez means son of Lope, Gomez is son of Gome, Masterson means son of the Master, and Johnson is the son of John. We're used to these by now. But why doesn't Juan Pablo adopt some Spanish surname like Gonzales or Lopez? Would he have to register it?"

"Yes—and pay seventy quetzales [$70]. He could never get that much money!" Sister said, "We'll keep on with the governor's system. It has made our records much easier."

I must say this: Maria, with or without a surname, was a magnificent cook. She set out chicken soup, fried chicken, mashed potatoes, beans, rolls and coffee. Sister Francis Christine seemed puzzled at the lavish meal at first, then comprehension dawned.

"Happy birthday, Maria!" she cried. "Happy birthday, and thanks for this wonderful dinner!"

It's the custom in San Miguel to celebrate one's birthday by making a feast for a friend. Maria had made the feast for us. No doubt she bought the chicken with her own money.

After dinner Maria posed for me. The long white huipile embroidered around the neck would have been enough, but she ran home to get a blue veil for her head and yards of costume jewelry. Her liquid eyes, smooth brown skin, rounded cheeks, black hair—what a lovely young girl she was!

Mateo left after dinner. He would be back the next day and pick me up for the return to Huehue.

Without more ado, we went, first, to the classrooms. The children, unable to afford uniforms, sat on stiff wooden benches in tattered, none-too-clean clothing, bare feet resting on the floor. A definite odor pervaded the atmosphere.

"Why that odor?" I asked, once outside the door.

"I wish I knew!" was the answer. "The pueblo has plenty of free water. Our people use it for laundry, washing their clothes once a week, but they don't like bathing. They prefer steam baths."

Steam baths? All of a sudden I remembered the dark, low little huts in San Miguel and also in Huehuetenango. They were fantastically small, with windows away down low in the walls. In them, water is thrown over heated stones, and the bather could well-nigh cook in the steam. I later saw the same custom in ancient Chichen Itza, and, even in modern America, our Indians have similar "ceremonial cleansings."

"What about sanitary facilities?" I asked.

"They have no sewerage system," Sister said. "Come, let me show you something!"

We crossed the main cobblestoned road to the school playground, as Sister explained Operation Outhouse. In a shed, we found cement toilet seats, rather hefty things, being constructed. Sister Jacinta Marie, it seems, has managed to interest Sanidad, the government health department, in the situation at San Miguel. From it she got wire for construction frames and cement for the seats. The people carried the sand a mile uphill from the river bank. Small stones came along the same route. Sanidad also supplied instructions for digging the pit, installing the seat and making a shed for privacy.

The men of San Miguel became enthusiastic. Most of them worked with such zeal that they dug pits deeper than required. In the school yard are the very first toilets this pueblo ever had. Father Edward Moore, M.M., put them in as a pilot project; the idea caught fire and is now blazing hygienically over the whole area. The outhouse, archaic as may be, is the latest craze here!

But toilets were not the only cement constructions in the shed. Even bulkier things were behind a table.

They were stoves, another of Father's ideas. He thinks homes cannot be cleaned up until people stop cooking over wood fires on the bare floor. Twice a week the Sisters serve a lunch to the children, made possible by food from the United States. The mothers take turns coming here to cook the food. Oh, wily scheme! Once they cook on the new cement stoves, they go home and tell their husbands they just have to have one.

I saw another of Father Moore's projects as we walked across the playground. It had once been a meandering stream, but Father deepened it at one spot and confined the stream. Then he filled in the area, made a bridge over the gurgling stream and, lo, the school had room for a playground.

In my esteem, the Sisters were growing ten feet tall. They shot up another foot when I saw their idea for sanitary dish-washing. A pretty wooden frame painted pink held two shining pans—no, they weren't metal pans but two halves of a five-gallon oil can, cut lengthwise. One was for washing dishes from the noon lunch; the other was for rinsing them. It was a very neat outfit; soon no bride in her right mind would consider setting up housekeeping without a Maryknoll double dishpan.

Across the playground was the clinic. Although Sister Agnes Miriam was away, Juana, one of the girls she has trained, took care of routine medical work. It did not seem so routine to me. She had two intravenous injections going, gave vitamin shots where needed and bandaged wounds. In the line outside the clinic sat a mother whose undernourished child was almost covered with draining sores.

In one of the two treatment rooms inside, a woman lay dying. An intravenous injection was relieving her last hours, but she had been beyond help when her husband carried her in. Now, after the long trek over the mountains, he sat dumbly beside her bed, holding her hand. Sister Francis Christine said a few words of comfort to him and adjusted the intravenous jar a bit. She asked Pablo to call Father. It was too late to hear her confession but the woman would not die without anointing.

In the storage room were crates of medicines, vitamins and food for the poor. Doctors and drug companies in the States are generous in sending sample medicines to Maryknoll Sisters in New York who crate them for the missions. Catholic Relief Services operated by the bishops of America pay for transporting the medicines to those who need it. Food had come from Care and Caritas, also.

"If only people in the States could see the good their donations are doing!" I exclaimed. "Often they have a vague idea of helping someone, but they can't realize that even a small donation can mean life or death for some poor person."

Sister agreed. "Every case that comes to us here is critical. If we have medicines to help, the person usually lives. If not, the person almost certainly dies. It's as urgent as that. You never ask yourself whether or not you are needed here. You just wish you were twins or triplets."

Preventive care is even more important although not so dramatic. Lessons start in first grade. During the first hours of the school day, each class comes out to the fountains in turn and each child cleans his teeth. One of the big girls puts the toothpaste on the brush and the child goes over to the fountain for a good cleaning job. The brushes are kept on special hooks in a clean place. On his way back to his room, each child gets a vitamin pill which he takes on the spot.

Sister Agnes Miriam gives pre-natal instructions to pregnant women. Some girls she has trained for it help her with this as well as with post-natal care. There is no doctor in San Miguel Acatan, so Sister serves as midwife, too. Sister Francis Christine, although not a nurse, knows enough to help out whenever needed.

Both she and Sister Jacinta Marie preach cleanliness and avoidance of infection, in season and out. Conditions have improved a good deal in San Miguel Acatan, but they are still a long way from ideal.

As Sister finished, an old woman came up with a friendly smile.

"How are you feeling now, Rosa?" Sister inquired.

"Much better, Madre. Thanks for taking care of me. I brought you this little gift." And Rosa took her hand from behind her back to hold out a live rooster, hanging head-down and most uncomfortable.

"But Rosa," Sister protested, "you should use this for your family. You really can't spare it."

"Don't worry, Madre. God will provide for us," Rosa insisted. "It is only right to show gratitude."

Reluctantly, Sister took the rooster. With a few startled squawks, his feet were shifted from Rosa's hand to Sister's. "Poor Rosa!" Sister said as we watched the old woman go down the street with great satisfaction. "It kills me to take this from her; she has practically nothing. But gratitude means more to her than this chicken."

Father Daniel Jensen, M.M., came to the convent after supper. A young Maryknoll Father with a zest for life, he is seeking new methods to aid his people. Together, we examined Sister Jacinta Marie's little museum.

The only thing "little" about it is the space it occupies. She has a collection of local woods, cut to show the longitudinal and transverse graining, together with bark and leaves. She has gathered many local minerals and rocks: azurite, malachite, cuprite, native copper, galena, calite, quartz, diorite, basalt, shale, limestone and some stalactites. The children, knowing Sister is interested, bring many specimens to her. Then she questions them as to where they found them. Soon she should know most of the mineral occurrences in the area.

"Here are the bowls," she announced. I dropped all else to inspect them. She has two almost completed. On one the domino design is outside and on the other it is inside. With painstaking work she has fitted together small pieces for the most part. Since that night, I have looked for that domino design in the Museum in Guatemala City, in Mexico City, in Merida, in illustrated pamphlets on Mayan art, in books, but I have not been able to locate anything like what Sister has. I photographed the specimens in color next morning so I would remember the design exactly as it is.

Just before he left that night, Father made an odd request—at least it sounded odd to me. "Will you turn off the electricity, Sister?" he asked. "You'll be up later than I tonight; you'll have plenty to talk about."

Sister Jacinta Marie explained. "The mission has its own dynamo here; there is no electricity in the pueblo. The last one up turns it off. Father usually does it for he's a night owl and we're larks."

We spent three delicious hours then, talking about people we had known at Maryknoll just a few years past; now they were scattered all over Asia, Africa, Latin America and in the less-settled places of the States. Some were speaking Chinese, Japanese, Filipino dialects, African tribal languages, Palauan, Marshallese and—in large numbers—Spanish. In a large mission order, this is one of the compensations. You can go to the ends of the earth, meet two other women dressed like you and spend hours recalling gay times and sad times, and enjoying the memories of both.

We also did a little work. Sister Jacinta Marie and I bent our minds to the task of identifying her specimens. Combining what I know from the books, with what she knew from on-the-spot observation, we managed to pin down the genus and species of everything she had collected. The rocks were classified and labeled; the pottery was put in order.

Eventually in the wee small hours, Sister Francis Christine turned off the motor and by flashlight we made our way upstairs. "Wait until you see the gadget in our rooms we undress by!" were Sister's last words.

On the windowsill in my room was a small box about six inches square, containing flashlight batteries. A flashlight bulb was screwed into a socket in front. It actually gave enough light to see around the room.

It was a pleasant surprise, next morning, to see so many people, men and women, at the big colonial church for Mass. "They're here every day," the Sisters said. "Since there is no work for them they have no schedule to meet."

At breakfast, Maria solemnly served poached eggs. "You rate!" Sister Francis Christine declared. "Maria thinks you're high-class company."

"How so?" I asked.

"She has borrowed Father's egg poacher for your breakfast. This is rare—only when notables visit." At this, I too joined in the laugh!

But Maria wasn't the only deluded soul who thought I was notable company. The children coming to school are supposed to bring pieces of wood, contributions of fuel needed to cook their lunch. Most of them also brought flowers for me. It gave me a quickie view of most of the flora in that region—single and double fuchsia, roses of tremendous size and rare colors, calla lilies, gladioli, dahlias, white and yellow ginger and various types of *Bromeliaceae,* which add vivid yellows, oranges and reds to the trees upon which they sponge a living. One little girl brought me a tremendous group of large white-and-red-striped lilies, all on one stem. Not knowing the specie, I photographed them for later identification. They reminded me of amaryllis, but were definitely lilies.

These are the Mam Indians, I learned from the Sisters. They

speak the Canojobal dialect. Their vocabulary is limited to what is within their experience. It is therefore a surprise to find that they have a word for "elephant."

"If I remember correctly," I told them, "both elephants and camels were in the United States before that last ice age. Both migrated southward, passing through Guatemala. That would have been some 25,000 years ago. Do you suppose the Mam Indians have been here all that time?"

Again, who knows? I recalled, however, what Senor Espinoza had said about a very old, pre-ceramic civilization at Kaminaljuyu. He dated it tentatively at 15,000 years ago. Maybe it's even older than that. Maybe, too, this civilization was all over Guatemala, all over Central America, all over America.

"Weren't 25,000-year-old campsites found on the banks of the Mississippi?" Sister Jacinta asked.

Again we came to another question mark—one that cannot be turned into a period today.

Mateo was honking for me at 2:00 P.M. In the Jeep with him were a Peace Corps man who had been helping Sister Rose Cordis in the Jacaltenango Hospital, and an Indian. Tons of baggage, it seemed, filled the back seat with the Indian. The Peace Corps man and I crowded in front with Mateo. Three men—and one Sister. Turning to Father Jensen, I said,

"I know one Sister doesn't go out with one man, nor do two Sisters go out with two men. But what about one Sister and three men?"

"I never heard the answer to that," he said, laughing. "However, in case of doubt, they told us in the seminary, genuflect. Not on the barranca side, however!"

It was a jovial send-off to the usual hazardous trip. The ruts that had held us steady yesterday were now filled with loose dirt and stones. We jolted and tipped dizzily on the narrow road. We lurched along like a drunken sailor trying to walk on the tops of the waves. Even after reaching Villa Linda where I thought the worst would be over, the road seemed just as bad, probably because I could never for a minute forget the drop at my side. Yesterday I had been reassured by the mountain wall rising on my side; today, I had nothing but the cliff beside me—a cliff we could roll over without a moment's warning.

As we approached Huehuetenango, a beautiful 180° rainbow

arched the sky. Entering the rain area, we crept along cautiously to avoid the slightest skid. Once we stopped at the very brink of the drop to permit a bus to pass. I did not breathe for ten full minutes, it seemed.

At one time, I thought nothing could compare with the mountains and skies of Hawaii. But now I'm not so sure. Guatemala is beautiful country, breathtaking in its rugged glory. But it is hostile; you pay for everything you get from it. The mountains demand a price from the traveler and the farmer, a price of sweat, blood and even life at times. More and more, I admire the Indians who live with it and live off it. Fighting for everything they take from the land, they live poorly, but they live. Only a tremendous people could do it.

MAYAN CALENDAR

Brace yourself, dear reader; you are in for an arduous journey. Not up mountains, across blistering deserts, through tangled jungles. You—if you stick with me through this chapter—will go back, back, back in time to millions of years ago. And we'll not do a hop, skip and jump by centuries nor even years. Rather we will do what the old Mayas did—painstakingly count days in the millions and billions. It's rather like heaping up a beach by carefully putting aside grains of sand.

In other words, you are warned. If you don't like hard work, skip this chapter.

In tracing the evolution of any civilization, we find a series of steps more or less common to all. Of course, one cannot say positively that such and such a thing happened in each specific case, but there are reasonable conclusions. For instance, when the social group consisted only of a small family, there might be little need for writing. Oral communication would suffice. Usually the family would be nomadic, hunting for food on the hoof.

Gradually, a clan would develop. If Big John was to get home from the chase before Little John, it might be convenient to tell him to start the camp fire. Or to let him know where Big John had gone. Or to warn him to go into hiding because the neighbors were getting ugly. So a message would be left on the sand in front of the cave's entrance. It would be a simple message, probably merely an outline of a fire with an animal cooking over it or under it. Or a footprint going off in a certain direction; or a warrior and spear. There could be no adjectives or adverbs—just the essential nouns. This is a pictograph, a simple drawing.

Later, more clans unite; the group becomes bigger. They feel need for a more permanent means of communication. A wedding is to be celebrated; the head clansman wants to invite all his relatives to the feast. But some live a long way off. A runner is to carry the message to them, so it must be written on something light—deerskin or papyrus or tree bark.

Then the group changes from hunting to agriculture. They can live in permanent homes, put up monuments and buildings. They discover stone as a medium. It was too heavy when they were constantly on the hunting trail, but now they like the durability of stone. They carve it, paint it and write on it. At first the writing is pictographic. Then, ideographic, combining a number of pictographs into a single symbol which stands for an idea. Eventually, the symbols no longer stand for ideas but for sounds, and the sounds are put together to form words. A phonetic alphabet has come into being.

The moment this happens is critical for the civilization. Language now becomes a tool for prose, poetry, history and study. It can be shaded and toned to the writer's whim.

Our first records of the Mayan people find them at this seemingly critical phase. Bishop Diego de Landa, who came with the Spanish conquerors, felt certain he discerned the phonetic element in their writings.

Where did the Indians come from? Most evidence points to a route from Asia across the Bering Strait and stretching south through both continents. The theory is that some stayed in Canada, some in the United States, others in Central America and the rest pressed forward to South America. There is evidence that they were in Tierra del Fuego at least 8,000 years ago. The Mayas spread through southern Mexico, Yucatan, Guatemala, Honduras and El Salvador.

They had Oriental blood, but that alone did not make them what they were. Their carvings, both in wood and stone, their pottery and designs remind one of Egypt, Greece, Assyria, and Japan and China as well. They were a virile people, ingenious, hardy, with high morals and great abstract intelligence.

They were self-made. They learned from observation and reasoning. Indeed in the world of their time, there were no teachers— even if they could have gotten in touch with them, who could have taught them much in either astronomy or mathematics. The Chinese had not yet devised numerical place value nor the zero symbol and they are credited with being first in that accomplishment.

Just when this great Indian migration occurred is not known. Possibly before the last glacial period, some 25,000 years ago. In both California and South Carolina, artifacts have been dated centuries before. They belong to "the Sweetwater Man," so named from the river in California beside which the first of these artifacts were found. The question archaeologists ask is: Was the Sweetwater Man one of the migrating Indians, or was he in California and South Carolina already when the Indian migrations rolled so majestically from north to south on our hemisphere? And the campfire sites, 25,000 years old, built on the banks of the Mississippi—did the migrating Indians build them? Or were other people already in this country when they passed southward?

Whenever it was the Mayas came to Central America, they were still a nomadic people. Some 11,000 years ago they were in the valley of Mexico hunting mammoths which had been forced southward by the great glaciers. Near San Miguel Acatan, a skeleton of an "elephant" was found recently, associated with human artifacts. Sister Jacinta Marie was not able to view it so she does not know if it was mammoth or mastodon. It might have been either. A mastodon, dated by geological strata at 30,000 years ago, has been found in Mexico near Puebla. Archaeologists say that there is practically no skeletal difference between the Indians who hunted the large hairy beasts then, and those whom the Spanish conquered in the sixteenth century.

Hunting through debris in the Tamaulipas caves in northeastern Mexico, scientists have traced the Indian as he changed from a hunter into a farmer. On the caves' lowest level is charred evidence of fire, wild plants and animal bones—food for a nomadic hunter. Above this are plant seeds and fibers of squash and beans. Next above, they found corncobs, carbon dated at 4000 B.C., plus or minus a couple of hundred years. Just as European agriculture developed around wheat, so American civilization depended upon maize. Where did maize come from? It may have been a sport resulting from fertilization of wild grasses. Who was the first Maya to eat it? Probably we will never know, but he was either a genius, a venturesome soul or someone so hungry he'd try anything.

Each individual seed was planted with a pointed stick in the few inches of soil which adhere to the sheer sides of towering mountains. While maize was developing, another ancient food, manioc or cassava (*Manihot esculenta*), was also taking hold in Central America. Its tuberous starchy roots, something like a sweet potato, substituted for the bread these Americans never knew.

In her *Gardens of Hawaii,* Mary C. Neal tells a Peruvian myth about these two age-old foods. It seems that a descendant of the sun created man and woman. When the man died, the sun felt sorry for the lonely woman and sent her a son. Later, the creator of the original man and woman killed the son. From his teeth grew maize and from his ribs grew the long roots of the manioc. Today, we still eat manioc and maize—tapioca and sweet corn.

Once assured of a continuing food supply, the Mayas settled into more or less permanent living sites. I say "more or less" because all through Mayan history they often reverted to their nomadic habits. They would pick up bag and baggage, wives and children, and leave stone cities which had been built with extraordinary labor and skill, to settle in untamed jungle and start all over again.

But farmers need to know the seasons, the timing of a year, when to plant and when to reap. Astronomy, mathematics and, above all, correct calendar are vital. Where could they learn these things? They worked it out, inch by inch, from observation and experience. They had no telescopes; Copernicus and Galileo would not be born for forty centuries. The Mayas could not wait. These "Greeks of the New World" arrived at a calendar and chronology excelled by none of their contemporaries in the ancient world nor by any civilization up to the present time. Their calendar is more accurate than our own as they approach closer to the sidereal year than we do.

Sidereal year	365.242,198 days
Gregorian year	365.242,500 days
Mayan year	365.242,129 days

They also used a calendar based on Venus. Whether or not they knew the full truth that Venus orbits the sun thirteen times while the earth goes around it eight times, or if they were aware that Venus is on an inner orbit and so passes between earth and sun five times for every eight earth orbits, I cannot say. But I do know that they used the results of such knowledge to determine that five apparent or synodical revolutions of Venus are equivalent to 2,920 earth days. Upon this knowledge, they built their Venus calendar.

Furthermore they had a lunar calendar, astounding since it is

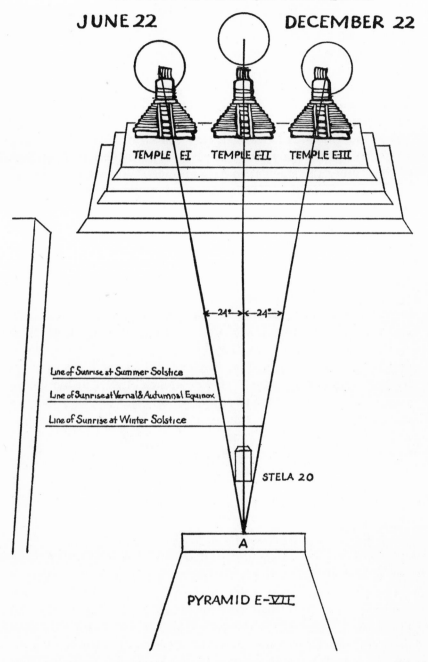

MARCH 21 AND SEPTEMBER 23

JUNE 22   DECEMBER 22

TEMPLE E-I   TEMPLE E-II   TEMPLE E-III

←—24°—→←—24°—→

Line of Sunrise at Summer Solstice

Line of Sunrise at Vernal & Autumnal Equinox

Line of Sunrise at Winter Solstice

STELA 20

A

PYRAMID E-VII

Observatories were constructed at temple sites by placing temples in a sighting line for the equinoxes and soltices. The plan above is the one used at Uaxactun, Guatemala (Peten State).

based upon the moon's apparent revolutions around the earth. The Mayas figured out that since the moon revolves around the earth while the earth is circling the sun, it must go just a bit further than if the earth were stationary while the moon swung around it. The lunation, calculated at 29 days, 14 hours, 44 minutes and 2.87 seconds, is slightly more than 29½ days. Twelve lunations amount to a little more than 354 days, 11 days short of the true year. The Greek Meton, Athenian astronomer in the fifth century b.c., arrived at the Metonic Cycle, an equation of 19 tropical years, 235 lunations or 6,940 days. Today, taking a lunation as 29 days 12 hours 44 minutes 2.8 seconds, 235 lunations total 6,939 days 14 hours 15 minutes and 58 seconds, so historians have reason for calling it a remarkable discovery by the Greeks. Yet the Mayas, by another route, had arrived at the same equation centuries earlier. In fact it was "built in" their calendar. One of the time periods they used was the katun, 7,200 days long. The tzolkin consisted of 260 days. One katun minus one tzolkin gave 6,940 days and this they found to be equivalent to 235 lunations.

In the Dresden Codex—one of three written Mayan records taken to Europe—there is evidence that the Mayas had a lunar calendar covering 505 lunations or thirty-three years. The calendar is divided into groups of five lunations (148 days) and groups of six lunations (177 or 178 days). This difference in days in the groups was possibly their attempt to adjust the calendar to events they observed, such as an eclipse at the end of five lunations or of six. It is rather simple to predict a lunar eclipse by geometry, knowing that it can occur only at full moon, when the sun is at a node or not over 12° 15' from a node (a point coincidental with the moon's orbit) but we have no evidence the Mayas calculated with geometry although we would suspect they had knowledge of it from the construction of their temples.

Eclipses do not follow the neat path the Mayas thought they did. Some years there are none; other years there are three. For instance, in 1962, there was a lunar eclipse on Feb. 19, 1962, another on July 17, 1962 (148 days) and a third on August 15, 1962 (29 days). However, the Mayas based their lunar calendar on lunations which they observed, and they calculated 505 lunations at 11,960 days. They then discovered (perhaps) that this number is exactly divisible by tzolkin (260 days) so they called it (the 11,960 day period) a cycle. Today with modern computations we say that 505 lunar revolutions amount to 11,959.888 days, so the Mayas were off .112 of a day. Had they written their lunar calendar for three hundred years, they would have been just one day in error. But they would have known they were in error and devised some means of correcting it.

Instead of being terrified over eclipses as some of the people of the Middle Ages were, they predicted them. They studied the heliacal rising and setting of Venus; that is, the first appearance of Venus after it had been in conjunction with the sun. They knew the true length of the tropical year a thousand years before the European world did.

Mayan writing has not been perfectly decoded. But so far as we can tell, they did not write fractions. This does not mean that they did not use fractions. Probably they worked them out mentally or on perishable material, but work them out they did. Just as we do, they added an extra day every four years to make a leap year. For longer periods, this would not do; it would upset the correlation with their three other calendars. So every 1,507 years, they added another year, making the period 1,508 years. They carried their correction along for 1,507 years before applying it. Imagine our remembering from the year 460 to 1967 to carry forward a correction, and then making that year 1968! This proves that the Mayan astronomers knew the sidereal (star) year as well as we do. The sidereal year is 365.242198 days. If we multiply its excess over the 365-day year—that is, .242198 by 1507—we arrive at 364.992386. The Mayas were short .0086 days on their adjustment. Using our calendar with a year length of 365.2425 days, we would be .4475 in error. As it is, even though we add a leap day every four years, we pile up .03 day shortage every four years, or 11.3 days every 1,507 years. This is partially corrected by not adding a day in the even-century years—1400, 1600, 1800, etc.

In calculating, the Mayas employed two sets of numerals. The first used dots for one's, dashes for five's and a symbol for zero. Three dashes with two dots meant seventeen. How the Mayas arrived at a zero we don't know.

They were able to calculate the period of time by abstract mathematics and abstract astronomy. In fact, they were using the modern arithmetic we are so proud of today at least five centuries before the Hindus began to use "arabic" notation. Using a vigesimal base (a base of twenty) they were able to proceed faster than had they adopted a base of sixty (the base we use in angles and time) which the Babylonians used. What tremendous spacemen these Mayas would have been. Maybe that is where they came from— from a super-civilization on some other planet.

The other set of numerals were glyphs of heads. While the

heads might differ with the artistic pleasure of the artist or develop into whole figures if the occasion was especially festive, there was always a certain feature associated with the glyph for each numeral.

0	1	2	3	4
5	6	7	8	9
10	11	12	13	14
15	16	17	18	19

A hand over the lower jaw was always "O." A forehead ornament of two or three pieces, an almond eye and a curl was "1." "2" always had a hand, open or closed, above it. A banded hat, a T-shaped ornament on the cheek or earplug meant "3." "4" was distinguished by filed teeth and a quadrangular, squinting eye; "5" by an old god wearing a headdress; "6" by an ax on the eye; "7" by a scroll under the eye and over the nose; "8" by grains of corn and a spiral out from the forehead; "9" by a number of dots on the chin; "10" by a fleshless jawbone; "11" by a query mark on the face; "12" by a projecting lower lip and a sky glyph as headdress; "13" either a bird-headed animal or the glyph for 3 with the fleshless jawbone of 10. From "14" to "19," the numerals are shown by adding the sign of ten, the jawbone, to 4, 5, 6, etc.

As we consider the glyphs, we are aware that the Mayan people were no longer using either pictographs or ideographs. Were they using a phonetic language? Or were they using associative symbols as we do? The fact that we allow "5" to stand for five is mere association and has no logical reality.

The astounding Mayas also discovered the value of place location of numerals, and used it centuries before Christ, and probably before that. We are so used to it that we never dream what genius it took to discover it. When we write the date 1776 A.D., we know the "1" stands for a thousand, the first "7" for 700, the second "7" for 70 and the "6" for six units. Added together we have the value of 1,776 years since the date of Christ's birth—a date we now know is erroneous.

Our numerical system is based on ten. Each figure to the left is multiplied by the next highest power of ten. For instance: 17,655 means

1 times	10,000	10,000
7 times	1,000	7,000
6 times	100	600
5 times	10	50
5 times	1	5
		17,655

We could express the relationship of the places as: ten units equal a ten, ten tens equal a hundred, ten hundreds equal a thousand, etc. The Mayas used a base of twenty, not ten, and they placed their numerals in a vertical sequence instead of horizontal. The following is a list of the names they used for the places, together with the value in our numeration.

Mathematical Calculations

20 Alau equal	1 Hablat	1,280,000,000
20 Kinchil "	1 Alau	64,000,000
20 Kabal "	1 Kinchil	3,200,000
20 Pic "	1 Kabal	160,000
20 Bak "	1 Pic	8,000
20 Kal "	1 Bak	400
20 Hun "	1 Kal	20
	1 Hun	1

Based on a twenty-day month, the Mayan dates make an interesting set of designs on any of their stelae.

For counting time, the hun became the kin (meaning "sun" or "day"), the kal changed to uinal ("month") and bak was called "tun." Furthermore, not 20 uinals made a tun, but eighteen. This was done to bring it in line with the 360-day calendar. By another adjustment they arrived at the 365 day year.

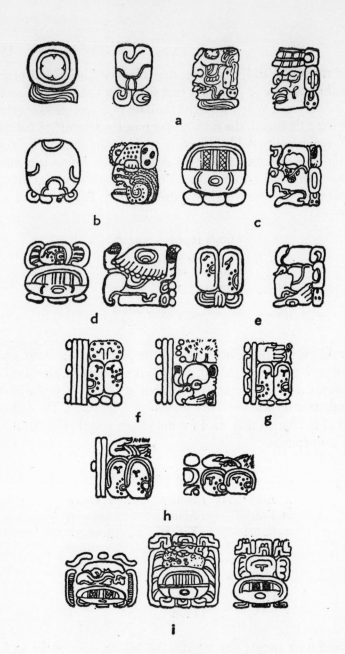

Nine Known Time Period Glyphs
Nine Known Mayan Time Period Glyphs
(a) Kin; (b) Uinal; (c) Tun; (d) Katun; (e) Baktun; (f) Pictun; (g) Ca-labtun; (h) Kinchiltun; (i) Alautun from Morley-Brainerd, *The Ancient Maya*

Kin = day
Uinal = twenty days or a month
Tun = 360 days
Katun = twenty Tuns or 7,200 days
Baktun = twenty Katuns; 144,000 days
Pictun = twenty Baktuns; 2,880,000 days
Calabtun = twenty Pictuns; 57,600,000 days
Kinchiltun = twenty Calabtuns; 1,152,000,000 days
Alautun = twenty Kinchiltuns or 23,040,000,000 days

So far, we are able to read only about 32 per cent of the Mayan glyphs; nearly all of these are numbers and dates. We know the glyphs for the twenty name days of the calendar, the nineteen months of the Mayan year, the face signs for numbers from zero to nineteen inclusive, the period glyphs in two styles, symbols for the four points of the compass, for colors and for several of the gods. There are other glyphs which the archaeologists merely skip when reading the dates. These may be history, although there is pitifully little of it, or they may explain the basis on which dates were calculated. As it is, we can count the years, but we do not know the date from which they were reckoned.

So far, some 400 different glyphs have been found. Of these, 90 to 95 per cent are ideographs; that is, they stand for an idea; at least, it is thought they do. Until scientists or linguists are able to read the glyphs, we cannot be certain. There are also approximately 200 glyphs made by combining individual glyphs.

The interpretation of what can be read is due in no small part to the labor of Bishop Diego de Landa. By contact with intelligent Indians, he was able to reduce some of the Mayan writings to Latin characters. There are also in existence three Codexes: The Dresden Codex in the Royal Library at Dresden, Tro-Cortesianus Codex in the Royal Academy of History in Madrid and Peresianus Codex at the Bibliothèque Nationale of Paris. None of these are thoroughly understood but at least they are something for scholars to study. All three codexes are written on both sides of long strips of amatl paper folded like Japanese screens. A coating of fine lime gave a finished surface for drawing. The glyphs appear in black, red, blue, yellow and other colors. In the Dresden Codex, the story of the world's destruction by water is told, but no other historical bits are recorded, so far as we know. Scientific observations are noted accurately; in this, the Mayas excelled the peoples of Babylonia, Nineveh, Memphis,

Thebes and even Athens and Rome. Yet, strange to say, although so gifted in abstract thought, they had no abstract glyphs. They seem to have written down only the results of their thinking, not the means to the end; this, again, is the mark of great intellect.

The Mayas used four measures of time:—a year of 365 days, a year of 360 days, a period of 260 days, and the lunar year. The 365-day year had eighteen months of twenty days each and a short month of five days called Uayeb. This short month was unlucky; anything begun then would fail. So the five days of Uayeb were spent in leisure as far as possible. The 365-day year was corrected every 1,507 years by making it 1,508.

The Tzolkin had 260 days, divided into periods of twenty named days and thirteen numbered days. The same day and number can occur together only once in every 260 days. Lucky and unlucky days were determined according to the Tzolkin. The Chichicas-tenango Indians use it so to this very day; they visit soothsayers to find a propitious day to cut down a tree, to start building a house or to erect the pole for the native pole dance.

The Mayan Calendar Round is an intermeshing of the 365-day and 260-day calendars. Pop is the first month; twenty numbers are added to it, just as we would say January 1, January 2, January 3, and so on. Thus we have Pop 1, Pop 2 and up to Pop 19. The last day of Pop was Pop completed.

Equivalent to this was the next month, Uo, seated, and written "O-Uo." According to this method, we could write April 30 as the last day of April, April completed or as O-May, the month that begins tomorrow.

To make this intermeshing of the Tzolkin and 365 year a bit clearer, I will let the letters from a to t stand for the twenty day names. With them were associated 13 numbers making in all 260 days. The same number could occur with the same day name once in every 260 days. Concurrent with the Tzolkin was interwoven the 365 day year.

Tzolkin (260 day year) 365 day year (18 months of 20 days plus the one
month of 5 unlucky days.)
For simplicity, I will use numbers for days
and letters for month names.

Numbers	Day name		Day of month	Month
1	a		1	A
2	b		2	A
3	c		3	A
4	d		4	A
5	e		5	A
6	f		6	A
7	g		7	A
8	h		8	A
9	i		9	A
10	j		10	A
11	k		11	A
12	l		12	A
13	m		13	A
1	n		14	A
2	o		15	A
3	p		16	A
4	q		17	A
5	r		18	A
6	s		19	A
7	t		20	A
8	a		1	B
9	b		2	B
10	c		3	B
11	d		4	B
12	e		5	B
13	f		6	B

No leap year correction was applied so the same day would occur in the same position every 52 years or every 18,980 days. Were we to carry the above table on for 18,980 days we would again arrive at our starting point 1-a-1-A.

The Mayas used still another means of dating, the Great Cycle of 29 times 52 calendar years or 1,507 tropical years in connection with the moon. In the calculation of 18,639 lunations, their error was approximately .64 of a day. In using the lunar calendar to double check the other measures of time, they stated how many days after a

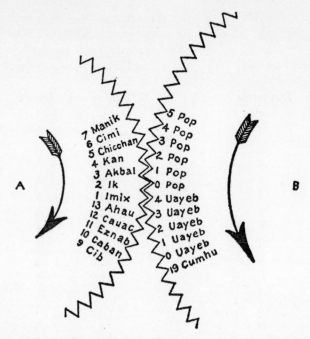

The Mayan Calendar Round: Intermeshing of the 365-day and 260-day calendars. Without leap-year corrections, this provided the same day would occur on the same position of the year every 52 years, or 18,980 days, from Morley-Brainerd, *The Ancient Maya*

new moon the date occurred, how many moons in the group had been completed and whether the last moon had been calculated as a 29- or 30-day period. We calculate the lunar period as a fraction over 29½ days. The Mayas adjusted their count by varying between 29 and 30 days and putting in an extra 30-day period when needed.

The planet Venus was probably an object of worship. I keep wondering why it was Venus and not Jupiter, which is even more beautiful. Possibly it was harder to calculate the revolutions of Jupiter since it is on so large an orbit that it takes 11.86 earth years to go around the sun once. Venus actually revolves around the sun every 224.7 days but because of earth's orbit, the planet appears at the same place in the sky in a little less than 584 days. Actually, the Mayas knew that 584 days was not correct; 583.92 was. To correct the error, they dropped four days at the end of every 61 Venus years. Had they continued this calendar for a thousand years, their error would have been less than a full day. Again, we are confronted by the tremendous intelligence of these people. The revolutions of

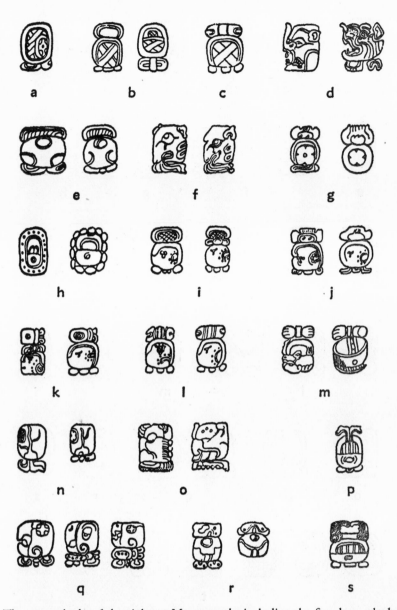

The name-glyphs of the eighteen Maya months including the five-day, unlucky Uayeb period. Each month had twenty days (360). The five-day Uayeb added to this made a 365-day year.

(a) Pop; (b) Uo; (c) Zip; (d) Zotz; (e) Tzec; (f) Xul; (g) Yaxkin; (h) Mol; (i) Chen; (j) Yax; (k) Zac; (l) Ceh; (m) Mac; (n) Kankin; (o) Muan; (p) Pax; (q) Kayab; (r) Cumhu; (s) Uayeb, from Morley-Brainerd, *The Ancient Maya*

The name-glyphs of the twenty named days of the Tzolkin
(a) Imix; (b) Ik; (c) Akbal; (d) Kan; (e) Chicchan; (f) Cimi; (g) Manik;
(h) Lamat; (i) Muluc; (j) Oc; (k) Chuen; (l) Eb; (m) Ben; (n) Ix; (o)
Men; (p) Cib; (q) Caban; (r) Eznab; (s) Cauac; (t) Ahau from Morley-
Brainerd, *The Ancient Maya*

Venus are not regular and it must have taken centuries of patient observation to collect all the facts needed for such accurate calculations.

Dates on most of the Mayan monuments are what we call the "Long Series," a double column of glyphs usually headed by an introductory glyph and a dedicatory symbol. They tell the exact number of days that have elapsed between the starting point (4 Ahau 8 Cumhu) and the date in question. This 4 Ahau and 8 Cumhu is the point of much debate. It stands as the starting point for all dates, as the Birth of Christ is for us. But just what happened then we do not know. It was some time in the past when Ahau was the fourth day in the week and the eighth day of the month Cumhu. J. Eric Thompson thinks it can be set in 3113 B.C. Other archaeologists place it 260 years earlier; still others hold that we do not yet have enough evidence to say when it was.

In date glyphs, the dot-and-dash numerals appear beside period symbols. A stela at Naranjo in Guatemala bears the date 9.12.10.5.12, which means 9 cycles, 12 katuns, 10 tuns, 5 uinals and 12 kins. From the table on a previous page, we get the value of the above periods. The cycle or baktun is a period of 144,000 days. We reduce all the periods to days, add the days and count forward that many days from 4 Ahau 8 Cumhu. The main difficulty, of course, is where we shall place 4 Ahau 8 Cumhu. But for the moment, let us agree with Thompson and let it stand at 3113 B.C.

The calculations are: 9 × 144,000 days = 1,296,000
12 × 7,200 " = 86,400
10 × 360 " = 3,600 (note use of 360-day year here)
5 × 20 " = 100
12 × 1 " = 1
Total 1,386,112 days

By a rather complex formula, this can be reduced to a certain day and month, but the Mayas usually put in the correct answer at the bottom of the column. The one given here is 4 Eb 10 Yak. We would place it around 684 A.D.

But this is only the initial series of the date-fixing business. They gave us the means by which they calculated the days and the answer they found. Now they also fix the date by the secondary series based on the lunar calendar. First they carve a glyph which means "Here we start the lunar count." Then they tell us how many days it was after the full moon, which moon it was of the group (there were groups of five and six between eclipses) and how long the previous moon count was (29 or 30 days). Finally they again give us their answer. It is 4 Eb 10 Yak.

Amazing people, these Mayas!

YUCATAN,
MEXICO

CHICHEN ITZA

One hour in a jet did it easily. The cabin was cool, the seats padded, the stewardess solicitous. Coffee or a cold drink whiled away the tedium of travel.

We were flying from Guatemala to Yucatan, that odd, square-shaped peninsula that juts out blunt-nosed into the Gulf of Mexico. It's odd because it is perfectly flat and has no rivers, lakes, ponds, swamps, streams, brooks, rills or trickles of water. The surface is porous limestone; any rain seeps through this to a solid rock floor below and then runs in underground rivers. Only here and there, the limestone crust has broken through and one can look down a deep well-like hole and see the water running far down. Nice—but not much use when you are staggering for thirst and your arm doesn't happen to be fifty feet long. These are the "cenotes" which play so large a part in Yucatan's history.

I was thinking much of Yucatan's history during that pleasant hour on the plane. We passed over the jungles of El Peten and I strained to see once more the white temples of Tikal, buried for a thousand years. We flew over other ancient cities deserted as they were in the eighth century. I saw hundreds of thousands—millions perhaps—leave the great stone cities and begin a trek of 300 miles if it were straight, possibly 500 or more along tortuous jungle paths.

They came from the forests where, at least, there was water, to the Yucatan peninsula and set up magnificent cities in this desert waste—Uxmal, Dzibilchaltun, Mayapan and Chichen Itza. I had seen the Old Empire at Tikal; I could see the New Empire in Yucatan.

The trek that had cost them months, if not years, of painful walking cost me only a pleasant hour. I felt, somehow, a little ashamed of myself that I got for nothing what they had paid so much for. As the plane door opened on the field at Merida, Yucatan's heat flowed in through the cabin, a sample of the climate they trudged in for months. Hot and humid. The peninsula is at sea level. Limestone is so close to the surface that only henequen can grow as an export crop. This hard, tough plant produces sisal fibers for making rope and coarse cloth. I did not think much of the Mayas' idea of good real estate for home-building.

A Jeep pulled up in a cloud of dust. Two young women alighted even before the third had brought it to a full stop. Soon the three of them were grappling with my bags and joyously pushing me into the Jeep. They were teachers at Rogers Hall, a beautiful new school of a thousand students, taught by these young Americans. I was to stay there while in Yucatan.

Merida, strange to say, is a booming city. Like Mexico City and Guatemala City, it is a happy combination of the old Spanish, the older Mayan and the modern American. It is a city of windmills; everybody has one in his back yard to pull up water from the underground channels. As a result, beautiful tree-shaded streets, colonial mansions and fountains in wide patios jostle with modern housing projects. All the time I was there, crews were tearing up streets and blasting for sewage, water, telephone cables and electric wires. It makes a New Yorker feel at home.

In the center of town stands a strange monument. Citizens of Merida regard it with mingled feelings of affection and pride that a family might have for Uncle Hezekiah's reproduction of Chartres Cathedral made entirely of matchsticks. It took a lot of time to make; it shows industry and devotion; nobody but Uncle could have done it. The man who carved this huge monument to the Mayan nation was Romulo Rozo, a Colombian by birth. He married a girl from Yucatan and came to love Mexico so much that he became a Mexican in heart. For fourteen years he worked at the monument, sculpturing every inch of it by hand. A history in stone, it depicts every event from Spain's conquest of Mexico to 1945, ending with President Avila Camacho. Some say the history goes back farther; they point out a figure they think is Columbus.

An Indian of heroic build dominates the center of it. To me, it seemed to be a warrior, but Rozo meant it to be Mother Earth. Serpents representing wisdom and fertility wind around her bosom.

She holds before her the Yucatan coat of arms, the only Spanishy carving in the whole tremendous piece. Below this is a thatched hut representing the Mayas; inside of this a votive light burns eternally.

On both sides of this huge figure, a mass of convoluted, involved, rugged symbols and figures build up to the central height. One can make out heads and hands offering bread, corn, buildings, statues of other gods, anything that was good. Two jaguar-headed human figures crouch in worship on either side. They signify courage.

Extending back in a semicircle, the sides of the monument are covered with carvings commemorating every law, reform and ruler during the last 400 years. If one walks around the semicircle to the opening, he sees that carved on the reverse side is the ceiba tree, the tree of life, which the Mayas called the yaxche. It is flanked on either side by four butterflies representing earth, fire, water and air, the earth's fundamental elements.

The semicircular arms enclose a small lake, Texcoco. On a stone base in the center of it is an eagle wrestling with a fire-breathing serpent. This recalls the sign given to the Aztecs showing where they should build their capital, Tenochtitlan. They did build it in the center of a filled-in lake.

Studying his work, I grew to admire Romulo Rozo. To sculpture this monument, he must have had a wealth of knowledge of Mayan history and art. He had to say things in stone as a Maya would have said them; to feel as a Maya felt. This man intuitively knew more of the Mayan soul than do some scientists who so painstakingly study shard after shard, stela after stela, temple after temple. Furthermore, as a man of his time, he could express the Mayan soul to the modern world. He certainly helped me to understand a bit more clearly the ruins I had come to see.

The road to Chichen Itza, oldest city of the Mayan New Empire, is a flat, monotonous highway flanked by field after field of henequen. Four of us made up the party—Clare Durant, a teacher at Rogers Hall, her parents from Easthampton, Mass., and I. Each of us had an abiding interest in Mayan civilization. On that long flat ride we compared notes.

Practically nothing, we decided, tells much about the real beginnings of the Mayas. We have only surmises that the first tribes were hunters. More than likely, they lived during the glacial period in North America and hunted mammoths forced southward by the great ice sheets. We have a shred of evidence for this in the fact that the Mam dialect of Mayan language has a word for "elephant," and, believe me, they had few words for things they did not see around them. We can guess, then, that the ancestors of the Mayas were here 25,000 or 30,000 years ago. Possibly before that. Indeed, not long ago, fossilized remains of a mastodon with human artifacts were found in Puebla near Mexico City by Cynthia Irwin, a Harvard graduate student. They have been dated at 30,000 years ago. Certainly, villages began to emerge around 2000 B.C. If it is true, according to some authorities, that the Pyramid of Cuicuilco, south of Mexico City, dates back to 6000 B.C., then cities were developing that early. Great temples of worship are not built by roaming hunters.

They were farmers by then, probably growing maize as the main crop. Maize is supposed to have developed somewhere in the highlands of Mexico by an accidental cross between wild grasses. Maize became the Indian staple from the Great Lakes to Chile. As the European diet developed around wheat, so the Indian diet developed around corn.

It could not replace meat completely but, combined with beans, it did. Black beans, called "frijoles," are high in protein content. Probably there were always a few hunters among the Mayas; in our own highly structured civilization, we have a few hunters, too. But when construction of pyramids and temples began, not many men could be spared to roam the forests in search of meat.

If villages existed by 2000 B.C.—and we are certain of this—then towns dominated by religion were being built by 500 B.C. People who perhaps lived in caves or thatched grass huts themselves built the great stone temples that survive to this day. Household utensils, ashes of fires, charcoal, stone and obsidian tools, fiber cleaners and ornaments such as jade, earplugs, noseplugs, beads and pendants —all the things people use in just plain living have been found in caves. But nothing remains of the huts—if they existed. Were the Mayan huts as perishable as those of their Indian descendants today, none would survive as evidence for any length of time.

Just the existence of a place like Tikal shows how highly developed was the agricultural civilization in the Peten. It also shows that the social organization had come a long way. Wandering clans do not undertake such great community projects. No longer were tribes the social unit. A city-state such as grew up in Athens and Sparta had developed. How early? We cannot say. By the time of Christ, the movement was well under way. Astronomical data for agriculture was needed; in some way the erection of temples was connected with this need. But the Mayas went further than practical astronomy; they studied the heavens for the sake of pure knowledge. The apparent movements of the sun and moon, Venus, Jupiter, Mars and Saturn were known. The Egyptians and Babylonians were not so good as they. The Mayas invented a chronology exact to the day, within a period of 374,400 years.

We can trace the Mayas distinctly between the fourth and eighth centuries after Christ. Temples and stelae are dated. Public buildings were made of stone, filled with stones and covered with cut stone highly decorated with sculptures and carvings. Towering pyramids—the ancestors of our skyscrapers—monasteries, palaces, observatories, ball courts, vapor baths were built. The Mayas made flat terraces which served as huge plazas they could group their buildings around. Where we would bring in a bulldozer to move a hill and fill in a gully, the Mayas carted fill and then covered the leveled area with limestone cement. They had a double purpose in this: It provided a large, flat space and also discouraged jungle growth from attacking their buildings.

"I sometimes think," said Clare, "that the Maya erected their stelae at Quirigua and Tikal because they were devoted to dates. That's all there is on them!"

"You have something there!" I said. "And others have said it, too. But I wonder if the stelae are not calendar corrections. After all, if we moderns did not have printed calendars, we might put up a sign in some public place every seventh day, stating, 'This is Sunday.' Then, all week we could count from that day. Four days have passed, so this is Wednesday. I have no evidence for this theory; it's only one person's idea."

At the highest phase of the Old Empire—that is, before the ninth century A.D.—the Mayas occupied territory from eastern Honduras, through almost all of Guatemala, to Chiapas in southern Mexico. At least one of the Yucatan centers, Dzibilchaltun, flourished at that time. If one was in such good state, probably others existed in Yucatan during the Old Empire years.

Then, one by one, the old cities in the south stopped building temples, stopped carving stelae, and whole population centers migrated to Yucatan. Many have wondered at this tendency to migrate; it was probably a throw-back to a nomadic past. At the end of the sixteenth century, Father Bernardo de Lazana told of the tradition passed along about this migration. "A few came from the east to Yucatan; this was the Cenial or Little Descent. Later, more came from the west, the Nuhenial or Great Descent." If he meant southeast and southwest, rather than east and west, we find it very credible. A line of dated cities stretches from the Peten on the southeast up through Yucatan—Ichpaatun, Tulum, Coba, Chichen Itza. They are much earlier than the string from the southwest—Santa Rosa, Xtampak, Etzna, Holactun, Jaina. Recent studies have thrown some doubt on this theory.

Another people lived in Yucatan before the Mayas came. The two cultures mingled; we find the Mayan pottery influenced by their new neighbors.

The climate was not very different from what they had left. While the highlands of Guatemala are cool, many of the Mayas came from lowland Guatemala and Honduras. The cities of Copan, Quirigua and Tikal are very hot and humid.

"I read somewhere," Mr. Durant spoke up, "that the Mayas sent scouts ahead of them—advance groups that stopped for a while in Bacalar, and reached Chichen Itza between 471 and 530 A.D."

"Oh yes," said Clare. "Quite a while ago Don Juan Perez, a famous Yucatan scholar, found an old document in the Town Hall of Mani not far from here. It said that the Mayas had left Nonoual in the land of Tulapan, spent sixty years in Bacalar, 120 years in Chichen Itza, 260 years in Champulin, then finally wandered around living in caves and woods for forty years and returned to their homes in Chichen Itza where they remained for 200 years."

"That wandering around for forty years reminds me of the Israelites in the desert," Mrs. Durant said. "Yet they tell us that there is no connection between the development of the Old World and New World cultures."

"Maybe so," Clare said. "Yet both have an account of the deluge. Just another unsolved mystery."

Chichen Itza was the earliest of the New Empire cities. In the sixth century, it was a frontier town; later it was the Mecca of the Mayan world. By the seventh century, it was a notable city. Uxmal and Mayapan were not founded until the tenth century. A stone lintel in Chichen bears on its face a date translated as August 28, 619 A.D. On the underside of this same lintel is the date, October

2, 618 A.D. It is part of a small temple in the southern part of the city, considered the oldest.

Sometime around this period, we come across the Itza people also living at Chichen Itza. There is no agreement among scholars as to who they were or from where they came. In what writings we have, the Itza are referred to as "holy men." The first leaders were three brothers who came "from the west" and lived very purely in an unmarried state.

The Itza were a Mayan people according to some authorities, or an American Indian people of Mayan stock as others say. They may have come from Mexico, or they were influenced by ideas traced to Tula in Mexico. In Yucatecan writings, they were considered foreigners.

A leader named Kukulcan was associated with the Itzas but we cannot be certain whether Kukulcan preceded, came with, or followed the Itzas to Chichen Itza. Later he was worshiped as the feathered serpent, essentially the same deity called Quetzalcoatl in Mexico. As a leader he was benign, a Solomon-type king. But as a deity, his appetite for human sacrifices was insatiable.

It seems certain then that soon after, if not before, the founding of the city, not later than 530 A.D., the Itzas were here and so mingled with the Mayas as to seem one people. Once more a migration took place. In 668 A.D., the people went southwest to found Chakenputun, near today's city of Campeche. They seem to have lived in Chakenputun for almost three centuries. Roughly at this same time —the eighth and ninth centuries A.D.—Tikal, Uaxactun, Nakum and other Old Empire cities were abandoned, but we don't know why.

After the centuries at Chakenputun, the Itzas trekked back to Chichen Itza. A fire in 844 had destroyed Chakenputun almost completely. If we are to believe the Mani manuscript, the trek took forty years, although some of them were back in Chichen by 964.

Among the city-states in Yucatan, two others were notable, Uxmal and Mayapan, both perfectly Mayan. In 1004 A.D., these formed a triple alliance with Chichen Itza, called the league of Mayapan. The three strong cities were to exert equal power, but from the beginning Mayapan sought sole control. While peace lasted, the land prospered, art flourished, architecture soared. This florescent period of the New Empire was like the Renaissance in Europe. Great pyramids, exquisite cut stone work, building façades covered with geometric carvings, great causeways connecting cities, all appeared in this period.

On the causeways, trade moved for hundreds of miles. Fine orange pottery from Vera Cruz traveled 650 miles by water and 75 miles by land. Fragile clay pipes came from Mexico City. Plumbate pottery traveled the precarious mountain trails from highland Guatemala. Gold came from Panama, jadeite from Guatemala and Mexico, turquoise from Mexico—possibly all the way from New Mexico, too.

Then in 1201 A.D., through the treachery of Hunnan Ceel, leader of Mayapan, the league erupted in civil war. Chac Xih Chac (the very red man), leader of the Itza, was too strong for Hunnan Ceel to conquer alone. He brought in Mexican allies, the Toltecs. With the newly invented bows and arrows, they defeated the Itza. In gratitude, Hunnan Ceel gave them Chichen Itza. It was a clever move; he no longer had to worry about a resurgence of conquered, crushed, captive Chichen Itza. To keep the other city-states subservient, he required that all the prince-rulers reside in Mayapan, governing from a distance through delegates.

The Toltecs introduced new customs, new religions, new art. From the thirteenth to the middle of the fifteenth centuries, Chichen became un-Mayan. Yet there was a vibrant quality to the Itza people which enabled them to adjust to a new environment and to achieve greatness through it. The Toltec feathered serpent deity Quetzalcoatl the Itza renamed Kukulcan and built a huge temple, El Castillo, in his honor. The Toltecs used the Atlantean design—small human figures with upraised arms supporting altars—so, in the new temples, every altar is held up by Atlantean figures. The Chac-Mool figures, reclining stone men with head turned to one side and a plate upon the abdomen to collect offerings, came with the Toltecs; they were placed at the temple entrances, at the altars and at the foot of the huge stairways which scaled the pyramids. The Itza people took up again the turquoise mosaic work they had once done so well, and turned out plate after plate.

In the "cenotes," the Toltecs saw a chance to make Chichen Itza a place of pilgrimage and to reap a pretty penny as well. These deep, well-like holes where the surface limestone has fallen into underground pools can be eighty or ninety feet deep. Chichen Itza had two such cenotes. The Xtoloc cenote within the city limits was a water supply for the people. The cenote at the north end of town was probably used for the same purpose originally, but the Toltecs made it the Well of Sacrifice where the tribe's treasures, human as well as monetary, were thrown to propitiate the gods. No doubt the curious came to see the maidens and babies thrown into the depths below, and stayed to toss in their gold and precious ornaments as well. It became a Mecca for the Mayan world. Even today tourists look on this cenote as a gigantic wishing well; American and European coins of recent date are brought up from the well's depths.

Over in Mayapan, all was not going well. The chieftains of the other city-states were virtual hostages there. In the fifteenth century, Tutul Xue, Lord of Uxmal, led the infuriated Mayas against Mayapan. The city was captured and sacked. The ruler and all his family, excepting one son who was away at the time, were killed.

Then the strangest thing happened. Both vanquished and victor abandoned Mayapan and established themselves elsewhere. The few survivors of the Mayapan people built a new city at Tibolon. Tutul Xue and his Uxmal people went to Mani. The Itza left Chichen Itza for northern Guatemala, retracing the trek of six or seven centuries before. These migrations are hard for us to understand, but they certainly help to explain how city after city has been abandoned in the course of Mayan history.

By this time, possibly the Toltec captors and the Itza captives had so integrated in Chichen Itza that they migrated as one people. At any rate, in the new capital of Tayasal near Flores on Lake Peten, there seems to have been no distinction. It was when he was fleeing from this city in 1695 that Father Andres Avendano came upon the ruins of Tikal.

Two years later Tayasal fell to the Spaniards, 150 years after Yucatan was subdued.

That's an interesting story. A father and son, both named Francisco de Montejo, did it. The father had come to Mexico with Cortez in 1519. Armed with permission from Charles V to conquer Yucatan at his own cost, he outfitted an expedition, landed in 1527, but failed. Four years later he came back—and again failed. But in 1540 and '41, he landed forces at Champoton on the west coast, seized the town in Kin Pech (now Campeche) and moved on to the ancient city of Ichcansiho, now Merida. With this city, the whole peninsula of Yucatan fell. Merida was founded as vassal to Spain the next year—January 6, 1542, according to the unrevised Julian calendar. Yucatan was a separate colony of Spain until 1821 when Mexico secured its independence. Since then, it has been a part of Mexico.

Part of the younger Francisco de Montejo's palace still stands in Merida, a continual insult to the Indians he vanquished. Flanking the doorway are two carved knights in full armor standing on the heads of Mayas.

"There!" Clare called out as we turned a corner and the ancient city of Chichen Itza stood revealed before us. First to meet our eyes, El Castillo reared its gleaming white against the blue, blue sky. History took a back seat as we scrambled out to visit the ancient city of Mayas, Itzas and Toltecs.

I stood before El Castillo and my mind went back to that day in 1914 when Edward Thompson stood on this same spot. Chichen Itza, under three centuries of decay and jungle growth presented "formless ruins and outlined ruins." Thousands of carved stones and square-cut stones littered the three-square-mile city as though giants had been throwing them around in a temper tantrum. He found the tops of seven massive structures still rearing above their skirts of greenery which trailed along a broad, level, artificial plain raised ten feet above the uneven earth below. El Castillo stood out then as it does now, for it is the tallest structure at Chichen Itza. However, as Mayan pyramids go, its 75 feet does not compare with the over 200-foot pyramids at Tikal. The base is square, 180 feet on each side. Thompson measured the inclined height and reported it to be 111 feet. In the center of each side is a stairway. Thompson counted 104 steps; there are now 91. Whether he miscounted due to jungle growth, or whether some steps were lost in the reconstruction is hard to say. Thompson found each stairway was almost one-third of the side width.

I can remember so clearly the first time I ever heard of Chichen Itza! I was in fourth grade, the kind of pig-tailed youngster who drops in at the public library on the way home from school to return an armload of books read in the past week, and to get out another. I had stumbled on bound copies of the National Geographic, 1912, 1913, 1914. I leafed through them quickly. And there it was—El Castillo, majestic in ruins, noble in decay, regal although men had forgotten her. I read Thompson's story of his finds—the ball court, the Temple of the Warriors, the Nunnery, the Market Place—and ran home to worried parents, late for supper. Now, more than forty years later, I felt Thompson was at my side telling me what to look for.

24. Citronella grows in shaggy clumps in the lowlands.

25. A swing of the machete and the green coconut is ready for a thirsty traveler.

26. *From the lowlands: long vanilla bean, round Copal seed pod, three part rubber seed pod, long grass of Citronella, mottled seed of Hevea brasiliensis.*

27. *After tapping the rubber tree, sap is collected and tested for both amount and latex yield.*

28. Flowers and leaves of Hevea brasiliensis, the variety of rubber tree used on the Firestone Plantation in Guatemala.

29. *Good Friday: As evening fell, the procession of the Dead Christ wound through the streets of Guatemala City.*

30. *The famous sawdust carpets of Antigua are made during Holy Thursday night by privileged families. Hours of work are wrecked in a moment as the anda of the suffering Christ is borne along.*

31. Clouds crest the summits of Toliman and Atitlan volcanoes as night descends on Lake Atitlan.

32. *Huehuetenango: The bull that escaped from the bullfight is safe…but what of the treed men?*

33. *Up the rough cobbled street of San Miguel Acatan walks Sister Jacinta Marie, one of three Maryknoll Sisters who work in this isolated pueblo. Convent is on the right, workshop and school on the left.*

34. *Chichen Itza: El Castillo, the Temple of Kukulcan.*

35. *Chichen Itza:* ABOVE: *Chac-mool seems to wait at the temple entrance for an offering.* 36. BELOW: *The red jaguar throne used to glare with jade eyes.*

37. *Chichen Itza: Each of the thousand carved columns depicts a different warrior.*

38. *Chichen Itza: Tzompantli or Platform of the Skulls.*

39. *Chichen Itza: Temple of the Warriors and part of its colonnade.*

40. *Uxmal: West building of the Nunnery.*

41. *Uxmal: North building of the Nunnery.*

42. Uxmal: Temple of the Magician.

43. Uxmal: Masks of the long-nosed rain god, Chac, border the steps of the Temple of the Magic

44. Uxmal: Framed in the corbeled arch of Nunnery's south building is the Palace of the Governor.

45. *Olmec head from Vera Cruz, Mexico. Weight, over sixteen tons.*

46. On the tilma of Juan Diego, Our Lady of Guadalupe painted her portrait.

His account of the undulating serpents marking each of the four corners had fascinated me. I could see no such serpents. But, as I caught glimpses of the nine terrace corners against the sky, I realized what must have misled him. He probably saw only the tips of the terraces showing above the tropical growth along the sides.

The main entrance was evidently on the north side, facing the cenote called the Well of Sacrifice. Kukulcan heads decorate the bottom step; on the top, the roof is held up by two serpent tails. On top of the ninth terrace, high against the sky, is the actual temple, 43 by 29 feet. There is just enough room on the terrace to walk around the outside of this small temple and see the view from all sides. The temple boasts no roof comb, as at Tikal, but the straight top of the temple is carved ornately. Inside the sanctuary, two stone pillars support twin beams of zapote wood—so hard that it has almost the endurance of steel. Richly carved, they in turn hold up a triple-vaulted roof. Everything in this temple is carved in low relief and, originally, it was painted. Thompson reported that the wood was finished naturally, all the stone work was painted in rich reds, greens, yellows, blacks and other native colors. What a brilliant sight this city must have been!

We had climbed those 91 fearsome steps—high in the risers and narrow in the treads with nothing but thin air to hold on to. Now, on the narrow ledge around that crowning temple, we surveyed the landscape. A 900-foot causeway to the north, which used to lead as straight as an arrow to the cenote, was visible only as a slightly winding path, wide enough for a single lane of traffic. The causeway had been at least 25 feet wide but the jungle claims most of it now. Thompson said he could see part of the surfacing on it in 1914.

To the northeast stands the Temple of the Warriors approached on west and south by the Group of the Thousand Columns. Now all these columns are white but eight or nine centuries ago they dazzled the visitor with a riot of color. Even today, small flecks of paint in pits in the stone attest to this fact. Just beyond the Thousand Columns, to the southeast, I could see the rounded columns of the Market Place.

Inching around the narrow space, I faced south and there saw the old part of Chichen Itza. It is pure Mayan and resembles its contemporaries of Uxmal, Kabah, Sayil and Labna, all built in the classic Mayan period between the seventh and tenth centuries after Christ. The unique rounded tower, the "caracol," or observatory, stood beyond the High Priests' Grave, the Deer House and the Red House. But this would never do! I had to see them all at closer range, so the four of us gingerly picked our way down the steep, dizzy stairway. How I longed for just one simple handrail!

Once down on terra firma, you would think us cured of Mayan pyramid climbing—but we noticed a doorway under the north stairway and investigated. It leads to an inner temple, much earlier in construction, which, like so many others in Mayan cities, had served as the stuffing for a much grander building. El Castillo had been built directly over this inner pyramid. Each of the outer nine terraces parallels an inner terrace; the temple on top of El Castillo stands on top of the inner temple. With buttressing and tunneling the archaeological restorers have made it possible to see this inner pyramid.

Obviously, it had been built before the Toltec take-over. Some decorations were added to keep in step with the new regime. Tigers, serpents, coats of arms and rosettes were sculptured on the exterior walls. In the top temple's antechamber, a Chac-Mool with shell eyes, teeth and fingernails begs for alms. These quaint Chac-Mool figures baffle me; one sees them everywhere in Chichen Itza. They look like men who had been lying flat on their backs on the ground with their knees doubled and their hands across their tummies. Then someone came alongside and, curious, they lifted up head and shoulders to look sidewise. A most uncomfortable position to hold for a thousand years or more! They seem to have served as a sort of collection plate at the temple entrance; the worshipers left their offerings on the Chac-Mool's abdomen. This particular one guarding the inner temple of El Castillo seemed to say as I passed him, "How about a contribution to building the new parish school?" I thought, "How Catholic can he get!"

The sanctuary of this inner temple holds a Mayan treasure—a sort of jaguar throne. Supported by stocky legs, it has a head on one end and a tail on the other end of its flat back. The jaws are open; the long incisor teeth of flint reminded me of those in the Copan carvings and the Kaminaljuyu tiger-priest mask. The whole beast was painted red and his spots are realistic inlaid jade disks. The eyes are jade balls, smaller but similar to those in the temple of Quetzalcoatl at Teotihuacan.

So much for the outer and inner temples at El Castillo. Possibly a third one is inside these two, and we may find it by the new X-ray technique, but so far we do not know for certain. We backed away from El Castillo, unconsciously acting as one does in a regal presence, unable to take our eyes from its majesty. Then Clare said, "Look! Everything is so symmetrical, so evenly balanced, and yet the carved mask over the doorway on this west side is off center."

Sure enough; it was a couple of feet toward the south. Yet on the other three sides, the mask was directly over the doorway. Why? Could this be an oriental influence? Chinese builders, I hear, always left some slight flaw, a misplaced brick, a stone out of alignment. They felt it would be wrong to turn out a perfect piece of work since the Supreme Being alone can produce perfection.

We turned westward to the ball court. Thompson had reported "two great parallel moles of solid masonry, 275 feet long, 34 feet wide and 25 feet high." Now the parallel moles no longer looked like breakwaters in a sea of greenery. Their stones were all in place, the low relief fitted into its pattern and one could almost imagine the teams of players marching onto the playing field. Now that the rubble has been put into place, the playing field looms larger than it did to Thompson. It is known to be 450 feet long. Spectators sat on the broad tops of two parallel walls running the length of the field. Some five feet from the base of the walls is a flat extension two or three feet wide, like a lower balcony. The wall of this structure slants into the playing field; a complex carving in low relief covers the side bordering the playing field. Players in feathered headdresses parade from either end, meeting in the center. Here, between the teams, is the death sign—a skull with vapor, representing speech, coming from his jaws. On the left is the first player of the victorious team, holding an unsheathed knife in one hand and a human head in the other. On the right is the first player of the defeated team, kneeling on one knee, and headless. Six streams of blood issue from his neck, in the form of upright serpents; a seventh stream takes the shape of a tree with flowers and fruit.

Players of both teams carry in their right hands a sort of large ring with a serpent's head where the jewel should be. Was it an instrument of the game, like a tennis racquet or a baseball bat? At the south end of the court, some of these rings seem to be set with birds' heads. I photographed one with a rooster's comb. Another seemed to be a quetzal head. Or an eagle's.

All players wore elbow, knee and hip pads. The object was to send a large, hard rubber ball through either of two stone rings set into the wall, eighteen feet from the ground. They could hit this ball only with elbows, knees or hips; they were not to touch it with their hands. Occasionally the players managed to put the ball through the ring, but not often. There were other handicaps; noseplugs and earplugs could have gotten in the way of a good shot. In the hot sun—and I have good reason to know that the sun is hot in Chichen Itza—the players frequently died of exhaustion running up and down the long field. But knowing that the losing team would be sacrificed to Kukulcan, they may have decided to die in the attempt to win, rather than under the priest's knife.

The ball court has three temples—Temple of the Jaguars and another near the southern end, and Temple of the Bearded Man at the northern. I stood under the overhanging roof of the southern temple, beside a headless player carved on a square column. It gave me a marvelous over-all view of the ball court. At the far end, 450 feet away, perhaps the umpire took his stance in the Bearded Man temple. From this vantage point—so perfect are the acoustics—his mere whisper could be heard through the length and breadth of the court.

The Temple of the Jaguars adorns the southern end of the eastern wall. Serpents' tails support the roof. The inner chamber is covered with a fascinating mural—the capture of a town. The houses are at the top, rows of square adobe huts. Women and children have come out to watch the fight which occupies the rest of the wall. Off center to the left, just behind a warrior fighting with a huge boar's-head mask, is a round thing surmounted by a perfect Roman cross. This mural, the experts say, depicts the Toltec conquest of Chichen Itza. It is completely non-Mayan. Did the Toltecs bring the round thing with the cross?

Underneath the Jaguar Temple, we discovered a break in the masonry and—of course—walked in. The inside was covered with exquisite polychrome bas-relief sculptures. Male and female deities, the rain god, aquatic plants and animals jostle for space on the crowded walls. At the door, stiff and disdainful, stands a jaguar throne. Only a hint of the original red paint is left; the jade eyes are missing. But his head is high. He doesn't mind that he isn't as colorful as he was six hundred years ago.

Tzompantli, or "Platform of the Skulls," lies east of the ball court. A gruesome, fascinating place. It's more like a wall five stones high in which each stone represents a human skull. These are sometimes thought to be the actual skulls of sacrificial victims embedded in the cement to preserve them and thus stacked up to make the wall. This is a little hard for me to believe. After teaching biology for years, I see nothing skull-like about them except their shape. My guess is that likenesses of the victims' skulls were carved in blocks and these blocks cemented together to form the wall. Each skull is different; most cheekbones are high; a few are low. Did some European wander into Chichen and end up with his head in this wall?

Barely giving a nod to the Platform of Venus, a low flat structure thought to have been a dance platform, I made a bee-line for the Platform of the Eagle and the Tigers. I knew that I would find there sculptures of tigers and eagles eating human hearts. Lighting was, for once, no problem. On all sides, the same sculpture is repeated. All I had to do was walk around the structure until I found an angle where the shadows were just right to bring out the low reliefs. With real glee, the tousled eagle, hair-like feathers standing uncombed upon its head, held a human heart in its talon just below the open jaws and protruding tongue. Facing the eagle, on the left, a spotted tiger, short ears erect, gripped a heart in his claw, with jaws already open to devour it. Bloodthirsty beasts, these. I wondered how these sculptures affected the Mayas who had been such a peace-loving people. The Toltecs who had lived with such symbols all their lives probably barely noticed them as they walked through the great plaza. But the Mayas, what did they think? Did they cringe with the thought that unless they did their captors' will, their hearts would be sacrificed? Did the Toltecs hold them in bonds by fear? By fear of terrible torture and death?

Across the wide plaza, the great Temple of the Warriors beckoned with its famous colonnade. Rows of topless columns massed in front and at the sides of the thick, squat pyramid. We started across the plaza, but in the middle made an abrupt left and went down the causeway to the Well of Sacrifice. We had picked up the car which had been parked by the ball court. For 900 feet, the old causeway led straight as an arrow from El Castillo to the cenote. But we did not drive straight as an arrow. Rather the car zigzagged around shrubs and small trees, detoured to left and right avoiding holes. Finally we parked ten feet away from the brink of the cenote, beside a low stone structure which might have been a purification steam bath or a small altar.

We peered over the grass-grown edge. Sheer, almost circular limestone walls rise forty feet above the water level in the cenote. The sides are watermarked at fifteen different levels, at which the water, moved by wind or breeze, ate into the sides and left a ledge. Below the dazzling whiteness of the sidewalls is the murky water. There is nothing lovely about it. Rather the dull muddiness seems to remember the gruesome murders it saw in the past. It is a haunted well, a well full of fearful secrets of man's inhumanity to man. It knew the screams of maidens at the threshold of life plunging into the abyss. Possibly, also, the horror of a priest pulled into the cenote by a falling maiden; a man's bones have been claimed from the rotten mud at the bottom. Historians write that this became a holy place, a place of pilgrimage. It was a Mecca, yes, not of worship but of horror.

It was hot and we rested on some rocks in the shade of a large tree. Tall grass hid the brooding cenote and I lifted my eyes to a warbling creature in a tree, a golden-yellow bird like a ray of sunlight. A nearer movement caught my eyes. An iridescent clock-bird waved his pendulum tail back and forth in perfect rhythm. A vibrant call trilled through the trees above me and golden-topped grass nodded beside me.

In this place that had known horror, there was peace.

That remarkable man, Edward Thompson, was first to dredge the cenote. As United States consul at Merida, between 1904 and 1907, he heard of Chichen and did some exploring. Then, for a song, he bought up the whole area early in the 1900's. Most of what he brought to the surface was taken to the Peabody Museum of American Archaeology and Ethnology at Harvard which financed the expedition. At the time, no Mexican law prevented such treasures from leaving the country. Later the Peabody Museum returned 94 pieces to Mexico. But Thompson was not able to explore more than a fraction of the 180-foot cenote; Mexico decided to find its own specimens.

Pablo Bush Romero, president of the Exploration and Water Sports Club of Mexico, known in Spanish by its initials, CEDAM, thought he could help. His group had been exploring old ships in the Caribbean just for the fun of it. They knew that the explorer, Link, who had worked on the drowned city of Port Royal in Jamaica, had used an "air lift," which acted like a powerful vacuum cleaner, pulling articles to the surface through a ten-inch pipe. Divers could do a little but the murky waters prevented their seeing very much.

The air lift was set up. Divers felt with their hands around the bottom of the pipe to remove any fragile objects that might be broken by its edge. Then the lift started sucking up the well bottom. On the barge's deck a gush of muddy water fell upon the screen set up to catch any object. A shout of joy rang out as a piece of copal, sacrificial incense from the Pom tree, stayed behind on the screen as the water ran through. Thompson had not exhausted the cenote's treasures. Hundreds of other things came up: potsherds, idols made of rubber and wood, a bone knife wrapped in gold foil, a portrait in jade, gold-plated beads, small ceramic masks, clay beads still bearing their original paint, death-bells from which the rattles had been removed to "kill" them. Modern coins from the United States, Mexico and Central American countries brought a light-hearted laugh from the scientists.

Divers brought larger things to the surface: bones of babies, fairly large masks, animal bones—jaguar, puma, alligator, deer and game birds. Possibly some had fallen into the cenote by accident; others may have been tossed in as an offering. A woman's skull was brought up. The bones were small and delicate. From the condition of the wisdom teeth, scientists said she was eighteen or nineteen years old. Her head had been flattened in childhood in accordance with Mayan custom.

Even today, people believe that the witch Hechiera has a cave down there in the water. If any unwary creatures come near, she pulls them down, drowns them and turns them into Alux people, small leprechauns. Once she loved a man and could not marry him, so forever she wreaks vengeance on others.

In four months, some 4,000 artifacts, enough to occupy scholars for years, had come up through the air lift. The last days were filled with surprises: a wooden doll wrapped in fragile cloth, rubber figurines, wooden spools decorated with black mosaic—could they be earplugs?—and two solid gold beads. The things had come from far places—Tabasco, Honduras, Panama, Costa Rica. From northwest Mexico, very close to California, had come a pottery like black cloisonné.

Those turbid waters hold more secrets. For years archaeologists have planned to pump the cenote dry and then excavate it. Not so easy! The water comes from the underground rivers and unless the source were plugged up, water would continue to fill it. The old cenote has much more to tell of the days when Toltecs held the Itzas captive. Someday it may give up those secrets.

In Chichen, the Temple of the Warriors is most characteristically Toltec. Almost a replica of the temple at Tula, it is a low building (thirty-seven feet high) but well proportioned. The Thousand Columns, square and elaborately carved, are massed in front and along one side. In an inner temple, similar columns are not only carved but painted in vivid hues. When the thousand outside columns were also bright with reds, greens, yellows and blacks, this temple must have been a staggering blaze of color!

The temple itself is built in four receding terraces on a base seventy feet on each side. Climbing the broad ceremonial stairway, we reached the top where the sanctuary and altar of sacrifice stood. At the head of the stairs, little standard bearers, looking for all the world like Smokey the Bear, stand at the head of the stairs behind open-jawed Kukulcan heads. A pair of great feathered serpent columns, fifteen feet high, held up whatever roof there had been. These serpents are everywhere at Chichen Itza where the Toltec influence is strong. They are L-shaped. The extension at the bottom is a serpent's head with fierce open jaws. The feathered body forms the upright. The rattles on the tail (Kukulcan is a rattlesnake) are bent forward and support the roof beams. It was daring construction; today, in the restored temples, such construction has to be supported.

My old friend, the Chac-Mool, is here, too. He looks down the steps, eying the worshipers as they toil up wearily, and silently asks a donation. Obviously beggars on the church steps were not a Christian invention.

The exterior wall of this topside temple is alive with carvings. A serpent-headed bird, and masks of Chac, the rain god, intertwine. Usually a human head looks out from the serpent's open jaws. I wondered if these strange beasts were all imagination or if these people had some record of flying reptiles from past geologic ages.

In a sanctuary at the back of the temple, the altar is supported by nineteen small human statues with arms upraised. These are the Atlantean figures, so named by excavators after Atlas who held up the world. The name has nothing to do with the mythical continent of Atlantis. Masonry benches with sloping backs line the wall. The priests could lean back and relax in comfort. I wondered if they had had padded seats, too.

As usual, another temple is buried under this Temple of the Warriors. The feathered serpent columns in it are still bright red and blue. Plumed serpents in green, yellow, brown, black, red and blue cavort over the walls. Yet the effect is not gaudy; rather, the colors blend perfectly here as they do in Indian costumes seen today on Guatemala streets.

A cylindrical jar, fourteen inches high and fourteen inches in diameter, was found under the altar in this inner temple. It contained a perfectly polished ball of jade, two inches in diameter. Mayan workers immediately recognized it as a "sastien," or conjuring stone, used by Mayan medicine men. Carved jade, the bones of a hummingbird and a strange turquoise mosaic plate were also found here.

The plate had been attached to a wooden back which had disintegrated. An expert on mosaic work, S. Ichikawa, came from the American Museum of Natural History in New York City. The plate was so delicate that it took him three weeks to repair its 8 inches, and three more weeks to paint a copy of it. The original is now in Mexico City's museum; the copy is in New York.

Leaving the Temple of the Warriors to prowl around the roofless colonnade of the Thousand Columns, we came across a shabby piece of work. Evidently, when the Itzas left Chichen to trek to Guatemala in the fifteenth century, some stragglers stayed behind. They converted the ancient majesty of the Warrior's Temple to make a crude dwelling place in the northeast colonnade. Bracing the roof with rubble fill, they made heaps of broken stones to wall off a few rooms. It was crude work done by hopeless people, or by people who no longer cared what they built. Remains of charcoal, poorly fashioned pottery, and a single jade chisel, show occupancy for some years.

Were these old people, too slow to travel, who stayed behind? Were they purposely abandoned because they hadn't the strength to work on the heavy construction jobs awaiting in Peten? What eventually happened to them? No bones are around. Did wild animals from the encroaching jungle finish them off?

The Market Place is to the south, an open square outlined by round columns topped by square capitals. Whatever roof shaded the area has long since disappeared.

Near here, a low stone building caught my eye. The door is no more than three feet high. Round porthole windows, also very low, are in the rear. (Any windows are rare in a Mayan edifice.) It looks like a playhouse, but it is a sweat bath with an intricate system of drainage running through it.

Old Chichen lies a few steps—and many centuries—away. We crossed the main highway to this old city, built long before the treachery of Hunnan Ceel. It is pure Mayan. There are rain gods but no feathered serpents, no Chac-Mools and no standard bearers.

Here is the Caracol, or observatory. Two concentric corridors circle an inner core, around which is a spiral staircase leading up to a chamber on the top. Through slots in the wall of this, one can observe the equinoxes and solstices. Because of this spiral staircase, the local people named the building the Caracol, or snail. This all sounds simple to us today but that building, extending seventy-five feet above the plain and thirty-seven feet in diameter, was a feat of great magnitude. It is easy now to build a spiral staircase, but imagine building one with nothing but stone blocks balanced one upon the other!

Old Chichen is a maze of small buildings. The Mayan prison, called "Chichen Chob" by Thompson, is now termed the Red House. This and other small edifices are covered with paintings of women grinding corn, men fishing or boating, warriors in battle, prisoners led off to torture or death, and human sacrifice. They were done by no amateur. He wielded brush surely as a true artist does.

The Nunnery, so much like the building of the same name at Uxmal, probably housed many priests. Thompson wondered about the chambers in the second story, where niches just the right size to store rolls of parchment were made in the walls. This could have been a library of Mayan history, a library future generations could never read. After the Spanish took over, there was a public burning in the Pueblo de Mani of 5,000 idols, thirteen altar stones, twenty-two small carved stones, twenty-seven rolls of deerskin (upon which the records of the people were written), 197 vases and a wealth of other material. The people wept as the fire swept away their treasures. Not only their works of art were gone, but the wisdom of their race and fathers had gone up in smoke.

Today, scientists could weep at the destruction of information they are searching for with every spadeful of dirt they dig.

UXMAL

Some people are smart. They can skip through a country—or a whole continent—and tell you all about the people, their virtues and failings, their political and economic prospects, everything! Books labeled something like, *Will Red China Dominate India?* could bear a subtitle, "Or, My Two Weeks in Asia"; magazine stories purporting to give authentic prognostications of world events are introduced by a bit of italic print: *"Mr. Snodgrass traveled through Vietnam and Cambodia and interviewed many political, religious and economic leaders. In the following article he reveals what our little brown brothers of Southeast Asia think of the United States."* As I put the magazine down, the conviction hardens, "I'll bet he never got within shouting distance of one little brown brother. He took big brown brother's word for what little brown brother thinks."

As a scientist interested chiefly in the relics of the past glorious ages in Yucatan, I visited ruins and interpreted them in the light of a lifetime of reading and study about them. But as a Maryknoll Sister, the plight of today's Indian people in Yucatan was never far from my heart.

The people I talked to were not political, religious or economic leaders. They were the children and parents of children, some rich, some poor, some in city schools, others in rural parish classrooms. They were teachers born and educated in Yucatan, and others from the States who could contrast the schools in which they volunteered to teach with the beautiful schools they themselves had attended in American cities.

These young teachers, all of them eligible for good jobs in city educational systems in the States, have come down to Yucatan, living in small villages, directing schools and living close to the people. This is real grass-roots technical aid; this is really keeping one's ear to the ground!

Three of us, Marie Lamond, Mary Schweiters and I, left Merida one bright morning at 8 A.M. bound for Peto, a tiny town just about dead-center in the Yucatan peninsula. For an hour and a half we drove south over the straightest road I had ever seen, and then southeast across the peninsula. There are only three roads which cut across this 200 x 250-mile chunk of land, east to west. Only one runs south to north and that's on the western edge. The eastern side, the Quintana Roo section, is blank on any road map.

We took the central east-west road. Fields of henequen stretched as far as the eye could see on both sides. Sisal, fiber from this plant, has been Yucatan's main export but now it is threatened by nylon. Still this fleshy-leafed relative of the century plant fills the fields; so far, no other economic plant has been found that can grow in the desert-like expanse.

Peto is a sun-baked pueblo with narrow streets and low adobe homes with some oval, palm-thatched huts here and there. Here we were to leave Mary Schweiters who was joining Elizabeth Nagel in conducting a flourishing school for about 250 pupils. The teachers' quarters were part of an old monastery left over from colonial days. Joined to a big, bulky church, its four-foot-thick walls keep out the glaring Yucatan sun, but do nothing to create a homey atmosphere. Elizabeth and Mary have put up drapes and done the thousand little things American women do to make a house feel like a home, but the twenty-foot-high ceilings defied them. Elizabeth had a good dinner ready for us. We sat down to it readily, but I could not shake off the feeling that we were dining in one corner of a museum.

Another pair of young American teachers conduct a school at Tzucacab, just a few minutes away from Peto. The Maryknoll Father in charge of the parish lives in a shack but he has built a lovely home for the teachers. The local market, hiding in the shade of a large tree, conducted business in eggs, bananas, black beans and onions; tightly rolled bills and battered centavos changed hands quickly. Between the market and the teachers' house was a vacant acre strewn with galvanized pipes ready to be assembled into the first sewage system for Tzucacab.

Alliance for Progress funds are making sewage systems possible in village after village. Big signs attest to this fact, generating friendliness for the United States in every pueblo I visited. To many people in the States, foreign aid means higher taxes and nothing else. It would make a lot of difference to them could they see what their tax dollars are doing for health and welfare in small places south of the border.

Having seen the present and glimpsed the future of this Yucatan area Marie Lamond and I set out to delve once more into the past. We set our sights for Uxmal, one of the oldest of Mayan ruined cities and one of the least excavated. Much of Uxmal's intricate yet massive stone carvings are still buried in the rubble of centuries and overgrown with high grasses. Yet what has been unearthed has earned for Uxmal the title, "most beautiful example of Puuc architecture in the Mayan world."

Entire façades of buildings—and by now you realize that Mayan buildings are not puny affairs—are stone mosaics of tremendous size. The pieces are not the inch-square bits used in mosaic work to which we are accustomed, but great pieces of stone, a yard square, weighing hundreds of pounds. The Puuc artist cut the edges sharply so they would fit neatly beside the next stone. He smoothly dressed the surface and carved intricate designs according to the part each stone was to play in the total pattern. In 1441, Ah Xupan Xiu, chief of Uxmal, led in revolt the rebellious chiefs who had been kept as hostages at Mayapan. The Mayapan royal family was overthrown and all killed except one son who was away. Uxmal was abandoned as were nearly all of the old capitals of Yucatan and the reigning Xiu established himself at Mani. When the Spanish conquered the land, Tutul Xiu was reigning in Mani.

Probably some of the Xiu dynasty are still living. Sylvanus G. Morley saw members of the family in 1940 and 1941 in Ticul, Yucatan. He witnessed the wedding of a son, Dionisio Xiu, and mentions that a daughter of Dionisio (his second child—the first was a boy) was born April 23, 1943. "Imagine!" I exclaimed. "These children are the fortieth generation from the founding of Uxmal by Ah Zuitok Tutul Xiu. What fun it would be to meet those people!"

"I'm sure they are simple farmers now," said Marie, "with only a memory of the greatness of their ancestors."

We turned off the road to the site. As Marie parked the car I looked at the distant buildings. The sunlight was taking on the orange-yellowish hue of late afternoon. Each cream-toned structure seemed to have a valance of delicate Valenciennes lace draped above the medial molding. What a fairy city it must have been when it came fresh from the stone workers' hands! Now, some thousand years later, in the midst of its fallen stones it was still a beckoning vision. Such is the deceit of great architecture! When the New Jersey buses swing around a ramp to enter the Lincoln Tunnel, one catches a glimpse of Manhattan's skyscrapers across the Hudson. Even though one may know all too well the hard cold truth of the businesses that go on in them, of the ruthless money deals, the petty ambitions, the lives reduced to a flicker that soon goes out—still the beauty of towers and jostling giants makes one think of noble aspirations. So it was with Uxmal as we walked across the grass-grown plain to the Pyramid of the Magician.

On the east side almost a hundred feet high, narrow steps tilt at what seems to be a 60° angle, straight up to the topmost temple which is really the fifth one constructed there. A barefoot Indian stood at the very top, outlined against the sky. I stood below fascinated to see him step gracefully and surely from his peak and descend the steep stairway sidewise. His foot just fitted on the narrow tread; he had no fear that a misstep would tumble him to the bottom in no time.

The base of the pyramid is elliptical and it rises in five humps. Even this, the most worked-upon building in Uxmal, is not yet completely restored. It is another example of pyramid built upon pyramid. There are at least five superimposed temples, each displaying a different architectural era.

Temple I, a long, low building at the base of the pyramid, stretches all along the west front. The outer wall is simply three round columns alternating with oblong pieces of stone. Five doors set in at equal intervals led at one time to inner rooms. When the next pyramid was built, these rooms were filled with layers of uncut stone. Some of this has now been removed and I glimpsed just a bit of the frieze of this early temple. One large mask of the rain god Chac above the second doorway is all that is left.

The later temples cluster around the top. Temples II and III cannot be seen from the outside. But Temple IV, known as the Chenes Temple, is a beautiful little thing at the summit of fifty perilous steps. The entire façade is a stone mosaic made up of one Chac after another.

"Why Chenes?" I asked Marie.

"The Chenes region is just north of the Old Empire cities in what is now central Campeche. At Uxmal, only two buildings show this influence—this fourth temple and a small building west of the Governor's Palace. The Chenes put stone mosaics all over the entire façade of a building. The usual decoration here at Uxmal covers only the part above the medial molding."

I climbed an elevation to get a shot of the entire temple, and found myself directly over a straggling group of tourists who appeared out of nowhere.

"What is that chain on the steps for?" asked a sweet young thing. Looking up, I saw what she meant. A heavy iron chain stretched from the Chenes Temple straight down to the bottom of those fifty perilous steps.

"Ah, that!" the guide said. "That was put in for tourists like you who like to climb to the top. A middle-aged lady once climbed those steps. She turned around to come down, lost her balance and we picked up her battered body at the foot of the pyramid." The group moved off, learning nothing else but this story. They did not notice the four-foot Chac masks which decorate the stairway on both sides, the Chenes decorations on the temple façade, the marvel of Temple I.

They did not even note Temple V which sits on a platform built up and over Temple IV, 89 feet from the ground. This is pure Puuc. I was interested to note that the artist had picked up the decoration motif used at the base of the original pyramid and repeated it in the base of the top sanctuary. How many centuries separated these artists who had constructed Temple I and Temple V, yet they recognized the same beauty!

In the frieze of Temple I was found a sculpture which has puzzled archaeologists for years. Popularly labeled "the Queen of Uxmal," it is rather the head of a young warrior with delicate features, looking out from between the jaws of a highly stylized serpent. Female figures were almost never carved in Mayan history. Marks that could represent tattooing or a beard are found on the cheeks. The hair is straight and rigid, bound with a headband of overlapping beads. Very Egyptian in its tone, it resembles a miniature sphinx with an Assyrian beard. I am certain those "tattoo marks" are very similar to the beard on a statue of Ashurnasirpal II, found in Nimrud. The bas-reliefs from Babylonia too are similar, representing the Babylonian King Baliddin and the great god, Marduk. The date of these has been set at 700 B.C.

The Pyramid of the Magician is very close to the Nunnery, a group of four buildings enclosing a central court, as four walls enclose a room but with the corners open. I had been backing away from the Magician's Pyramid and going up a rocky slope to elevate myself to get the photos I wanted. Suddenly, turning around, I found myself on a level with the eastern flank of the Nunnery. A few more steps up revealed the entire courtyard, 200 x 250 feet, spread before us flanked on the four sides by ornate buildings. There were scrolls, squares with beveled sides, latticework so lacy that each strip of stone appeared to have tatted edges. Before me was a corner of the east building decorated with stone Chac masks. The long nose characteristic of the Chac flowed out gracefully into space, one nose above the other. I gazed in wonder at the 52 feet of façade. Below the medial molding was a row of miniature columns and from there to the bottom, evenly placed, smoothly dressed stones. A stairway ran the entire length of this east building; we picked a spot that looked in good condition and descended to the grassy court.

At the center we could see the north, west, south and east buildings enclosing this spacious court. The east building we had just left stretched its full length, with a carved façade that took one's breath away. Over the central doorway, three Chac masks rested one above the other like figures on a totem pole. Flowing from this on either side, a stone latticework continued out to each corner. Six triangular designs, three on each side, were spaced equally on the latticework. Eight narrow parallel bars crossed the triangles and on the seventh bar was a serpent's head. The perfection of the geometric design contrasted sharply with the ornate and flowing façades of the north, south and west buildings around the court.

The north building was most imposing. A stairway of twenty-three steps spread out ninety feet along the front. The stairway is flanked on either side by low buildings, also temples. That of Venus on the left is so called because a motif over the main doorway is believed to be the sign of the planet. However, it certainly looked like a variant of the Chac mask to me. The temple consists only of three dark rooms.

The building at the right of the great stairway is also a temple. Its two-pillared portico opens into just one room. The frieze has completely disintegrated and the stones which once braced it from the rear now support grassy intruders. It must be discouraging work to excavate these temples! Grass grows on the sides of the Magician's Temple, on the friezes of the Nunnery, from every spot where it can get a foothold. It's one thing to excavate these places, and another to keep them excavated. They should be sprayed with weed killer every year!

The north building is all of 270 feet long. Doors open into eleven rooms and each of these in turn opens into an inner room. Two other rooms are entered by doors in the lateral façades.

Not much of the original frieze is left but what can be seen is exquisite. Over every other door are four overlapping Chac masks, which reminded me of the headdresses of the figures on the large stelae at Quirigua. Over the other doors are miniature stone "huts." The beautiful stone latticework with "tatted" edges alternates with scroll-like designs in smooth, finished stone. The plain and the ornate alternating in this manner is most pleasing to the eye.

"Some of this frieze is like the designs at Teotihuacan—the year's signs, for instance," Marie observed.

"But not the serpents," I said. "At least not as they were originally."

"No, none of them is feathered. They are just plain wiggly snakes. Probably there were plenty of them around when this city was built."

The west building, 59 feet long, is still seven feet longer than the east building. Seven doors lead into seven double rooms, and they into inner rooms. Chac masks rise above the second and sixth doorways. The latticework, plain scrolls, huts and three-part molding are just as those on the north building. But there is one difference. A feathered rattlesnake slithers across the lattice design. A Toltec invader must have reached Uxmal and added that touch.

A mythological figure of a man with a turtle's body stands on a throne under a feathered canopy, above the central door. These sculptures added to the original design spoil it. The snakes are put together like the sections of a horsetail plant and the human figures lack both stability and grace. Later sculpture did not follow the severe symmetry of the original designs, with the result that it irritated me as when some jangle prevents the flow of music.

Seeing the great south building, we realized that we had investigated these Nunnery buildings enclosing the central court backwards. The main entrance was from the south, through a high corbeled arch. On the outside, facing south, were eight doors leading to eight rooms. The rooms were not connected in the center of the building. The visitor, having come through the arch, finds the whole expanse opening out to him. Directly in front, across the green court, he sees that magnificent north building with its broad stairway. The smaller east and west buildings hem in the grassy court on either side.

Where he stands, if he turns around, he can see the stone frieze which stretches the length of the south building. A stone hut stands above each door and bears a Chac mask on its roof. The frieze on either side is made up of individual X's so perfectly joined that the effect is that of a stone lattice. Sections of plain-cut stone, with perhaps a few small columns, divide the sections of lattice.

Looking through the arch, I saw framed in it the Governor's Palace standing on a natural elevation some forty feet high, and raised another twenty-three feet by a man-made platform. It was an impressive sight.

Between me and the palace was the long ball court. I had seen pictures of it partially reconstructed but they must have been scientific projections into the future. Only long green humps with a pathway between them indicated where once the valiant had died because they could not bump a ball through a ring. Off to the right there were more mounds, some of them quite high. Temples, no doubt, pyramids of colossal size. But they have not even been touched by the excavators. At Uxmal, even more than in other sites, the work still to be done staggers one.

The Governor's Palace is another huge building. It rests on a terrace 600 by 500 feet in area and forty feet high—equal to a four-story building at home. On this huge area, the Mayas constructed another terrace twenty-three feet high, and, on top of that, still another one about three feet high. All of this is to prepare you for the size of the building itself—320 feet long, forty wide and twenty-six high. This, in any man's language, is a big building.

Morley wrote that this building was the most spectacular construction erected in pre-Columbian America, and well he could. Catherwood brought its beauty to the world in his drawing of one of the two corbeled arches, surrounded by delicate stonework in geometric designs.

The palace is box-like in line but the façade is one of the finest examples of Puuc architecture in existence. The main design is the

Chac masks which are not superimposed but placed in diagonal line. The scrolls and latticework also follow this diagonal line. It is estimated that 20,000 individually cut stones were used to complete this remarkable façade.

I was especially struck with the perfection of small details in the carved stone. The delicate design on the scrolls, the inset latticework behind the scrolls, the looped ribbon effect on the top of the frieze, all are lovely. I wonder what artist planned this building with its perfection of parts and symmetry. I wonder who the stone workers were who so expertly executed the design. They must have been unruffled people with time on their hands and peace in their souls.

The House of the Turtles is a few feet northwest of the palace, so called because of the turtle heads peeping out in the listel, or narrow fillet border of the cornice. Extremely simple, the façade recalls the early Greek architecture. The frieze is decorated with a row of slender stone columns which reminded me of bamboo screenwork. The column sections were joined by the sort of nodes that exist in bamboo. A turtle in the round rises above the space between every ninth and tenth column. Being an amphibious creature, the turtle was associated with water cults which seem to have obsessed the Mayas.

Many buildings remain to be excavated and restored at Uxmal. The southern group of buildings may be even more imposing than the Nunnery quadrangle. Judging by bits of cornice and frieze showing above the rubble, the whole must have been most impressive. The court measures 200 x 66 feet, and is entered by a vaulted passage. In the court is a wall composed of pillars made of cut stone and surmounted by nine triangular crests resembling church belfries; spaces have been left in which could hang a carillon of bells. Of course there is nothing to indicate bells were ever hung here, but this wall of potential belfries is like the view one gets driving along the Yucatan highway and seeing a colonial church in the distance. Some unromantic soul named these triangular structures "dovecots" as they looked like pigeonholes to him.

East of the dovecots is the Great Pyramid, a mass of rubble except for a cursory attempt of excavation at the very top. About 600 feet farther to the east is the Temple of the Old Woman. It is completely overgrown and very little of the top rubble shows above the greenery. It is said to be the home of the old witch. The legend goes that an old woman succeeded in hatching a child from an egg.

When this child was a year old, he was a fully mature man but had the stature of a dwarf. The woman sent him to the king of Uxmal to challenge the king.

The dwarf was so successful in every test the king could devise that the king became irritated. He ordered the dwarf to build a great palace in a single night, a thing he felt certain the dwarf could not do. Death was the penalty if he failed. With the witch's help the dwarf did build the palace overnight. The king was beyond himself with anger; he devised another trial which he felt certain would kill the dwarf.

"We'll get some hard nuts," he proposed, "and we will put them on your head and have somebody crack them there with a hammer. You do it first."

The dwarf was in a panic. He ran to his mother witch. She gave him a magic, invisible plate to cover his head. The nuts were hammered open but he was not harmed. Then the king submitted to the same test. His head was split wide open. The dwarf was proclaimed Lord of the Land. The Great Pyramid of the Magician was built for him. As for his mother, the witch, she was not seen again, but they say she still lives in her house with a pet serpent for whom she steals children. Someday, archaeologists will excavate her house and see how much foundation there is to this story.

One of the green humps I had seen from the Nunnery, although unexcavated, is called the Cemetery. Probings into the ruins have outlined a square patio, a pyramid and a low platform. Four small platforms found at the base of the pyramid bear sculptures of skulls and crossbones and these have given the place its name.

If excavation and restoration is ever completed at Uxmal, it will be one of the most imposing of the Mayan ruins because the structures are crowded together in a small area. There are more buildings at Chichen Itza but they are so spread out that one cannot view the whole city. At Tikal, the temples are extremely high but the jungle prevents an overall view of the immensity of the place. Here at Uxmal, it could be possible to stand at the top of the Great Pyramid and see all the beautiful buildings almost at arm's length.

Stelae were carved here as at other Mayan cities. One, covered with date glyphs, weathered and undecipherable, stands on the third lowest step of the northern building of the Nunnery. Some 300 feet west of this building is a platform which serves as a base for a number of carved stelae. They range in height from five to ten feet and are carved on a single face. There are possibly fifteen of these stones. Some are only fragments and it is difficult to say if each fragment is the only remaining stone of a single stela, or if many fragments belong to a single stela. All are lying on their sides as Morley placed them for study twenty odd years ago. Many of the sculptures have been so thoroughly weathered that they are lost. The rest are ornate, almost gaudy in their wealth of detail. In fact I thought them a jumble of human figures, feathered headdresses, legs, shields, animal heads and miscellaneous clothing. Modern Mayan art of a decade of centuries ago. I wonder if some rebellious soul, tired of making exquisite temples, let himself go by carving these stelae as a hobby. Had they been used as commemorative stelae, they would have been dated. Or maybe there was a contest to produce a stela for some purpose and these were the "also ran."

This group of stelae brought the ancient Mayas closer to me than those I had seen at other sites. Here I saw, not the perfect thing, set in its place and complete with dates upon dates, but flamboyant things which had been strewn around the platform without any real purpose. Not every Maya was an exceptional artist. Some tried and did not attain excellence. Possibly in future excavations, these ideas of mine will prove untrue. Be that as it may, I will always feel closer to the ancient Mayas because I thought these thoughts.

DZIBILCHALTUN

"Take your choice," said Marie Lamond, as she pulled the car to the side of the road and draped her arms over the steering wheel. "Today, will you be an archaeologist or a conchologist? We can continue down this sun-baked road and get to Progreso where the beach is littered with the most marvelous shells; I can see you going out of your mind, wanting to scoop up the whole beach and take it in toto to Maryknoll for your fabulous shell collection.

"Or, we can turn off to the left here, bump down a rocky, hot road and be at Dzibilchaltun, where the Mayas lived for an uninterrupted 4,000 years. It's up to you."

We were nine miles north of Merida. The day was young, even if I wasn't; the camera was loaded; my stamina seemed equal to any strain upon it. I made up my mind.

"I'll be both, Marie. We can go around Dzibilchaltun. This old archaeologist has studied about it for years and knows just what she wants to see there. Then we'll be off to Progreso beach, and I'll turn into a conchologist."

Marie sighed, knowing what a day was ahead of her, but she bravely turned left down the side road.

Dzibilchaltun is now being excavated, studied and restored under the direction of Dr. E. Wyllys Andrews of Tulane University. As a young man, he had come there in 1941 with Dr. George W. Brainerd of Carnegie Institution and resolved to study every bit of it. But World War II intervened and it was not until 1956 that he was able to return. Since then, he has been doggedly at it, surveying, matching up jigsaw puzzles of fallen temple stones, plotting palace floor plans and studying thousands of pottery shards.

I saw him once, several months after I had seen his work at

Dzibilchaltun. Leaving a Pan American plane at New Orleans, I caught a glimpse of his youngish, bearded and mustached face. The fleeting view gave me the impression of a man of unbounded energy.

Dzibilchaltun's importance lies in the fact that it is the only Mayan city we know which was never abandoned. In unbroken line, the Mayas lived here from at least 2000 b.c. until after the Spanish conquest. During all this time, it was a trade center for the whole hemisphere. Pottery from all the Mayan cities found its way here. It was used, discarded or broken, and can now be picked out of foundations, walls and debris. Thus, a complete sequence of ceramics and architecture covering those 4,000 years is here, waiting to be pieced together. Such a broad spectrum of history provides a good background into which cities of shorter duration can be fitted. Tikal, Palenque, Chichen Itza and most of the other Mayan cities of both New and Old Empires can be given a place in this time sequence, for their pottery appears here at Dzibilchaltun.

The city covered between twenty and thirty square miles. The central "downtown" area of ten square miles was densely populated, judging by the number of structures built. Outside of this center, there seems to have been a "suburban" area, less populated but dotted with many ruined buildings.

I had read some of Dr. Andrews' accounts but I was not prepared for what met my eyes. An old colonial church was near the entrance, a cenote was at the right and a nice little museum at the left. Off in the distance I saw heaps of stones peeking through green vines and bushes. Nothing else. I had expected a temple or two of Tikal proportions or at least one big stela like those of Quirigua, or a small but beautifully proportioned pyramid as at Zaculeu. They were not here. Where were the temples and courts and palaces Dr. Andrews described so accurately? He saw them all in the heaps of stones. They were visions of things to be brought to light in years to come. A dedicated archaeologist sees visions of what once was, long before the plodding workmen have pieced together the stones.

A path stretched down through the bushes to the left.

"The Temple of the Seven Dolls is about a mile down this ancient causeway," Marie suggested.

It may have been an ancient causeway and, at one time, it may have been sixty feet wide. They say, too, it was long enough to cover Pennsylvania Avenue from the White House to the Capitol. Originally, it was built of stone blocks, leveled with gravel and smoothed with white cement. But I failed to see cement or gravel and, as I trudged along, the huge stone blocks made me fear for my ankles at every step.

Hot. Blistering hot. The sun beat down on us from above and, doing double duty, glared up at us from the limestone. My eyes stung, even through dark glasses.

"What a place to live in for 4,000 years!" I moaned.

"What a place to dig and study Mayan history!" Marie re-proached.

Hundreds of white stones, about two feet long, were heaped up along the road; each bore a number: 501, 503, 507, 511.

"This is a jigsaw puzzle being worked out. Those heaps will be reconstructed into a temple," Marie explained. "The masons on the job have been working at different sites for so long, they know what the building will look like before they start. They number the stones and fit them together as they are found. Some will never be found; rock thieves stole load after load to be crushed into gravel. Also, seven fincas and two cities have used these stones, nicely cut already, for their buildings."

I remember a quip in something Dr. Andrews wrote in 1959. Speaking of his head mason, Juan Chable, he said, "Born at least a thousand years too late! He would have been one of the ancients' greatest architects. As it is, he can now reconstruct Mayan temples so well that, a season later, I cannot tell what is early Mayan and what is late Chable." I had chuckled to read it then, but a year in Mayan America taught me to appreciate not only the past but also the present ability of these people.

After an eternity of stumbling along on those boulders, fearing a cracked ankle at every step, we came to a small temple at the right. It was little more than a low platform with a stela mounted on top. But a short distance further on, we passed between low ruins and found ourselves facing the Temple of the Seven Dolls. I moved around a bit, angling for a good shot as usual and was surprised to feel Marie push me away from a heap of rubble. I had almost stepped on a big black tarantula with a three-inch body. We made certain it was thoroughly dead before I again looked into the camera finder.

The temple we now saw had been the first building on the spot, hidden under later construction and filled with rubble. All but one corner of this temple had been buried under 10,000 tons of uncut stone. Many more tons had been stuffed into the interior so that it could hold up a higher edifice. The later buildings must have collapsed, or so many stones may have been stolen that the whole edifice was dismantled. The earlier, smaller temple was freed from its mantle of debris.

In the excavations, great excitement prevailed when it became evident that this Temple of the Seven Dolls possessed true windows. No other Mayan building has been found with square windows. The steam baths at Chichen Itza and other sites have small porthole-like openings for ventilation, set in the wall. But the Seven Dolls Temple windows were square and at normal height; panes of glass would look at home in them.

The temple itself was made of great slabs of crudely cut stone, covered by a thick coat of stucco. An ornate frieze, cut in full relief, almost encircled the top. Walls four feet thick, mortared with mud, kept the heat out of the interior.

How old was this Temple of the Dolls? It was in use off and on for at least a thousand years. In the original construction a beam of hard subinche wood was used in a doorway. Now, using a saw for metals, since no wood saw would make a dent in this hard wood, slices were cut from it. Two independent Carbon-14 dates were secured from two laboratories. Results: The tree was cut in 458 A.D. plus or minus 200 years; or it was cut in 508, plus or minus the same amount. Thus, the earliest the tree was cut was 258 A.D., and the latest 708 A.D.

At some time in the past, this temple was buried. It was not demolished but carefully preserved under the rubble. Whatever was built over it may always remain a mystery; it was completely removed later.

In the thirteenth or fourteenth century, the Indians became archaeologists and excavated their own temple. They cleaned out the sanctuary and rededicated it. In almost the exact center, they dug a tube-like hole, plastered its sides and dropped into it seven clay dolls, each with a notable deformity. Two steps back from the top of the opening, they built an altar bearing a medallion in the center. Three times this medallion had been reworked with stucco and repainted, making four layers in all. Andrews managed to take off the two top layers and record them. It seemed imprudent to attempt to remove the third layer and thus uncover the bottom medallion as it was crumbling, so both lower layers were carefully lifted from the altar front together and now rest in the Mexican museum. Both Layers II and III bore inscriptions of the fourteenth century A.D.

We walked around the temple to get a good look at it from all sides. There, in the burning heat of this desolate place, a young Mayan woman had spread out her hand-made huipiles for sale, hoping that a few tourists might come by. They were lovely—sheer white cotton with colorful hand embroidery. We talked to her and took pictures. Then Marie bought a small huipile. The price, fifty centavos. When Marie added another fifty centavos, the woman looked at her in thankful disbelief. But—the labor on that huipile deserved more than fifty centavos.

When Dr. Andrews began his excavations, only one building was more than a heap of rubble. This was named the Standing Temple and restoration was begun. At the same time, surveys of the whole area were made. Four hundred ruined buildings were discovered, as well as deep piles of debris left from long living in the city. Pottery remains were found in temples as well as in open land which might have been dotted with perishable grass huts. From these remains, it was evident that this had not been just a ceremonial center. It had been "home" to 10–15,000 people. This conclusion upset the usual opinion that the temple areas were merely places of worship and administration but did not form a city as we know it, supporting a permanent population.

The question in my mind was, "How did a large population eke a living out of this barren, dry, limestone earth?" Our farmers would never consider working a tract if "hard-pan" were a few inches under top soil. This is nothing *but* hard-pan. True, there is underground water and there were cenotes within the city limits, but what a task to irrigate by hand every inch and every seed! I could see no evidence of irrigation channels; the work must have been done manually. However, the city did survive. It was here when the Spanish arrived in the sixteenth century, so somehow they managed to raise the food they needed. Possibly, as the excavations continue, we may learn how they did it.

In the foundations of the Standing Temple, pottery from Uaxactun in Guatemala was found. This could be an important step in the effort to correlate Mayan dates and our modern calendar.

Dated temples and stelae abound in every Mayan city, but all of them begin to count from a mythical date somewhere in the distant past. To know that a certain stela was erected 900 years after that uncertain date is no help when one tries to fit it into our calendar. Dzibilchaltun's record of continuous occupancy for 4,000 years shows a definite sequence of types of architecture and pottery. Not only local pottery but pieces from practically every point in the Mayan world came over the trade routes here. Dzibilchaltun serves as a tremendous filing system in which it is now possible to fit all the miscellaneous pieces collected over years of excavation. This alone justifies the long periods spent in the laboratory at the site, classifying pottery and reconstructing vases, bowls, idols, figurines and jewelry. A wealth of material has come from the diggings. In one cut, sixteen feet wide and fourteen feet deep, 250,000 fragments of pottery were found.

Another fertile source of material is the cenote near the center of the city. The day I was there, local people were splashing in its cool waters, pushing aside water lilies as they swam. It is approximately 100 feet across at its widest and 144 feet at its deepest. Formed like a sock, the opening is at the surface, the foot and heel 144 feet down. Professional divers, from both Mexico and the United States, have brought up worked stone from sixty feet, fossil scallop, clam and cockle shells from 100 feet, jewelry from 144 feet. Pail after pail full of earthenware pots were hauled up. Clay flutes, pottery with the famous Mayan blue finish, obsidian knives and flakes, bone noseplugs, a bone awl carved with hieroglyphics, bones of cows, rodents and humans, flattened skulls, one large femur which may be all that is left of a Spaniard who fell in. At first it was thought that these things had either fallen in or were tossed in during the years but when jewelry and non-utilitarian objects were found in abundance, it became clear that this was the center of a cenote cult similar to that of Chichen Itza.

The fossils at the 100-foot level and a piece of a sea fan at the 90-foot level are interesting finds indeed, for a geologist. Those animals live only in salt water. At one time back in geologic ages, did the ocean cover this area and deposit enough limestone to build up the level 100 feet? Is this part of the recently raised sea bottom?

Another mystery is this: Starting at around sixty foot depth in this cenote which slants down to 144 feet is a cascade of stones, all carved and shaped for construction purposes. The stones are found all the way to the bottom. An old tradition says that the castle of a "cacique," or head man once fell into the cenote. Was the castle on the cenote's edge when the land level was sixty feet lower than it is today? Did the sea knock it over into the water when it transgressed this area?

The museum had many fascinating things pulled from the cenote. One was a small wooden mask wearing two topknots and puffing his cheeks out. Others were a rock crystal cylinder, jade beads and a clay jaguar. Of the dozen or more cenotes on the site, only this big one has been studied so far. The rest may be simply water supplies, or they, too, may yield archaeological treasures from their depths.

The work to be done at Dzibilchaltun is enormous. Dr. Andrews knows the task ahead of him. He estimates that it will require ten to fifteen years to restore the rambling palace area which covers a dozen acres. The work can't be glibly done. Archaeologists must meticulously record the level, the associated pottery and architecture of each object as it is found. Only thus can the time sequence be perfected.

Burial places with skeletal remains, found in various architectural periods, may tell us what races inhabited this region in the different centuries. Pottery left in the graves as offerings determine the periods fairly well. Thus we can equate cultural achievements with the people responsible for them, a thing we have only guessed at up to now.

Dr. Andrews has formulated a sequence of cultural periods for Dzibilchaltun, as follows:

1. Dzibilchaltun "Formative" Stage 1   1000 B.C.–700 B.C.
   [When the evidence is complete, he will carry it back to 2000 B.C.]
2. Dzibilchaltun "Formative" Stage 2   700– a little after 500 B.C.
3. Dzibilchaltun "Formative" Stage 3   Approximately 500–300 B.C.
4. Dzibilchaltun "Formative" Stage 4   Approximately 300–10 B.C.
5. Transition   10 B.C.–90 A.D.
6. Early Period, First Phase (Tzakol)   90–350 A.D.
7. Early Period, Second Phase (Tepeu 1–2)   350–600 A.D.
8. Transition   600–700 A.D.
9. Florescent Period, First Phase (Pure)   700–900 A.D.
10. Florescent Period, Second Prase
    (Modified)   900–1150 A.D.
11. Transition (Black-on-Cream Pottery)   1150–1300 A.D.

12. Decadent Period, First Phase
    (Monumental)   1300–1450 A.D.
13. Decadent Period, Second Phase   1450–1600 A.D.
    (Post-monumental)
14. Colonial Period   1600–

Because, for the first time, it has been possible to study a complete sequence, this time schedule differs from those of Morley, Thompson and other archaeologists. Here, transitional periods come to light, as well as the non-permanent effect of ceramic changes brought in by conquering tribes. Art expressions changed while conquerors were in control, but when they had left, the Mayas reverted to their own style and techniques. The Puuc in Uxmal and the Toltec at Chichen Itza had no lasting effect on Mayan culture.

In a way, this was too bad. The "better" never grew to "best." For instance, in Mayapan's decadent period just before the Spanish came, the Florescent techniques were abandoned and Early Period architecture resumed. Some builders tried to imitate the Florescent style, but they had lost the knack. They tried to carve and ended up by filling in with crude stucco. They even tried to use the old ceremonial calendar which the Florescent age had discontinued. Attempts to copy Florescent pottery produced only a coarse, crumbly, grey ware of no artistic value.

The Mayas seemed not to resist change; apparently they adopted every new idea that came to them, wrapping it in their own personality. New designs, new pottery shapes, new building plans were expressed as a Mayan artist would express them. But, underneath, they clung stubbornly to their tribal art; it came to the surface when the glamor of the new had worn off.

The marvel is that new generations should know about the old art. Were techniques of the past passed on as part of a ritual? Did the Mayas "absorb" their conquerors just as the Chinese did in their long history? Long ages ago, tribes from the north and west invaded and conquered parts of China. The Mongols took the north; the Hakka invaded part of the eastern coast. But after a time the invaders had melted down so that they blended with the people they had conquered. Was it so in Maya-land? Perhaps, with this difference. They may have adopted the conquerors' art for a time, but they returned to their own art forms eventually, although with a loss of techniques and proficiency.

Cross-dates with other Mayan cities may be the Rosetta Stone furnished by Dzibilchaltun. For instance, Tepeu pottery from the Peten was found in Structure I here, and a lintel from Structure I has been carbon-dated at 483 A.D. Ceramics from various places were found at the base of Structure 226, a lintel of which is carbon-dated at 300 B.C.

As we got into the car, Marie and I took a backward look at the mass of grass-grown stone heaps which had been a trade center for 4,000 years. "Dr. Andrews is a courageous man," I said. "I had no idea of the vastness of the work yet to be done."

"Yes," agreed Marie. "Along with everybody else interested in the Mayan peoples, I'll follow his work here with great interest. It may be that among these piles of rubble, he will find answers to a goodly number of our 'Why's' and 'Who's' and 'When's.'"

After the stifling heat at Dzibilchaltun, it was a treat to be back on the main road to Progreso. Miles before we could glimpse the Caribbean, or Gulf if you want to be prosaic, the sea breezes tempered the glaring sun's heat.

It was a Sunday; the seaport of Progreso was just a drowsy little town. Not much business in the dark little stores, although they were open. No ships anchored at the mile-long pier of concrete and steel. We turned down a side street—unpaved, of course—and soon came to a small beach house, shaded by coco-palms and bright with bougainvillea. It had been lent to us for the day.

Marie started to boil water for coffee. I wandered down to the water's edge. That was my undoing. Ten feet up from where the blue Caribbean lapped the white sand beach, shells lay where high tide had left them. Was I dreaming? For years, when friends visited islands in the Caribbean, I had asked them to bring back shells for our Motherhouse collection. Among our three thousand varieties, we had shells from the Philippines, Hawaii, California, Mauritius, China and Japan, but still practically nothing from this area.

Now, here I was surrounded by *Polinices, Ostreas, Nassariums, Lucinas, Arcas, Chiones, Trachycardiums, Tellinas, Semeles, Astraeas.* There were varieties of *Murex* with spines or nodules or both; large heavy cones so ground by the water that no pattern was visible; small, delicate cones, middle-sized ones and tiny, lovely ones with immature patterns. The banded tulip (*Fasciolaria tulipa*), *Xancus angulatus,* delicately spiked *Spondylus,* great *Strombus gigas* and smaller *Strombus costatus,* were piled on top of left-

handed welks (*Busycon contrarium*) and their right-handed brothers, *Busycon carica*. Here and there a Baby's Bonnet (*Semicassis
testiculis*) was partly covered with gaudy pectens. Tuns (*Tonna
galea* and *Tonna perdix*) bedded down with *Patellas* and *Fissurel-
las*. Long, slender, pointed *Terebra* merited their name of auger
shells. Stuck upright in the sand were a number of long, delicate
Atrina rigida (rough pen shells). Many were broken but three or
four were perfect and looked as though some Victorian scribe had
just put them aside to dry.

I looked around with avaricious eyes, taking stock of the treasures on the beach. Slippery Sam with the Crown Jewels? A book-
worm loose in the Vatican Library? A safe-cracker prowling
through the United States Mint? Pick your own simile and it will be
right!

Then I began to collect, telling myself over and over again to be
cautious. "You'll have to carry the delicate specimens yourself," I
talked to Greedy Me. "The others you can ship, but remember
there's space on the shelves for only one sample of each variety."
What a struggle it was! I was surrounded by shells the like of which
I had seen only pictured in books or stowed in the drawers of the
Smithsonian Institution when Dr. Harald Rehder had shown me
the vast collection there. And they were mine, all mine, just for the
trouble of picking them up.

I don't know how long I was there, I forgot about food and the
coffee Marie was making. Finally, she came to me with a deal. If I
would come back to the house and eat something, she would help
me collect shells. So we did.

We combed the beach for the perfect specimens, used the cookie
box for the pen shells, the cracker box for the Tuns, wrapped tiny
immature shells in Kleenex so they would not be lost, used old
newspaper to keep the *Strombus gigas* from wrecking the Ficus.

The sun was low when we called a halt.

"You have yet to see a sunset from the end of the pier," she reminded me. With a prayer, "Dear Lord, please let me again see a
Caribbean beach," I picked up the large package of shells and struggled to the car while Marie brought thermos, luncheon basket, food
we had not eaten, and empty Seven-Up bottles.

Inching along the pier, we had to make way for the family
groups fishing over the sides. We parked the car just outside the
door marked "Aduana" (Customs House) and were in time to see

the sky go from a deep blue to orange and red, Mayan orange and Mayan red. The water caught the color from the sky and soon we were in a sea of brilliant color which deepened moment by moment until, just before darkness, the fishermen along the pier were black silhouettes against a shimmering carmine backdrop.

Lights in small buildings along the water's edge dimly flickered on the softly rippling waves. I said to Marie, "Had I sought a site for a city, it would have been here, not at Dzibilchaltun."

MEXICO

AMERICAN "PYRAMIDS"

If you live in the United States anywhere in the great trough that scoops through the continent, known as the Mississippi Valley, you may be sitting this very minute on an ancient Indian "pyramid." It may be a long-forgotten temple; it may be a burial mound. Under your house there may be nothing but rubble, or there may be hundreds of skeletons. Not a cheery thought but, for archaeologists, an interesting one.

Many a stalwart citizen snorts in disbelief at the idea that there are ancient pyramids buried under the mounds which dot this land from the Great Lakes to the Gulf of Mexico, from the western edge of the Mississippi Valley straight across to the Atlantic. "Pyramids?" he says. "They were in Egypt! The Mayas built a number, I know, and there is at least one in China. But in New Orleans, St. Louis or Cincinnati? Don't be silly."

It is hardly silly. Not every tribe of Indians built pyramids, but enough piled them skywards to leave thousands of mounds over the central states to tantalize archaeologists. They could tell so much, if there were only time and money to dig into them!

Our mounds differ from the Egyptian pyramids both in construction and in use. American pyramids are heaped-up piles of rubble or earth, faced with stone, if it was handy, or with adobe bricks. The Egyptians built geometrically perfect structures terminating in a point; their sole purpose was to entomb kings or priests. The American Indians also built burial cones with a point, but they made pyramids, too, in which the top was flattened to provide a platform for a regal dwelling or an altar of sacrifice. The pointed

247

conical burial mounds far outnumber the truncated pyramids. The American dead were not mummified. Just the opposite. The bodies were buried in earth or treated in some way to remove the flesh. Then they were interred in a jar, an ossuary or communal pit. Sometimes the bones were joined in alignment and thus left with hundreds of other skeletons.

Because of their bulk, the "pyramids" in the United States are generally classified as earthworks. The Aztecs leaned to the colossal, too, but they used stonework which gave sharp lines to their pyramids. Tikal filled the structures with rubble, but the exterior had definite outlines, tall and graceful. The United States pyramids just sprawl.

The whole area in and around St. Louis was once filled with mounds. In fact, St. Louis was named Mound City at first; there is still Mound Street, Big Mound and Old Mound Market. In 1819, after many had been demolished, twenty-seven still remained. Then, after the city was built, only one mound remained within the city limits. The tragedy is that they were leveled without adequate study. In 1869 a burial chamber containing twenty-seven bodies with pottery and flint artifacts was found under the city. It, too, disappeared under the wreckers' shovels and into souvenir collectors' pockets.

Across the Mississippi in East St. Louis were the Cahokia Mounds, clustered into a great ceremonial center. At least 67 major mounds and many smaller ones marked the site.

In 1882, Great Cahokia Mound was 99 feet high. Its north-south bases were 998 feet long; the east-west, 721 feet. It covered more than sixteen acres with a bulk of twenty-two million cubic feet of dirt. It had been accumulated basketful by basketful. Again and again, each man and woman must have trudged up the ever-lengthening slope with his meager load of earth. Random tunnels, sent down through the mound for curiosity's sake, disclosed layers of black humus, lenses of sand, deposits of yellow clay and loess. It must have been back-breaking work to carry the loads upward. But finally, after ten, fifteen, twenty years, the pile reached as near the skies as man could take it. Then it was crowned with the temple, the purpose of it all.

Great Cahokia is still a giant. Its top has been sliced off and its sides have been trimmed but it is still the most colossal mound in the United States.

Both Creeks and Cherokees of the Southeastern States were mound builders. They laid out their cities around a central plaza as the Mayas did. They played their ceremonial games, especially a game called "chunkey," with a rubber ball about as big as a bowling ball. Some genius in Middle America had found the sap of the rubber tree and arrived at a knowledge of what it could be used for. Inventive minds! The balls were black; obviously, after the sap had dried, it was smoked. Soon rubber balls were carried throughout all America. Columbus took the first rubber ball to Europe where it performed amid cries of, "It jumps and rebounds!" Some say that these Indian ball games were the great-grandfather of soccer, basketball, tennis and golf.

The game, as played by Creeks and Cherokees, is so like that of the Mayas in Tikal, Chichen Itza, Uxmal and other Central American places, that it leaves little doubt that these tribes had common origins.

Teams of nine to eleven players played so well (their lives were often at stake) that, for an hour or more, the ball would not touch the ground. A good deal of gambling preceded the game and often the gamblers took the ball to the gods for a special blessing to insure a winning game.

No one knows when the ball game became a part of Indian life. An archaic figure representing a ball player, found at Tlatilco, Mexico, has been dated at 1500 B.C. The first real ball court in existence is the one at Copan, Honduras, 200–300 A.D.

Many of the mound-building tribes in the United States constructed their cities around a central plaza as did the Mayas, Aztecs and Toltecs. In the southeastern United States are remnants of once fairly large cities built by Cherokee and Natchez tribes.

Around the central plaza of the Cherokees were grouped the principal buildings. The town house or palace was on a circular elevation at one end. At the opposite end, on a rectangular pyramid, was the temple. The lesser structures faced the plaza, and in doing this faced the four points of the compass.

This layout and building scheme was followed in the Natchez towns of southwestern Mississippi. The Natchez were sun worshipers as were the builders of the Illinois mounds, the pyramids at Teotihuacan, near Mexico City, and the rest of Maya-land. In honor of the sun, a flame burned continually in the Natchez temple atop the pyramid.

When the Spaniards arrived, mounds were in use. De Soto, for instance, was accustomed to them. Landing at Tampa Bay in Florida in 1539, he found the Timucuan chief, Ucita, living in a house built on top of a pyramid near the beach. It fronted on a great open square decorated with a carved wood fowl, complete with glaring, large, grotesque eyes. Later, when he visited Tuscaloosa, "the Black Warrior," he had to climb the high stairs in his heavy armor (no mean feat!) to the level of the chief who sat languidly on his balcony.

In Middle America, archaeologists have given names to structures without knowing just what they were used for. They have called one a nunnery, another a palace, a third a council chamber and so on, without any real proof that they were nunneries or palaces or temples or what-not. Had Tuscaloosa not been sitting on his balcony watching, probably with amusement, the Spaniard valiantly climbing up his front steps in cumbersome armor, scientists might have conjectured that the pyramid had supported a temple. Again, we might have thought Ucita's house in Tampa to be an ancient fortress.

Ohio could well be called "the Mound State." No less than 10,000 were counted there. As far back as 1788, General Rufus Putnam surveyed the mounds at Marietta and set them aside for preservation. One rectangular earthwork enclosure at Chillicothe formed part of a World War I camp, and the city itself is on the site of an ancient village. Circleville takes its name from a large circular earthwork. Miamisburg is marked by a gigantic conical mound.

"Effigy mounds" were built to resemble various animals. The likenesses, too large for a man on the ground to see as a whole, are easily seen from a plane. In Ohio, Newark has its eagle, Granville an opossum; Warren and Adams counties have serpents. The great serpent mound northwest of Portsmouth, Ohio, is 1,300 feet long. The mounding is so well done that rain and snow have not been able to beat down its sculptured effect. At Hopewell, excavation has brought to light copper objects of beautiful workmanship—a swastika, a serpent's head, and a quatrefoil. This last may be an adaptation of the kin sign which Middle American stone engravers used to represent the sun.

There are mounds near New Orleans. On April 15, 1732, Alexander de Batz, a French engineer, visited the last temple of Acolapisia, forty miles north of the city, and sketched it.

In Oklahoma, what was probably the last communal burial in the Mississippi Valley took place near Spiro. The place was marked with a large conical mound flanked by three lesser ones. In 1933 this was pillaged without its ever having been studied by scientists. All we know is that three burial mounds had been built one on top of another. At least 2,500 skeletons—the lower ones dating back into the dim past—were buried with fabrics, feathers, rabbit fur, buffalo fur and other treasures which might have given us an insight into history we now can only guess at. Today, however, universities are sending out teams to many Indian sites. The scientific work done now may give us answers to many puzzling questions of Middle America.

According to present opinion, the main stream of Indian migration came across Bering Strait and flowed down the western coast through Canada, United States, Mexico, Middle and South America. It reached Tierra del Fuego by no later than 6000 b.c. Families or clans broke from the common stream to penetrate eastward to the Gulf of Mexico and the Atlantic Ocean.

Possibly there were several waves of migration. If so, at least one came from northern Asia because, even today, Mayan babies are often marked by the Mongoloid spot at the end of the spine. It is a blue to purple spot, small as a dime or large as a dinner plate, which usually disappears by the tenth year. It is found only on those whose ancestors were Orientals.

When man came to the Western Hemisphere, he came as a full-fledged man. Whatever evolutionary stages he had gone through had been accomplished in another land. He brought his weapons and primitive tools with him. He was a hunter, a man of great ingenuity and adaptability. Wherever he went, he could use the materials at hand for the task he wanted to do.

He was a trader and an almost insatiable traveler. He paddled distances in his light canoes on the rivers, lakes and oceans, traded his handiwork in far villages and brought back the results of his barter.

Our first Americans had arrowheads and spears made of flint and quartz, but these could scarcely pierce the tough hide of the beast. Somehow, they got around this difficulty. Did they lure him into a pit and hurl stones down to kill him? We do not know. But we conjecture that they did kill mastodons, for the animals' bones are found in proximity to charcoal and human artifacts.

The mastodon was here a long time before the first Americans arrived. He may have stayed on after the Ice Age. Certainly, mastodons were here during the Pleistocene Period and as late as 10,000 years ago.

Cynthia Irwin, a graduate student at Harvard University in 1962 claimed she found 30,000-year-old Mastodon remains associated with human artifacts ten miles from Puebla, Mexico.

Ten thousand years ago, a special group of hunters roamed what is now the United States. Using exquisitely wrought spearheads, they killed bison, American camels, deer and rabbits. These spearheads are known as "Folsom Points" because they were first found at Folsom, New Mexico. They are more oval than arrowshaped. Not only were they chipped to shape but the edges were fluted by a secondary chipping until they were razor sharp. We call the man who made these Folsom Points, "the Folsom Man." Some of the fluted points were found associated with charcoal which could be carbon-dated. The campfire had burned into charcoal 9,883 years plus or minus 350 years ago, so Folsom Man had been there between 9,000 and 10,000 years ago. Judging from other artifacts found with Folsom Points, we know the women could sew and weave. Woven sandals with a C-14 date of 9,000 years were found. Folsom Man also painted his body. He wore lignite, bone and red hematite beads. He had stone knives, hide scrapers, hammers and engraved bone-disks.

I have seen the fingerprints of a Folsom Man. In fact, I photographed them. Ever since then, I feel kinship with him over the thousands of years. A few years ago, I was in Illinois looking for traces of ancient beasts. Near an abandoned quarry in which children were swimming, I found the fossilized footprint of a prehistoric animal. A young man who had been diving into the quarry came by and stopped, interested. Then he brought me a white ball of something like clay. He had seen children playing with it and, when he showed interest, they gave it to him as they would any stone. Were a man to take clay, roll it between his hands and shape it into a roundness, it would be like this ball. There were fingerprints and palm prints which had been left in the soft clay and then hardened.

"What is it?" he asked me. "How old is it?"

I had an idea what the answers to these questions were, but I hesitated to say so without expert opinion. I photographed the ball and sent it to the Smithsonian Institution for identification. "Folsom Man made that ball," the answer came back.

The young man kept his ball but I have another treasure—a

lump of clay that Folsom Man did not quite shape into a ball. I found it near Batavia, New York. It is the same kind of clay and covered with fingerprints just as the ball was, but the shape never became a ball.

Another relic of an even greater past is a piece of fossilized coniferous wood. In the early 1800's Dr. James A. Whitney secured it in barter from the Indians in the southwestern United States. It has on it the mark of a saw which bit into the wood. The interior of the cut is stained with a metallic stain, as if the saw were a bit rusty. Certainly the saw-mark was made before the wood fossilized because bits of the soft wood were pulled by the saw. Was a metal saw used? By whom? How long ago? How long did it take the wood to fossilize after it was sawed? 25,000 years?

Even prior to Folsom Man was another inhabitant who has come to be called "Midland Man." Maybe he was Folsom Man's ancestor; maybe he belonged to another tribe. A skull has been found in Texas, narrow and very like skulls of modern Indians. You or I might think it was a local Indian buried in an ancient spot, but the C-14 date of the skull is approximately 12,000 years ago.

Then there are "Clovis Points," very like Folsom Points, but a little cruder in workmanship. Material found in association with the Clovis Points has a C-14 date older than 12,000 years and less than 15,000. Man was here to make them that long ago.

In the Sandia Mountains southeast of Albuquerque, New Mexico, a cave has been excavated. Three layers of strata in the cave give us a further time schedule of the first Americans. The uppermost layer, dated 1,000 years ago, contains the usual remains of Indians who lived around 900 A.D. Then there is a hard crust of limestone and, under it, a layer containing Folsom Points associated with bones of the bison, mammoth, ground sloth, camel and wolf. Under this is a still older layer of material impregnated with yellow ochre. Mixed with rocks and pebbles are bones of mastodon, mammoth, an extinct horse and camel. There are hearth remains, charcoal, ashes and burned bones, javelin heads, and "Sandia Points," also resembling Folsom Points but different, more primitive. There are stone knives, scrapers, grooved stone balls like the "bolas" once used on the Argentine pampas for killing small animals and birds. How old are these things? Older than Folsom Man because the deposits are under those of Folsom Man.

Another First American is "the Tepexpan Man," found in Mexico where he probably fell 15,000 years ago. It had been known man hunted in the valley of Mexico during the last Ice Age but no actual human skeleton had been found. Hans Lundberg, a Canadian geophysicist, argued that somewhere there must be a skeleton. With an electrical sounding-device, he began examining the area. Any lengthening or shortening of the time required to return the electrical signal meant something different in the path of the impulse. With infinite patience and determination, he found three significant areas. Digging in two, he discovered nothing more than underground pools. Just as in the story books, he then dug in the third spot and found the skeleton of the Tepexpan Man. Although the skeleton appears to be a very recent type and shows no primitive characteristics, the date of his burial is fixed without a shadow of doubt. He was under a layer identified with the rainy climate of the Ice Age. This layer was put down 10,000 years ago. He is older than that. 15,000 years old? Older? Possibly.

Through carbon-dating, we have learned that man has been in America a long time. We had a date, November 4, 291 B.C. (Spinden correlation) on a monument in Yucatan; now we know that this is rather a late date in man's history in our hemisphere. The following are just a few of the Carbon-14 dates already obtained. Many more are on file but these impress upon us how old Americans really are.

> Danger Cave, Utah—basket—9,000 years
> Fort Rock Cave, Oregon—sandals—9,000 years
> Tule Spring, Nevada—charcoal from a fire set by man—23,800 years
> Lubbock, Texas—carbon associated with Folsom Points—9,500–10,000 years
> Midland, Texas—skull—12,000 years
> Cape Denbigh and Brooks Range, Alaska—artifacts—8,500 years
> Chile—organic remains—8,000–9,000 years
> Hearth near Lewisville, Texas—37,000 years
> Southern California, Santa Rosa Island off Santa Barbara—Red Heads—8,000–10,000 years
> Eleven miles away from above—Black Bottoms—8,000–10,000 years

The last two are especially interesting. On Santa Rosa Island there was discovered a whole cemetery of skeletons with heads painted red. If you remember, at Tikal the whole skeleton of a young priest had been dyed red. The bodies had been buried sitting upright with knees under chins, in a sociable group. There were seventy-five skeletons in all and three were 7½ feet tall. All had been big people. Associated with the burial were bone whistles, red abalone shells, bones of sea lions, seals and whales.

Eleven miles away, 129 people were buried, in what is now known as "the Cemetery of the Black Bottoms." After death, the abdomens of the bodies were filled with black clay which stained the end of the spine and the pelvis. They were all buried on their sides. Steatite beads, barbed spears and green abalone were found in the graves. Perhaps they had a sort of Jack Sprat agreement with their neighbors, the Red Heads: "You eat the red abalone; we'll eat the green."

Russell Cave in Jackson County, Alabama, may be useful in cross-dating American remains. The deepest level so far uncovered bears a C-14 date of 8,160 years ago plus or minus 300 years; it was occupied from 6000 B.C. to 1600 A.D. Six feet above the lowest floor is a skeleton approximately 4,000 years old. Some arrowheads are here, chipped with deer antlers, but not so well worked as the Folsom Points made some 2,000 years earlier. Had the Folsom skill been lost?

These people of Russell Cave decorated their pottery by pressing designs into the wet clay with a small wooden paddle. They used mats and baskets to give a woven pattern to the wet clay, too. The Mayas also used the basket-weave pattern but they carved it in stone. However, they did make sample designs in clay and when hardened pressed them to decorate bowls. A number of these sample designs are on display in the archaeological museum in Guatemala City. The first Russell Cave pottery was found at the 3,500-year-old level.

Digging down farther into the past, excavators came across late archaic fishhooks, two bones lashed together to form a V, a type that Eskimos use today. Also, by 5000 B.C., some ancient Edison had devised a light for his living quarters. He took the humerus of a bear, cut it smoothly and cleaned out the marrow, then filled the center with bear fat and inserted some sort of wick. It would give a smoky but good light.

Tunnels dug below the present floor, dated at 8,000 years ago, reveal charcoal and evidence of a fire fourteen feet below. At sixteen feet below the present floor, there are points like the Folsom Points. At twenty-three feet, more charcoal has been found which is carbon-dated at 9,000 years. I wonder what man cooked 9,000 years ago. Bear steak?

Artifacts found in Russell Cave show that it was on a crossroads of migration from north to south. Another city on the trade route is the Ancient Buried City of Kentucky, marked by mounds overlooking the confluence of the Ohio and Mississippi Rivers. Conch shells from the Gulf of Mexico lie side by side with copper from the northern Great Lakes region, mica from the pegmatite veins in the Appalachians, fluorspar from southern Illinois, and lead from Missouri or Illinois. The trade materials were worked by skilled artisans.

Largest of the nine mounds of Ancient Buried City is a burial mound for some 150 persons. Articles left with the dead show designs very similar to those used by the Mayas—human figures, bears, fish, frogs and even the plumed eagle. Large wooden earplugs are very like the Mayan ones. Some were buried in baskets, akin to the Mayan burials in pottery bowls.

The tallest mound here supported a temple made of hard clay like that at Kaminaljuyu. It has been excavated from five feet of earth which had formed on top of it. On the altar platform are the remains of a thatched roof shelter made of split cane bound with grass. There were three rectangular altars of burnt clay. Evidently, the temple had been filled with inflammable material, a sacrifice, animal or human, tied to the altar and the whole set on fire. Another temple which had been burned in the same way was found buried under this upper temple.

Another of the nine mounds of Ancient City held the council house, twenty-one by twenty-five feet. Post holes show there had been a temporary roof. An ancient engineer had made a drainage ditch outside the walls. In the kitchen debris were corn cobs and bones of deer, fowl, squirrel, raccoon and terrapin.

Excavation of the site began in 1932 when Mr. Fain King of Paducah purchased the mounds. Trowels, orange sticks, hairbrushes and fingers have all been used to free delicate carvings found there such as tiny shell jewelry and a thumbnail portrait sculptured in fluorspar. This is the same technique needed at Kaminaljuyu. Indeed, this ancient City of Kentucky has so many things in common with Kaminaljuyu that it provides a link between the ruins in North and those in Middle America. Could some of the same people who built Kaminaljuyu have migrated to the United States? I wonder. There is more than a suspicion that the Hopewell Indians who flooded through Illinois by the thousands, came from the south. They brought shell artifacts with them, too.

In dim ages past, a people whom we call the Olmecs migrated into Vera Cruz, Mexico, and founded their sacred city and the "La Venta" culture. When they came, we do not know. Where they went, they left no trace. But seven centuries before Columbus sailed for the New World, they had vanished into near oblivion.

They were gifted both in arts and in intellectual power. They carved twenty-ton stone heads and made delicate mosaic masks and precious jadeite ornaments. When their works of art were finished, they buried them. Why? To give their most precious works to their gods?

At La Venta, they built a great pyramid, a gigantic pile of clay and sand 100 feet high. Five huge stone heads with flat noses, round eyes, full lips and headgear like a cap adorned the site. These were not Mayan faces, yet the heads resemble the great stone heads at Copan which are definitely Mayan. Oddly enough, sculptures very similar to these were found in the ruins of the Fifty-Three Towers in the Bayan ruin of Angkor Tom, Cambodia. They were made by the Khmers, another people whose origin and ending are clouded in mystery. One head found in Cambodia has a definitely Mayan nose. Were the Khmers descendants of the Olmecs, or from a parent stock? Did they originally come from India as an old Chinese legend states? Was it true that a young prince of Delhi led his followers to Cambodia, subdued its people and set up the Khmer State?

The Olmecs used a Mayan calendar or, perhaps, the Mayas improved the Olmec calendar and then used it. They cut serpentine into pavement blocks and polished what must have been the first antique verd floor. Basalt columns, tall and weighty as those at Stonehenge, were capped with Stonehenge-type vaults weighing tons. One mosaic shows a stylized jaguar face or possibly a Chac face like the old, old shrine up on the back wall at Tikal's acropolis.

Later in Mexico's history, a great white city was built on a lake, the city of Tenochtitlan, now Mexico City. On November 8, 1519, Cortez saw the gleaming temple tops above the trees, as he rode over the wide causeway from Ixtapalapa. A teeming population of 300,000 gave no hint of the orgies of human sacrifice that went on day after day. The city was predominantly white, a shining, glaring white under tropical sun, softened only by a bit of purple volcanic ash which, used sparingly, lent a pink tone.

Tall pyramids, topped by temples, hemmed in the central plaza and ball court. There were the usual gladiatorial stone and the rack of skulls adorned with the heads of sacrificed enemies.

The greatest pyramid bore twin temples, one to Tlaloc the rain god, the other to Huitzilopochtli, god of war. They had been dedicated in 1490 (or some give the date as 1484) in ceremonies unmatched for ferocity. For two years, war was waged against Oaxaca to secure hordes of captives to sacrifice at this dedication. Twenty thousand were dragged up the steep stairs, laid backward over the altars, their hearts torn out and burned with a horrible stench. The stairs ran with the blood of their discarded bodies. Even the priests must have wearied as they plunged obsidian knives into body after body. Part of that ceremonial stairway can be seen today just a block from Mexico City's cathedral.

The amount of slave labor exacted from the populace can be judged by the 77 lesser pyramids and many other constructions around that central plaza.

The Aztecs partially rebuilt Tenochtitlan and made it again a great religious center. It finally fell to the Spanish who razed the beautiful pyramids, burned the writings and works of art and rebuilt the city from the ground, calling it Mexico City.

A mile north of Mexico City is Tlatelolco, built on several floating islands. The chief temple there, atop a high pyramid, was dedicated to two gods—Huitzilopochtli, god of war, and Tezcatlipoca, the "Smoking Mirror," or god of earth and sky.

Four days after Cortez entered Tenochtitlan, he asked for an escort to visit Tlatelolco. Montezuma did not like the idea but he dared not refuse him. He stalled for time, saying he would precede the Spaniard to the temple and offer a sacrifice in reparation for this invasion of the gods' privacy. Bernal Diaz was with Cortez on that visit; years later, details were still fresh in his memory. The two Spaniards mounted the 114 steep steps to the twin temples on top of the pyramid. There they saw two arched stones wet with war captives' blood. Two stone idols with glaring eyes, covered with gold and pearls, wore necklaces representing human hearts and heads. Eight hearts freshly torn from living breasts burned before the two idols. Freshly splashed blood was still wet on the floor and walls. The stench was horrible.

Perhaps this experience accounted for Cortez's cruelty to the Indians, especially to Montezuma. He may have thought that a people so inured to bloody sacrifice would not understand a gentler approach. He set out to show them that he, too, could demand human lives in abundance. The friars and priests with him saw that this was an aberration in a fundamentally admirable people. The Indians were so ignorant of the true God, they imagined He would be influenced by human sacrifices. The missioners put their faith in the Indians' basic humanity and set about teaching them of a reasonable, loving God. They were right; Cortez was wrong.

Five miles farther north is Tenayuca, the Place of the Serpents. Today, children play among the stylized snakes. They run their small hands over the rattles on the reptiles' tails. But once this was a horrible place where the hearts of living men were wrenched from their bodies and burned. It must have been a nightmare then to see serpents' heads protruding from walls and stairways, with long teeth and licking tongues demanding more and more blood. Two rattlesnakes crowded each other on the temple altar on top of the pyramid.

Tenayuca must have gorged itself on blood for centuries. It was rebuilt at least five times and every rebuilding meant the end of a long period of use.

Long centuries before the Spanish came to Mexico, the Nahuatl people had established a ritual of renewal. At the beginning of every fifty-two-year cycle, everything from temple furnishings to kitchen pottery was thrown out. The old was broken and the new put in its place. Life began anew; the old was buried in the past. What I have learned of these renewal ceremonies reminds me of our Easter vigil service. A new fire was kindled in the temple and smoldering charcoal was taken to each home to enkindle its hearth fire. In the semi-darkness, the light of spiritual renewal was borne from the temple to the home. Was it a presage of the time when they would all light their tapers from the paschal candle?

It would not have been the first time a pagan people had been prepared by their own customs for the advent of Christianity. Homer's *Iliad* and *Odyssey* is a case in point. The Trojan Hector stood head and shoulders above the Greeks who conquered him and above Achilles, whose sword ran him through. He, the true hero of the *Iliad*, went down to defeat. Later, when the Greeks heard the Christ had been killed in disgrace, even so they were ready to accept Him as Hero of the World. They had read of it before.

Penelope, too, was a figure of things to come. She remained faithful to her husband while he wandered for ten years. She suffered the importunities of suitors who would convince her that Odysseus was dead. Thus, through the faithfulness of the great woman, Penelope, the Greeks were prepared for the suffering of Mary, the greatest of all women.

The last New Fire ceremony was held at Tenayuca in 1507. The next one would have taken place in 1559 but by that time the Spanish had sacked the land, the temples were destroyed and nearly all the rulers killed.

The State of Puebla, Mexico, has a pyramid which covers a greater area than any other pyramid in the world. Although only half the height of Al Giza, the famous Cheops monument in Egypt, it is spread over 3½ times the acreage.

This is Cholula Pyramid, dedicated to Quetzalcoatl, the Feathered Serpent, God of Learning, Bringer of Civilization. Originally, Quetzalcoatl was a legendary white man who came to help the peoples of Middle America. Through the centuries, his identity became foggy and distorted; he changed from man to reptile. Instead of bringing good, he demanded sacrifice. This very fact seems an indication of how far in the past his original visit must have been—probably centuries before Christ.

Cholula was a Mecca. Shrines jostled one another. Altar stood beside altar on adjacent pyramids. As the centuries scampered after one another into the limbo of time, temples overlay earlier temples like the layers of pearl on an oyster's grain of sand. By the time the Toltecs invaded the Mexican valley around 500 and 600 A.D., the temples had been in use for a great space of time.

The rubble-filled early temples supported later ones built over them. This went on until a single colossal pyramid sprawled over forty-five acres. The slopes are irregular, the terraces offset; no master plan existed. The work ambled on through generations and centuries.

On the summit of Cholula Pyramid now stands the church of Nuestra Senora de los Remedios and, beside it, a walled churchyard 178 feet above the natural plain below. Once again Cholula is a Mecca for pilgrims who visit the holy place.

When the friars first came, they established a school for poor Indians. In telling the story of the Tower of Babel, they had a ready-made visual aid in the huge misshapen pyramid. Since then, the Indians have incorporated the idea into their legends. They tell their children that Cholula is the spot where tongues became confused.

A man-made mountain of mud and bricks, Cholula grew like Topsy under different generations and races. It does not have, of course, the unifying structure of an Egyptian pyramid, nor is its purpose the same. The Americans built pyramids to lift their temples closer to the sky; the Egyptians made them to mark tombs.

Bernal Diaz del Castillo, mentioned earlier as companion to Cortez when he visited Montezuma's pyramids in Mexico, had a habit of counting steps, even as you and I. He later wrote that the Temple Pyramid of Texcoco had 117 steps; Cholula, 120; Tlatelolco, 114. Diaz was counting steps while Montezuma oversaw the human sacrifices at the top. Possibly he checked his count as the bodies bounced down step by step.

Just twelve miles south of the great modern city is one of the most mysterious and provocative structures of them all, a great truncated cone, probably the oldest formal architecture on the western hemisphere. The present exterior is faced with unworked stone; the interior is built up of rubble and earth. Cuicuilco is the only pyramid whose antiquity can be checked by geologists, for it was inundated by lava thousands of years ago. Other pyramids are dated by guesses at the stratification and pottery sequences, or by actual dates.

Ten miles southwest of Cuicuilco is the volcano Xitli. Thousands of years ago it spewed out a great volume of lava, flooding over the whole ten miles between it and the pyramid and burying the base a depth of twenty-five feet. It must have been an eruption of great violence and long duration. I, for instance, remember the 1960 eruption of Kilauea Iki in Hawaii in the Puna rift zone. It lasted a month, covered 600 acres to a depth of twenty feet, and built a half-mile peninsula into the water. We thought that was devastating. In comparison with this eruption of Xitli, it would have been pretty puny. This lava flow was much greater than the flow in Hawaii.

Dr. George E. Hyde of the New Zealand Geological Department dated the lava flow of Xitli as 7,000 years ago, or 5000 B.C. But the pyramid must have been built, used and even abandoned before these dates. In fact, a thousand or more years of dust had collected and now forms a layer between the temple and the lava.

Near the modern village of San Angel nearby, there is a very old cemetery which also was buried under the same lava flow. In coarse gravel lie skeletons, perhaps of Cuicuilco's builders. In the gravel with them are their bowls and pots, baked clay dishes, obsidian knives and figurines. If we accept Dr. Hyde's dating, these people lived and worked here 1,000 years before the Great Pyramid of Pharaoh was built in Egypt, and 5,000 years before the Assyrians constructed their palace of Sennacherib. However, other scholars say that the remains are no older than 700–1000 B.C. Carbon dating may settle the argument.

In Indian lore, there are no traditions of this terrible volcanic eruption so it must have taken place in the far distant past. It was a disaster that would have been long remembered. The roar of exploding lava, the searing heat that burned everything in its path could not soon have been forgotten. The fact that it is, indicates how long ago it happened.

The Pedregal, meaning "Stony Place," is a great tongue of black, flinty lava, fifteen miles long, three miles wide and five- to thirty-feet deep. The Mexican government has tunneled under it and brought to light skeletons of people very much like today's Indians; also, stone implements and pottery of a Neolithic culture. One almond-eyed female head and a chalice-shaped bowl had been buried for 7,000 years.

Cuicuilco had been a truncated cone, 52 feet high, 412 feet in diameter at the base. The top platform was 290 feet in diameter. An outer wall, inclining at an average angle of 45°, is made of large blocks, three to four feet in length, of a previous flow of lava. I marveled that they could cut these blocks. Hardened lava is extremely hard. I once tried to divide a piece of lava from the Puna eruption in Hawaii, so as to leave a lava specimen in the Kaneohe school. Not having a carborundum saw, I could not do it. These ancient people supposedly had nothing but stone implements. How did they achieve those neat blocks of lava?

These lava rocks were placed on their sides with the smaller end toward the core of the building, buried in smaller pieces of lava. Rough blocks of dense basalt and andesite faced the sides. No attempt was made to smooth them; such a process was far beyond any tools they had.

On the top platform was eighteen feet of volcanic dust and pumice. Both this dust and all the lava used for building ante-dated the Pedregal flow. The altar upon this top platform was 22 x 9 feet and made of water-worn boulders fitted together with clay and resting on large lava boulders bedded in clay and sand.

And still another mystery! The builders of Cuicuilco seem to have departed before the Pedregal lava engulfed the area. In fact the structure had already started to decay. A platform on the eastern side, thirty by seventy feet, had fallen and crumbled into dust before the Pedregal lava buried it under ten feet. There is eight feet of loam on top of the summit altar. Some fifteen to seventeen feet of sand, clay and rock had accumulated on the pavement of the original temple before the lava covered it; this strengthens the theory that the builders lived and worked thousands of years before the Pedregal flow. If so, this temple was built 8,000–10,000 years ago. However, some argue the flow may have been only 1000 years B.C. If true, it will be difficult to reconcile this date with other known facts.

Certainly, it was an organized society that built this enormous temple. The population had turned from hunting to agriculture. Master planners and community engineers worked under a strong government. The art was crude but it was art. The lines were solid and vigorous with a severe beauty.

This conical pyramid was used mainly as a temple; burials were incidental. Were these the same peoples who, farther north, built conical mounds for burial and rectangular ones for temples? Did these same people later build Teotihuacan? How do these two step-pyramids—Cuicuilco and Teotihuacan—fit into the history of the world's other pyramids?

Teotihuacan, "Home of the Gods," is twenty-five miles northeast of Mexico City. The Toltecs, we know, kept this place as their principal religious center until 1200 A.D., but whether they built it or not is a question. Figurines and pottery on lower levels date back to 300 A.D. or earlier. Kaminaljuyu traded with Teotihuacan over the years; that pottery was interchanged is quite evident.

The Street of the Dead, more than a mile long, is the main thoroughfare there. Marking the mid-point is the magnificent pyramid known as "El Sol" (The Sun); at the north end is La Luna. The Street of the Dead is flanked along its entire length by small pyramids, topped by sacrificial areas, thirty or forty steps above the street level. As the victorious troops returned from battle, the warriors with their prisoners marched down this avenue, beating wooden drums, shrilling on clay flutes and hoarsely sounding conch-shell trumpets. Feather headdresses waved in the breeze; brightly colored loin cloths and heavy jade jewelry made it a brilliant sight. As the procession neared the altars, a priest or attendant grabbed a prisoner and dragged him up the stairway to the sacrificial form to tear his heart out.

According to legend, at the time of Montezuma, there was a celebration at Teotihuacan every twenty days and, borne to the spot on a gilded litter, he often took part in the human sacrifices.

The huge Temple of the Sun covers eleven acres. No two sides are of equal length but the average is 692 feet. No less than 35,067,-596 cubic feet of fill is walled in by adobe brick and overlaid with dark purplish-red volcanic stone. Patches of the original pink-painted plaster are still visible. Three times, the pyramid was enlarged by the simple expedient of laying a new wall and veneer over the old one, thus making it higher and wider at the truncated top. When El Sol was restored in 1905-10, the outer veneer was completely removed since it was beyond repair. This made the bases twenty-five to thirty feet shorter.

It's an awesome thing—El Sol—with its tremendous bulk rearing upward. Just to get it all into camera range, I had to back and back for yards. The four triangular sides are so big, they seem to be rounding upward, although one knows they are plane faces. Five terraces divide the slope. Standing at the foot of the pyramid, I could not see the top steps.

The top platform where the sun temple stood is 212 feet above the base. On this 5,000-square-foot platform stood the idol Tona-catecuhtli, "Giver of Life." Six feet wide, six feet thick, and eighteen feet high, it was carved from a single block of porphyry. No matter how much slave labor was available, it must have been a major engineering feat to raise this huge idol from the level of the plain to the temple platform, a height equivalent to a twenty-story skyscraper.

Halfway up the pyramid, a stairway leads down into its dark recesses, tunneled through the bulk to discover mementoes of the past. Strange idols, grotesque forms, small figures, jade, obsidian, arrowheads of flint, small heads of burnt clay, antique earthen jars and others with forms like those in use today, skulls, skeletons and one precious piece of woven cloth were excavated from the depths.

From the summit of El Sol, the quiet valley is visible for miles. The small village of San Juan Teotihuacan nestles in the shadow of the great pyramids that have made it famous. Popocatepetl, eternally rearing its great, snow-covered peak skywards, stands beside the volcano Iztaccihuatl and it is easy then to believe the legend concerning the two. "Popo" went off to war, leaving his beloved Iztaccihuatl behind. Malicious tongues told her he had been killed in battle and she died of a broken heart just before Popo returned to claim her as his bride. Finding her dead, he erected a high throne for her and another for himself. Eternity after eternity, Popocatepetl stands beside his Iztaccihuatl, guarding her. So the people talk of Popo and the Sleeping Lady.

In 1911, the Chinese Minister to Mexico climbed El Sol and to his astonishment saw on the summit an inscription common to burial places in China. Had migrants from his country built this place?

I walked from the Sun to the Moon along the famous Street of the Dead, feeling the ghostly presence of thousands of warriors marching their wretched captives beside me. I thought, what a terribly black-and-white world it was in ancient times. The strong were so strong, the weak so weak. The victors were so victorious, the defeated so horribly worsted. A man who might have trodden the necks of his enemies yesterday is himself mutilated and torn apart today. No "cease fire," no period of negotiation, no mild swapping of territories, no courteous cover-up of the fact of conquest and defeat created a grey half-win and half-lose atmosphere. No, it was winner take all—or nothing.

The Moon Pyramid is almost completely restored. Four terraces are visible and, when the summit is completed, another may take shape. Like El Sol, it is a truncated pyramid, but smaller, with a base 170 by 142 feet and the summit 150 feet above the plain.

Some 180 smaller mounds surround the major structures. Little by little, these are being restored. One of the newest to emerge from the neglect of centuries is the Temple of the Butterflies, completed in 1964. A low building abutting one of the smaller temples near La Luna, it has seventeen steps leading up to a long platform. Here slender, squarish columns support the stone lintels (originally wooden) which, in turn, support the roof. Large serpents' heads embellish the top step.

Under the overhanging roof of a side altar, an original painting can still be seen. It seems to be a great jaguar with long claws, done in outlines of red and blue. I took it with a movie camera and in 35 mm. slides. A guard came up gesticulating furiously.

"What firm do you work for?" he asked.

It took some convincing that I merely wanted pictures to show to friends.

A temple dedicated to Quetzalcoatl is partially restored. On either side of the wide staircase are large, heavy serpents' heads. It has been necessary to prop metal rods under the lower jaws, to hold up the heads, because some have been broken. I wondered what leverage the original workmen used to balance them so that they jutted into space firmly. Originally, the eyes were pieces of carved jade and obsidian but I saw only a few in the sockets. Most have gone into rubble or into pockets.

The serpent motif is everywhere on this Quetzalcoatl temple. Three curious bands of decorations cross the façade. This pattern repeats itself endlessly—a fanged serpent's head with a ruff around his neck like daisy petals, then several stylized rattles, then a face like a Chac mask, then three things that seem to be vertebrae, then the serpent's head wearing the daisy-ruff again and the whole sequence follows along. I puzzled over some stonework near the ground. What seemed to be waves were carved, rolling over various rattles from the snakes' tails. Then it seemed more probable that what I took to be waves were really serpents' bodies. When the temple is fully reconstructed, there will be continuous designs to the top. It will be well worth going back to see.

Today, people of the United States are surprised to learn of the archaeological wealth of their own country. In the early half of the nineteenth century, Stephens and Catherwood created the same surprise when they made known their finds in Middle America.

Somehow, we think of ourselves as a new people and we cannot believe we have a past more extensive than yesterday. We know that the first Americans were Indians, or some ancestors of the Indians, but we tend to think that those who landed on Plymouth Rock are the real Americans.

Nothing could be more untrue. We are but the most recent wave of immigrants to these shores. We are adding our puny bit to the great history of America, the America which has known resourcefulness, intellectual acumen, architectural progress long before Europeans touched these shores. And after us? What wave of migration will follow us?

GUADALUPE, UNION OF THE CONTINENT

One summer at the beach, I noticed a half-dozen baby sandpipers playing on our lawn near the water's edge. They did not seem to notice the clouding sky nor the urgent calls of their mother. When she finally got them together, the storm broke with deluging fury. Mother Sandpiper tucked them together into a feathery heap, and sat over them with protecting wings covering each downy head. She took the full force of the storm as she sat in the open, head bent to catch the least peep of her little ones. As the sun broke through and the rivulets of water ceased plowing routes to the ocean, Mother Sandpiper stood up and started to dry her drenched feathers, while her fluffy, dry babies ran around the lawn on the foolish business of little things.

The incident seemed trivial, yet it gave me an understanding of God's love for all mankind, as He expressed it:

"How often would I have gathered thy children together,
as a hen gathers her young under her wings but thou
wouldst not." (Matt. 23, 37.)

When Cortez entered the beautiful city of Tenochtitlan in 1519, he was lost in admiration at its man-made mountains of stone but he was sick at the horror of the human sacrifices he saw.

Since the large cities had developed, the majority of Indians had been little more than slave laborers, building tremendous temples and palaces for the ruling priests. Then came the Spanish—war, bloodshed and another variety of slavery. The Indians had lived in fear of their grotesque gods who demanded more and more human sacrifice. Now they lived in fear of their new masters and the punishments they meted out. Aside from the love they knew for one another, there was no love in their lives.

In my human way, I like to imagine God in heaven deciding upon an ambassador to tell these people of His love for them. Not an angel, not a prophet, not an apostle. He wanted an ambassador who would portray the tenderness of His love. In Bethlehem, Nazareth and Jerusalem, Christ had lived under foreign rulers and with His human heart knew what it entailed. Who would be able to tell His understanding love for these people? Who? His mother. She had lived with Him all those years. They had gone through the sorrows and agonies together. She could tell these beloved Indians of His love. Now for the first time, they were learning of the true God from the Dominicans and Franciscans. Lest God seem as remote as their false gods, He would send Mary to them. He would make the first approach.

He meant to show His love for the whole western hemisphere, so Mary would come to His beloved people in the very heart of the land. In 1531, there were no divisions into countries. It was one vast expanse of land peopled from Alaska to Tierra del Fuego by Indians, interrelated by blood. The whole land and all its people must know of His love.

The Indians had placed their temples on man-made mountain tops. He would choose a God-made mountain for His Mother. Tepeyac, meaning the "Sharp Summit of the Hills," is the highest of the high mountains which surround Mexico City. One morning as dawn was breaking, a devout Indian named Juan Diego was hurrying the short distance from his dwelling in Tolpetlac to the church of Santiago el Mayor to hear the Saturday Mass in honor of Mary, Mother of God. As he reached the foot of Tepeyac, he heard sweet music and saw a great light coming from the summit. While he looked upward, scarcely believing his eyes and ears, to his utter astonishment, he heard his name called in a woman's sweet, delicate voice, "Juan." Quickly he climbed the slope.

In the center of the brightness stood a beautiful woman. Later, Juan said her robe "shone so brightly that its glory shone around the rough rocks on the hilltop, and the stones appeared to be precious gems and transparent, and the leaves of the thorns and cactuses, which grow very small there, and meanly because of the dryness of the place, appeared to be clusters of fine emeralds, their twigs and stems and thorns of burnished gold and shining; and even the ground of the level plain which was there on the summit appeared like jasper with many colors blended together."

Just as later Mary spoke to Bernadette in her patois, so now she spoke to Juan in his native dialect. Both she and Juan were perfectly at home with each other from the start. Her dark Jewish complexion was much like his own. Her dress, similar to the ones she used to wear in Nazareth, was not unlike that worn by his dear deceased wife.

With a serene countenance and an endearing tone in her voice, Mary said:

"Juan Diego, my son, whom I love tenderly, like a little and delicate child, where are you going?"

"Noble Mistress and My Lady, I am going to Mexico City to hear Mass which the ministers of God, His substitutes, offer for us."

Juan had been well instructed by the Franciscan Friars. Both he and his wife had been the joy of the Fathers who were working under difficult circumstances to teach the Indians and to protect them from the demanding Spaniards. Since Juan's wife had died, he made the journey alone each week.

Mary told Juan she was the Mother of the ever True God and that she wished a church to be built on the summit of Tepeyac in her honor.

"My very dear son, you must know that I am the eternal Virgin Mary, Mother of the True God, Author of Life, Creator of all and Lord of the Heavens and Earth, Who is present everywhere, and it is my desire that a church be built here in this place for me, where, as your most merciful mother and that of all your people, I may show my loving clemency, and the compassion that I bear to the Indians, and to those who love me and seek me and to all those who seek my protection, and call upon me in their travail and afflictions, and where I may hear their sorrows and prayers and give them consolation and help. And so that my will may be accomplished, you must go to the City of Mexico, to the palace of the Bishop who lives there, to whom you will say that I have sent you, and that it is my pleasure that he build me a church in this place; and tell him all that you have seen and heard; and you may be sure that I will thank you for all that you do for me in this that I put in your care, and you will be noted and exalted by doing this. Now my son, you have heard my wish; go in peace and be sure that I will repay you for the work and diligence you employ, so spare no effort in doing this."

Juan replied: "I go, most noble Lady, and my Mistress, to carry out your command as your humble servant; wait a little while for me."

Love begets love. Although Juan styles himself as "your humble servant" he adds in a familiar tone, "wait a little while for me."

Mary knew to whom she was sending Juan Diego. The Bishop-elect of Mexico City, Don Fray Juan de Zumarraga, was one of the truly saintly men of the New World.

Charles V of Spain had become more and more concerned about the stories reaching him from the New World. He had been told of cruelties to the Indians. Guzman was a tyrant. The Indians were being robbed of the little they had. It worried Charles.

During Holy Week, Charles left his court and spent the holy days in the monastery of Abrojo where one Fray Juan de Zumarraga was Friar Prelate. Upon leaving, Charles left a most generous, really a lavish alms. Fray Juan immediately gave it all away lest it harm the austerity of the monastery. Charles heard where his money had gone and he wondered at the clear vision of the Friar Prelate. A short time later, as the need for a strong leader and a protector of the Indians in Mexico became more evident, he determined to send Fray Juan. On December 12, 1527, he ordered his ambassador in Rome to secure the erection of a new diocese in Mexico with Fray Juan as its bishop. Not waiting for the papal bulls to come through, he insisted Fray Juan leave immediately for the New World. Fray Juan neither wanted the post, nor did he think it right to act as Bishop-elect until word came from Rome. His community thought it better for him to obey the king so he took this to be the Will of God and left. The four-month ocean voyage left him so ill it took him a month to re-cover. At that, he was one of the lucky who had not died at sea.

In January, 1529, he presented his appointment as Bishop of Mexico and Protector of the Indians. Guzman, who considered him-self dictator of the land, refused to cooperate with Fray Juan. In fact, he put every possible obstacle in the path of the zealous friar. Fray Juan was not only a holy man but a patient, determined one. He did all he could for the Indians with rare courage. He bided his time until he could do more. When he could do no more than listen to the Indians and weep with them, he did that. In 1532—the year after Juan Diego saw Mary—Dona Isabel, then ruling Spain, sent for him to be consecrated. Six years after he was appointed Bishop-elect, he was consecrated Bishop on April 27, 1533.

Returning to Mexico, Bishop Juan de Zumarraga continued to live the life of a humble friar. He always journeyed on foot and barefoot. Every night he rose at midnight to say Matins, fasted rigorously on all the Church and Franciscan fast days and often went to the monastery of San Francisco where for a few short hours he could be just a friar among his brethren.

It was to this man that Mary sent Juan Diego on her mission. Juan waited a long time to see the Bishop. The servants who guarded the entrance took it upon themselves to make poor Indians wait for hours, even for a whole day. And the Bishop who gave himself untiringly to all was unaware of the delay. Juan, being very poor, waited most of the day. When the attendants became tired of the sport, they finally ushered him into the presence of the Bishop who received him with great kindliness. He listened with interest to Juan's story of his talk with the Lady. Being a holy man, he did not discredit what Juan said but he needed more evidence. If it were really Mary who sent Juan, she would not mind sending some sort of a sign. I wonder if, in his heart, the Bishop did not dream of Castile roses as a sign. It would be so nice to see the lovely flowers again.

The Bishop told Juan to return again in a few days. Trudging along homeward, Juan felt he had failed his Lady. There on the top of Tepeyac she awaited him and he immediately fell on his knees, explaining:

"My very dear Daughter, my Queen, my Lady Most High, I did what you asked, and although I was not given entrance right away to see and talk with the Bishop, after a long time, I did see him, and gave him your message in the way you commanded; he heard me quietly and with attention, but from what I saw in him, and from the questions he put to me, I do not think he believed me, because he told me to come back again, so that he could inquire of me at length about the business on which I came, and examine it to the roots. He presumed that the church you ask to be built is a fiction of mine, or a fancy of mine, and not your will; so I pray you, that you send some noble and chief person for this purpose, one worthy of respect and to whom credence will be given; because you see, my Mistress, that I am a poor country man, a humble villager, and this matter on which you send me is not for me; pardon me, my Queen, for my boldness, if in anything I have exceeded what is fitting and owing to your greatness; I do not wish to fall under your indignation or to have displeased you with my reply."

These very words have been handed down to us in the historic writings of the Indians and translated from the original Mexican dialect without any alteration.

Mary replied to Juan:

"Listen, my well-beloved son, be assured that I do not lack for servants or people to command, for I have many whom I could send if I wished who would do that which I ask them; but it is fitting that you attend to this matter, and I ask it of you, and through your intervention my will shall be accomplished, and my desire; and so I pray you, my son, and command you, to return tomorrow to see and talk with the Bishop and tell him to build me the church that I ask of him; and that she who sends you is the Virgin Mary, Mother of Very God."

After waiting all day at the Bishop's house, poor Juan might have drawn a long sigh and murmured, "Not again!" but he did not even mention it. One can sense he was used to waiting, used to being last—for he was an Indian.

Juan replied: "Do not be displeased, my Queen, and my Lady, with what I said, because I will go with a very good will and with all my heart to obey your command, and to take your message; I did not want to excuse myself from it, nor did I consider the road a task, but it was only that perhaps I would not be accepted nor heard well, or if the Bishop did hear me, he would not give me credence. I will do all that you command me; wait for me, Lady, tomorrow in this place, at the setting of the sun, and I will bring back to you the reply which he will make, and so I leave you in peace, my exalted Daughter, and God keep you."

At the setting of the sun—Juan knew he would again be made to wait, that was his lot. What a revelation of the treatment of the Indians these few words signify!

The next day, Sunday, Juan attended Mass at the church of Santiago Tlatelolco. Then Juan made his way to the Bishop's palace as his Queen had requested. It was a long time before the Bishop was told he was waiting. When finally he knelt before Bishop-elect Zumarraga, tears came to his eyes as he recounted that he had again seen the Mother of God. She had told him to return to the Bishop and renew her request for a church. The Bishop really believed Juan and questioned him over and over to secure all the details that must have been dear to his saintly heart. However, much was at stake. Prudence told him he had to be absolutely certain it was Mary who sent him the message. The devil can be clever and harm might come to the Indians' faith were it Satan who had hatched a plot. So the Bishop asked for a clear sign such as no one could mistake, a sign that only Mary could send. Juan said he would bring the Bishop whatever sign he wished.

The Bishop was taken back at Juan's utter confidence in the Lady of his vision. Juan seemed to have no doubt Mary would know what sign the Bishop wished to have. He was certain Mary would give the sign. How well Juan knew his Lady! And how well she was fulfilling her role of ambassador of God's Love! She was asking for a church, but it would be hers only in name. It would be God's church and in it God would strengthen, console and love these poor Indians.

The Bishop sent two of his household after Juan to report on whom he saw and where he went, but they lost him as he approached the spot upon which Mary awaited her messenger. To her he reported the day's visit and the request of the Bishop for a sign. Mary thanked him for his trouble in her behalf and told him to return the next morning for the sign.

When Juan reached home that night, December 10, 1531, he found his uncle, with whom he lived since his wife died, very ill of "cocoliztli" (typhus). The fever was so malignant that all day Monday, December 11, Juan stayed by his side nursing him, but the illness progressed. Early on the morning of December 12, 1531, Juan Bernardino, the uncle, begged Juan Diego to run to Tlatelolco to get him a priest that he might receive the Sacraments before he died. Juan set off in haste. When he came to Tepeyac, he dared not cross the summit as was his wont because he did not want to be delayed by Mary. His first duty was to his uncle—after that he would do her bidding. So he took the lower road, bending a little to be hidden by the low bushes as he trotted along. But Mary had everything under control. At a turn in the road, Juan saw Mary coming down the hill to meet him. How well she understood his heart and his motives!

"Where are you going, my son? And what road is this you are taking?" Juan was torn and twisted by worry over his uncle and duty to his Lady. He dropped on his knees before her and in the midst of his confusion poured out his soul.

"My beloved daughter, and my Lady, God keep you. How did you waken? Is your health good? Do not be angry with what I have to say. Hear me, my Lady, and know that a servant of yours, my uncle, is dangerously ill of a sudden sickness and mortal; and because he is very weak, I am hurrying to the church of Tlatelolco in the city to call a priest to come and confess him and give him the unction, as we are all born subject to death. And after I have done this duty, I will come back here to this place to obey your command. Forgive me, I pray you, my Lady, and have a little sufferance, as I am not trying to avoid doing what you have commanded your servant, nor am I making a false excuse. Tomorrow I will return without fail." Juan was not even going to take time to bury his uncle. He would return as soon as he had taken the priest to his home and back to the monastery.

Mary understood fully. She did not scold Juan for failing to come the day before nor for putting his uncle before her.

"Listen, my son, to what I tell you now. Do not be troubled, nor disturbed by anything; do not fear illness, nor any grievous happening, nor pain. Are you not under my shadow, my protection? And am I not life and health? Are you not in my favor, and do you not go on my errand? Do you need anything else? Do not be troubled, or take thought of your uncle's illness, for he will not die of this seizure, and is well even now."

As the words fell on Juan's ears, the tumult and confusion in his heart ceased. Perfect peace enveloped him and he knew he could fully trust the words of his Lady. He sank down into the embrace of her kindness and her love for him and for his uncle. From the fullness of his grateful heart he said:

"Then send me, my Lady, to see the Bishop, and give me the sign, as you said, so that he will give me credence." What a miracle Mary had worked in his simple, noble soul!

With affectionate accents, Mary said:

"My very dear and tender son, climb up to the top of the hill where you have seen me and talked with me, and cut the roses that you will find there, and collect them together in the skirt of your cape, and bring them here to me in my presence, and I will tell you what you have to do and to say."

As every other Indian who climbed the slope of Tepeyac knew, Juan was aware no roses could possibly grow on its summit. Even the scraggly cactus clutched with desperation at the rocky soil. The hard, sterile earth had never known a flowering thing. And yet Juan immediately climbed to find the roses Mary said would be there. And they were, a whole garden of exquisite, fragrant roses fresh from the pampered gardens of Castile. The delicious fragrance set his nostrils a-tingle as he stroked the cool, dew-covered flowers. He cut as many roses as his "tilma" (mantle) could hold and then on sure, sandal-shod feet ran to Mary who was standing under a Quancahautl tree, a forest tree often called the "prayer tree." Its ancient trunk was still in existence in 1666 when Luis Becerra Tanco wrote the account I am using for this narration.

Mary took all the roses out of Juan's tilma and arranged them one by one, herself. Then helping him fold the tilma over his precious burden, she told him to show the flowers to no one until he reached the Bishop. Little did Juan guess at the surprise Mary had placed on his poor maguey tilma.

Again, the attendants kept him waiting in the Bishop's courtyard. Filled with curiosity, they pulled at his tilma to see what he carried but Juan, with Mary's help, was stronger than them all. Finally, the Bishop was told of Juan's presence and called him in. Even the heat of the sunny courtyard had not wilted the roses and so, when the Bishop asked what sign he had brought, they tumbled onto the floor as a cascade of freshness from a beloved garden in Castile. And then the Bishop, lifting his eyes from the roses to Juan's face, saw what Juan had not seen, the portrait of Mary painted on his tilma. Dropping to his knees, the Bishop murmured words of love for her who loved the Indians so much. Rising, he gently untied the knot behind Juan's head and reverently carried the tilma to his oratory in the first of thousands of processions.

All that day, the Bishop entertained Juan and wanted him near. Next day, he and a group of officials went with Juan to the top of Tepeyac to mark the exact spot designated by Mary for the church.

Still accompanied by the officials, Juan returned home to his uncle and found him well as his faith had told him he would. Mary had even appeared to Juan Bernardino, telling him news of his nephew and adding she wanted her image on the tilma to be called Santa Maria de Guadalupe. She did not say why, woman-like, and to this day, no one knows the reason of her choice. But Guadalupe has become a household word of love in all America.

I had loved the story of Guadalupe for longer than I care to say and now that I was in Mexico City, the Basilica was the first spot I wanted to visit. A great fenced-in patio fronts the Basilica and the Tuesday morning I entered its iron gates, large bouquets withered in the sun from the thousands of pilgrims who had been there the Sunday before. They had come as so many others come, two and three days' march away. They had camped in the open, prayed at their Mother's shrine, assisted at the Eucharistic Liturgy and received sacramental grace. They had found comfort and consolation.

I had been saving some Ansco 200 color-film just for this visit as I hoped its speed would pick up the beauty of the interior. At the entrance, I started taking movie shots. The shrine was filled with people of all stations in life. Among the wealthy fingering their expensive rosaries, the poor Indians mingled and were at ease in their Mother's home. Rich and poor alike made their way up the long aisle on their knees, praying for all the needs of their hearts and souls. Here and there, a tourist stuck out like a sore thumb while others mingled as one with the devout group.

As for me and for all the pilgrims, one thing in that vast church riveted our attention, Juan's tilma over the central altar. The golden candlesticks on the altar reached to it. The golden shaft of sunlight through the high window pointed to it. Thousands of eyes were lifted to it. There was Mary's portrait.

For years it was said Mary had painted her image as an Indian girl. Fray Jose Francisco de Guadalupe Mojica, O.F.M., after years of study, thinks she did not. She painted a true portrait of herself as she walked the streets of Nazareth, Bethlehem and Jerusalem. Her dark skin made her one with the Indians and yet it was the dark complexion of a Jewish girl. In northern Palestine, the women wore a long tunic lined with fur for warmth and Mary, who came to Juan in the Mexican winter of December, reveals the rabbit-fur lining of her tunic at the wrists. The shape of her hair under her veil is that of the Palestinian woman with plaited hair worn in a circle around the back of the head. Her mantle is the Judean semicircular cloth which covers the person from head to foot. And in her eye is the image of Juan as she saw him when she painted her portrait.

The tilma was made of maguey cloth and woven coarsely like a burlap bag, but the portrait shows none of the unevenness of the cloth. Maguey cloth lasts a very short time, so it is a miracle this tilma is as perfect as it was three hundred years ago. It has never been restored. In fact, it is impossible to add to the portrait. Some soul added a gold crown and it peeled off. Others painted the moon silver. It blackened and is peeling, too. Angels were added and they have disappeared.

Although Mary's face is turned to the side, I felt she was looking at me. Her sweet expression is filled with compassion and understanding of the woes of the world. For those moments at her feet, heaven is no longer a thing of faith but of knowing.

Mass after Mass followed each other at the altar below Juan's tilma and thus it is day after day. Hundreds flock to receive Christ during the Masses. Her love surely has led America to her Son. Those of us from the United States have been slower to find she is the Mother of all Americans, not just the possession of Mexico. Her shrine is in the heart of America and she belongs to all on the western hemisphere.

Europe may have its Lourdes, its Fatima, its La Salette. We have our very own Guadalupe.

EPILOGUE

All books must come to an end sooner than the author wishes because of the limitations of size. Even the encyclopedist cannot say all he wishes about every subject. So I suppose I should not feel too great a sense of frustration in being obliged to omit much from this volume. There are literally hundreds of Mayan ruins I have not even named. I have merely touched on the flora and fauna of Guatemala. Volcanoes have been named, nothing else. Very little has been said of the wealth of Indian costuming, use of native dyes, intricate weaving. There is the whole field of Mayan folklore I have used in but few instances.

I have said nothing of my trip to El Salvador and the tropical beauty of the country together with the heart-breaking slums in the Maryknoll Fathers' parishes in Santa Ana, an hour from the capital, San Salvador. I have omitted a description of the modern metropolises taking over the old Spanish in Guatemala City and Mexico City. I sincerely hope you, the reader, will not be too disappointed when you cannot find topics you wished to read within these pages.

There are also things I would have included if it were possible to do so. It would have been a joy to tell from whence the peoples of Mayan America came. We can be certain some came from Asia, but from where did the Olmecs come? And where did they go? Why are sculptures from thirteenth-century Cambodia similar to Vera Cruz Olmec heads, older than 600 B.C.? Why do carved stones from Tiquisate, Guatemala, have a laughing and a sad side, reminiscent of Greek stage decorations? Why do statuettes from fifth-century

Oaxaca resemble Shakespearean jesters? Why do figurines from the Gulf coast make one think of effervescent movie actors? Is Dr. Sidney Edelstein right in thinking the similarity of dyes used in Mexico and Israel (I might add, in Pliny's Rome) has a bearing on Mayan migration? If so, which way did the migration go, from Israel and Rome to Middle America or vice versa?

I would like to know when the first migration came to the shores of America. With carbon-dating, we have evidence of the age of remains containing carbon, but what of stone Folsom Points and tools? Tree-ring data in the southwestern United States has helped a little. Dr. Edward V. Sayre's atomic analysis has clinched pottery trading in Mayan America but has not given us dates of that trading. Possibly now, with the technique developed by Fleischer and Price of dating minerals by chemical etching of fission fragment tracks, we may, after it is perfected, find a way of telling when an arrowhead was cooked in a mammoth carcass. As we learn more about methods of dating, we may have an expanding time schedule to go with our theory of an expanding universe.

As has been remarked before, the first migrants to America were nomad hunters. But I suppose we could have called the young men who went west in colonial times nomads, too. For the time, they had no real homes or farming culture, living off the animals they shot and the plants of the wayside. At any rate, our first Americans had tools and were very resourceful. Even the oldest skeleton found so far bears no primitive characteristics and most of us would find it hard to believe that it did not belong to a man of our generation.

The first Americans had an amazing abstract intelligence. They developed mathematics, astronomy and chronology within their own culture centuries before such abstract science was known anywhere else. Their architecture and art were matched in other countries years later. Only China surpassed them in carving jade. Their sculpture and paintings of the human figure were proportioned and natural. From the beginning of stelae carving, they used the difficult profile to depict their gods and leaders.

Morality among the Mayas was very high and their purity in single life and in marital relationships is attested by the sacred books which have come down to us, especially the Popol-Vuh. So far, not a single nude figure has been found, nor has a syphilitic bone been uncovered in ancient Guatemala. European histories of medicine state that syphilis originated in America. Since Guatemala, Yucatan and Honduras are almost certainly the center of the first American Mayan civilization, and since no syphilitic bones have been found in the archaeological diggings, one might guess syphilis was brought to the Mayas some time later. It occurs in the Inca skulls, in bones from New Mexico and in one from Mexico. Excavations continue, so someday evidence of syphilis may be found even in Guatemala.

A ceramic of an old hunchback (600–900 A.D.) shows Pott's disease and demonstrates the length of time tuberculosis has been in America. It also demonstrates the accuracy of Mayan ceramics.

Surgery was practiced by the Mayas, using scalpel-quality obsidian knives. Dr. C. Martinez Duran, Professor of Medicine at Guatemala University, thinks the sculptures called "Life and Death" by some archaeologists are really unilateral dissections. Today we might preserve such a dissection in formaldehyde. Then they preserved it by carving it in rock. Other sculptures show tumors which appear to be metastasizing sarcomas. Another illustrates a bilateral exophthalmos, probably caused by thyrotoxicosis. Did medical students carve these as homework? Or were they used in religious ceremonies to avert like sickness?

No matter where we turn in Mayan America, there are unanswered questions. As excavations continue, bit by bit is added to the little knowledge we have of the first Americans. There is a long history and a proud one to be unraveled on this continent. How wrong Montaigne (1533–1592) and Descartes (1596–1650) were when they wrote that the American is an example of a man without a history— and Marcellin Boule (died 1942) who failed to recognize antiquity in the western hemisphere.

In order to appreciate our past, we have to get the right perspective. Years ago when I studied history and geography in grade school, I imagined the Pilgrims landing on an uninhabited land, vacant and waiting for them to do something with it. I knew there were a few Indians here and there but I visualized them as campers temporarily hunting for this or that. It seemed only natural to me that the "real" Americans from Europe should push the Indians together as one would the objects on a shelf, to make room for the new people.

It took years for me to realize that this land of ours had known waves of population centuries before Europe was civilized enough to travel across the Atlantic Ocean. The Pilgrims, or even Leif Ericson, were latecomers to these shores, the current migration. Since then, I have seen the Irish, the Italians and the Mexicans migrate to the United States, work themselves up from common laborers to influential, valued leaders. The same migrations have been assimilated in Middle America and South America.

The western hemisphere was a united whole when the First Americans flooded over it from Alaska to Tierra del Fuego. It should still be a united whole. Some of us speak English, some Spanish, some Portuguese, but the barrier of language is breaking down through travel, aid missions, tourism and the Organization of American States. We of the western hemisphere, we of America can present a united front to the rest of the world. United, we have the vigor to be a tremendous power for good in the world. But to be united, we must realize America stretches from Alaska to Tierra del Fuego. All of us are Americans.

While we are striving for the goal of unity, we can make Tiny Tim's Christmas prayer our own: "God bless us every one!"

APPENDIX

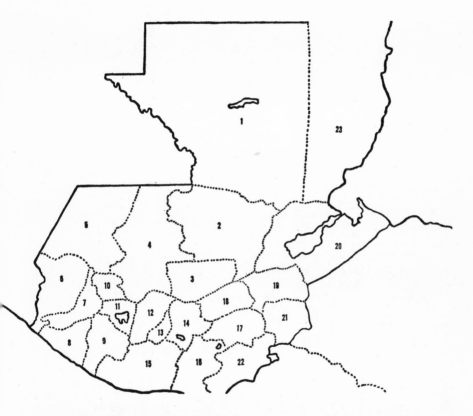

1. Departments or States of Guatemala followed by Capitals and Distance in miles of Capitals from Guatemala City

1. Petén, Flores, 294. 2. Alta Verapaz, Cobán, 156. 3. Baja Verapaz, Salamá, 112. 4. Quiché, Santa Cruz, 103. 5. Huehuetenango, Huehuetenango, 150. 6. San Marcos, San Marcos, 160. 7. Quezaltenango, Quezaltenango, 125. 8. Retalhuleu, Retalhuleu, 157. 9. Suchitepéquez, Mazatenango, 155. 10. Totonicapán, Totonicapán, 110. 11. Sololá, Sololá, 74. 12. Chimaltenango, Chimaltenango, 30. 13. Sacatepéquez, La Antigua, 28. 14. Guatemala, Guatemala, 0. 15. Escuintla, Escuintla, 35. 16. Santa Rosa, Cuilapa, 40. 17. Jalapa, Jalapa, 110. 18. Progreso, Progreso, 75. 19. Zacapa, Zacapa, 120. 20. Izabal, Puerto Barrios, 237. 21. Chiquimula, Chiquimula, 125. 22. Jutiapa, Jutiapa, 77. 23. Belice, Belice, 400.

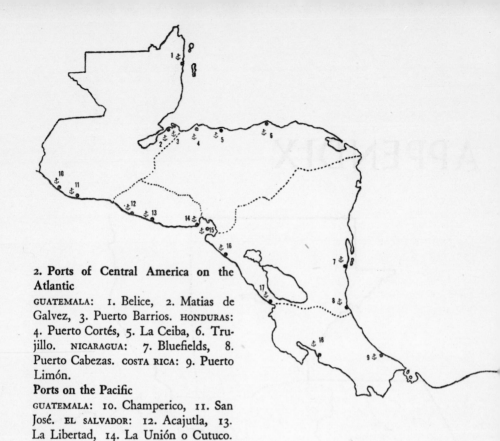

2. Ports of Central America on the Atlantic

GUATEMALA: 1. Belice, 2. Matias de Galvez, 3. Puerto Barrios. HONDURAS: 4. Puerto Cortés, 5. La Ceiba, 6. Trujillo. NICARAGUA: 7. Bluefields, 8. Puerto Cabezas. COSTA RICA: 9. Puerto Limón.

Ports on the Pacific

GUATEMALA: 10. Champerico, 11. San José. EL SALVADOR: 12. Acajutla, 13. La Libertad, 14. La Unión o Cutuco. HONDURAS: 15. Amapala. NICARAGUA: 16. Corinto, 17. San Juan del Sur. COSTA RICA: 18. Puntarenas

3. Rivers of Central America Which Empty into the Atlantic Ocean

GUATEMALA: 1. El Chiapas or Tabasco, 2. El Usumacinta (boundary with Mexico), 3. El Hondo or Azul (boundary with Mexico), 4. El Belice, 5. El Sarstun, 6. El Polochic, 7. El Dulce, 8. El Motagua (boundary with Honduras). HONDURAS: 9. El Chamelecón, 10. El. Ulúa, 11. El Lean, 12. El Aguań or Romano, 13. El Tinto, 14. El Patuca, 15. El Wans Coco or Segovia (boundary with Nicaragua). NICARAGUA: 16. El Prinzapolca, 17. El Grande de Matagalpa, 18. El Escondido, Bluefields or Mico, 19. El Indio, 20. El San Juan (boundary with Costa Rica). COSTA RICA: 21. El Colorado, 22. El Tortuguero, 23. El Reventazon, 24. El Matina, 25. El Sixaola or Tarire (boundary with Panamá).

4. Rivers of Central America Which Flow into the Pacific Ocean

GUATEMALA: 1. El Sushiate (boundary between Mexico and Guatemala), 2. El Naranjo, 3. El Tilapa, 4. El Samala, 5. El Nahualate, 6. El Madre Vieja, 7. El Coyolate, 8. El Guacalate, 9. El Michatoya, 10. El de los Esclavos, 11. El Paz (boundary with El Salvador). EL SALVADOR: 12. El Jiboa, 13. El Lempa, 14. El San Miguel. HONDURAS: 15. El Goascorán (boundary with El Salvador), 16. El Nacaome, 17. El Choluteca, 18. El Negro (boundary with Nicaragua). NICARAGUA: 19. El Estero, 20. El Leon. COSTA RICA: 21. El Tempisque, 22. El Barranca, 23. El Grande de Tarcoles, 24. El Grande de Pirris, 25. El Grande de Terraba, 26. El Diquiś, 27. El Coto.

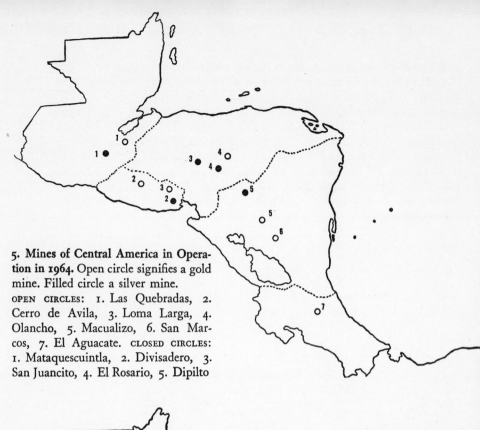

5. Mines of Central America in Operation in 1964. Open circle signifies a gold mine. Filled circle a silver mine.

OPEN CIRCLES: 1. Las Quebradas, 2. Cerro de Avila, 3. Loma Larga, 4. Olancho, 5. Macualizo, 6. San Marcos, 7. El Aguacate. CLOSED CIRCLES: 1. Mataquescuintla, 2. Divisadero, 3. San Juancito, 4. El Rosario, 5. Dipilto

6. Volcanoes of Central America and feet above sea level

GUATEMALA: 1. Tacaná, 13,411. 2. Tajumulco, 15,147. 3. Quezaltenango, 10,490. 4. Zunil, 11,659. 5. Santa Maria, 12,434. 6. San Pedro, 9,979. 7. Atitlán, 11,633. 8. Tolimán, 10,405. 9. Acatenango, 14,190. 10. Fuego, 13,695. 11. Agua, 12,382. 12. Pacaya, 8,415. 13. Tecuamburro, 6,435. 14. Jumaytepeque, 5,993. 15. Suchitan, 6,739. 16. Amayo, 3,465. 17. Moyuta, 5,557. 18. Chingo, 5,874. EL SALVADOR: 19. Apaneca, 5,576. 20. Santa Ana, 7,772. 21. Izalco, 6,221. 22. San Salvador, 6,227. 23. San Jacinto, 4,775. 24. San Vicente, 7,178. 25. Tecapa, 5,257. 26. Chinameca, 4,627. 27. San Miguel, 6,999. 28. Conchagua, 4,122. NICARAGUA: 29. Consigüina, 3,861. 30. Viejo, 6,300. 31. Momotombo, 6,155. 32. Masaya, 2,805. 33. Mombacho, 5,280. 34. Ometepe, 5,379. 35. Madera, 4,214. *Small Volcanos:* 36. Guisisil, 37. Palma, 38. Juigalpa, 39. Pan de Azucar, 40. Picara, 41. Ventanillas. COSTA RICA: 42. Orosi, 7,689. 43. Rincon de la Vieja, 4,950. 44. Miravalle, 4,732. 45. Poas, 9,174. 46. Barba, 9,570. 47. Irazu, 11,491. 48. Turrialba, 11,197. 49. Chiripó, 12,646. 50. Ujum, 9,702. 51. Pico Blanco o Kamuk, 9,616. 52. Picacho, 7,125.

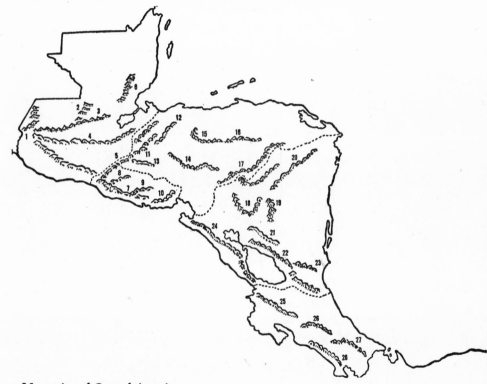

7. Mountains of Central America

GUATEMALA: 1. Sierra Madre or Cuchumantanes, 2. Chamá, 3. Santa Cruz, 4. Minas, 5. Merendón (boundary between Guatemala and Honduras), 6. Cockscomb. EL SALVADOR: 7. Cadena Costera, 8. Apaneca and Lamatepec, 9. San Salvador and San Vicente, 10. Tecapa and Chinameca. HONDURAS: 11. Celaque, 12. Puca or Opalaca, 13. Montecillos, 14. Comayagua, 15. Sulaco, 16. Misoco, 17. Dipilto, Colon or Chile (continuation of same mountains in Nicaragua). NICARAGUA: 18. Yalí, 19. Datanlí, 20. Yeluca, 21. Amerrique, 22. Huapí, 23. Yolaina, 24. Las Tablas. COSTA RICA: 25. Guanacaste or Tilarán, 26. Central Range, 27. Talamanca or Dota, 28. San Blas, 29. Brunqueña.

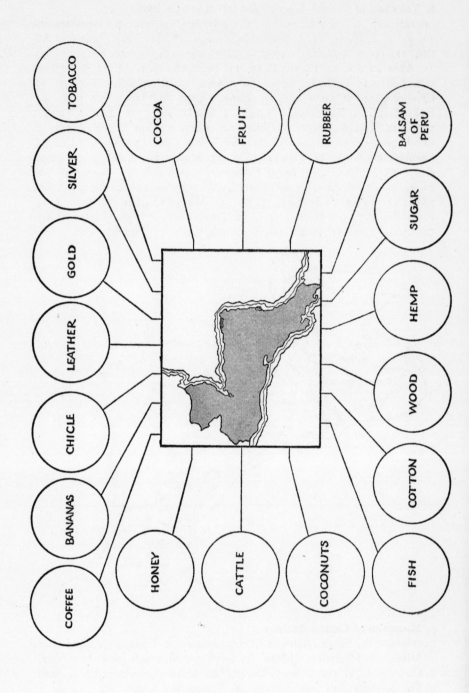

POSSIBLE CORRELATION OF MAYAN DATES WITH THOSE OF THE CHRISTIAN ERA

Classic Period (Early)

Long Count	Gregorian A.D.	Event
8.14.3.1.12	Sept. 17, 320	Leyden Plate engraved at Tikal
8.14.10.13.15	April 11, 328	Stela 9, Uaxactun date
8.16.0.0.0.	Feb. 3, 357	Stelae 18 and 19, Uaxactun
8.18.10.0.0.	May 17, 406	Stela 5, Balakbal
8.19.0.0.0.	March 25, 416	Stela 18, Tikal
9.2.0.0.0.	May 15, 475	Lintel at Oxkintok, Yucatan
9.4.0.0.0.	Oct. 18, 514	Chichen Itza occupied by the Itza
9.6.10.0.0.	Jan. 29, 564	Stela 1, Tulum, Quintana Roo
9.8.0.0.0.	Aug. 24, 593	Stela 1, Ichpaatun, Quintana Roo

Classic Period (Late)

Long Count	Gregorian A.D.	Event
9.11.0.0.0.	Oct. 14, 652	Stela 1, Island of Jaina, Campeche
9.12.10.0.0.	May 10, 682	Stela 1, Coba, Quintana Roo
9.13.0.0.0.	Mar. 18, 692	Chichen Itza abandoned, Itza-Chakanputun
9.16.0.0.0.	May 9, 751	Stelae 5 and 7, Santa Rosa, Campeche
9.16.13.0.0.	Mar. 1, 764	Temple of Initial Series, Holactun, Campeche
10.2.0.0.0.	Aug. 17, 869	Xiu history—arrival at Nonoualco
10.2.10.0.0.	June 26, 879	Temple of Initial Series, Chichen Itza
10.3.0.0.0.	May 4, 889	Last stelae of Classic period, Stela 12, Uaxactun, Stela 10, Xultun, Stela 1, Xamantun, Campeche
10.4.0.0.0.	Jan. 20, 909	Latest certain date of Classic period, Jadeite gorget from Tzibanche
10.6.0.0.0.	June 24, 948	Chakanputun abandoned, Itza returned to northern Yucatan, Xiu left Nonoualco for east
10.8.0.0.0.	Nov. 27, 987	Chichen Itza reoccupied by Itza, Mayapan founded by Kukulcan

Postclassic (Puuc Period)

Long Count	Gregorian A.D.	Event
10.9.0.0.0.	Aug. 15, 1007	Uxmal founded by Ah Zuitok Tutul Xiu, League of Mayapan began
10.18.10.0.0.	Nov. 22, 1194	Plot of Hunac Ceel, Itza driven from Chichen Itza by Cocom of Mayapan, League of Mayapan ended

Postclassic (Mexican Period)

Long Count	Gregorian A.D.	Event
10.19.0.0.0. to	Sept. 30, 1204	
11.11.0.0.0.	April 21, 1441	Ascendancy of Mayapan

Postclassic (Disintegration)

11.12.0.0.0.	Jan. 6, 1461	Destruction of Mayapan, all large Yucatan cities abandoned. There were exceptions to this as at Dzibilchaltun but certainty awaits further excavations
11.13.0.0.0.	Sept. 23, 1480	Devastating hurricane
11.14.0.0.0.	June 11, 1500	Pestilence, Spanish first seen (1511), smallpox epidemic, Mayacimil (easy death)
11.17.0.0.0.	Aug. 1, 1559	Spaniards arrived, Merida founded (1542), conquest completed (1546)
12.1.0.0.0.	June 7, 1638	Padres Fuensalida and Orbita visited Tayasal (1618) to convert the Itza in Peten
12.4.0.0.0.	July 27, 1697	Tayasal, last capital of the Itza, destroyed by Martin de Ursua

The above list is according to Morley-Brainerd in *The Ancient Maya*. It differs from new discoveries in Dzibilchaltun but is still useful as it shows the succession of events.

SELECTED BIBLIOGRAPHY

Adams, Richard E. W., Broman, Vivian L., et al., Tikal Reports Nos. 5–10, *Museum Monograph,* The University Museum, Philadelphia, 1961.

——, and Trik, A. S. Temple 1 (Str. 5D–1): Post-constructional activities. Tikal Report No. 7, *Museum Monographs,* The University Museum, Philadelphia, 1961.

Aldrich, L. T., et al., Radioactive Ages of Micas from Granite Rocks by Rb-Sr and K-A Methods, *Trans. Am. Geophys. Union,* 39, 1124, 1958.

Alva Ixlilxochitl, Fernando de, *Obras Historicas,* ed. by Alfredo Chavero, Mex., 1891.

Alvarado, Pedro de, *An account of the conquest of Guatemala in 1524,* ed. by Sedley J. Mackie; with a facsimile of the Spanish original, 1525. N.Y., The Cortes Society, 1924.

Ancient Maya Paintings of Bonampak, Mexico, Carnegie Institution of Washington, Pub. S46, Washington. n.d.

Andrews, E. Wyllys, The Archaeology of Southwestern Campeche, *Contributions to Am. Anthropology and Hist.,* Vol. 8, No. 40, Carnegie Inst. of Washington, Pub. 546, Washington, 1943.

——, Excavations at Dzibilchaltun, Yucatan, 1956–1962, *Estudios de Cultura Maya,* UNAM, Vol. 2, Mex., 1962.

——, Progress Report on two seasons work at Dzibilchaltun, Northwestern Yucatan, Mexico, *National Geographic Mag.,* Washington, 1959.

—— Dzibilchaltun: Lost City of the Mayas, *Nat. Geog. Mag.* 115, Jan. 90–109, 1959.

——, Excavations at Dzibilchaltun, Northwestern Yucatan, Mexico, Proc. *Am. Philos. Soc.,* 104, No. 3: 254–65, Phila., 1960.

Annals of the Cakchiquels, The original text, with a translation, notes and introduction, by Daniel G. Brinton, Phila., 1885, 243p. (Library of aboriginal Am. Literature, No. 6, ed. by D. G. Brinton)

Anonymous, Mayan Stone Monument Bears Date 32 A.D., Tikal, *Science News Letter,* Vol. 76, 9, July 4, 1959.

——, Mastodon and Man Kept Company in Mexico, *Science Digest,* 61, Oct., 1962.

Avendana y Loyola, Andres, *Relacion de las dos entradas que hize a la conversion de los gentiles Ytzaes y Cehaches* (Peten-Itza), Merida, 6 de abril de 1696, Ms. Newberry Library, Chicago.

Barrera Vasquez, Alfredo, El misterio de Dzibilchaltun, El angulo historico-filologico del problema, Univ. Yucatan INAH, *Centro de Estudios Mayas,* Pub. 1, Merida, Yucatan, 1959.

Batres, Leopoldo, *Teotihuacan,* Mex., 1906.

Becerra Tanco, Luis, *Origen milagroso del Santuario de Nuestra Senora de Guadalupe,* Mex., 1666.

Berlin, H., *El Templo le las Inscripciones VI de Tikal, Antropologia e Historia de Guatemala,* Vol. 3, No. 1, 33–54, Guatemala, 1951.

Beyer, Hermann, The Analysis of the Maya Hieroglyphs, *International Arch. Ethnog.,* Bd. 31, S1–20, Leyden, 1930.

——, On the Correlation between Maya and Christian Chronology, *Maya Res.,* Vol. 2, No. 1, 64–72, N.Y., 1935.

——, Studies on the Inscriptions at Chichen Itza. *Contributions to Am. Archaeology,* Vol. 4, No. 21, Carnegie Inst. of Washington, Pub. 483, 37–175, pls. 1–14, Washington, 1937.

Blom, Frans, Notes from the Maya Area, *Am. Anthropologist,* 1924.

——, The Maya Game *pok-ta-pok* (called *tlachtli* by the Aztecs), *Middle Am. Research Series,* Pub. No. 4, 486–530, Tulane Univ., New Orleans, 1932.

——, Commerce, Trade and Monetary Units of the Maya, *Middle Am. Research Series,* Pub. No. 4, 532–56, Tulane Univ., New Orleans, 1933.

Bowditch, Charles, P., *Mexican and Central American Antiquities, Calendar Systems and History,* Washington, 1904.

——, *The Numeration, Calendar Systems and Astronomical Knowledge of the Mayas,* Privately printed, Cambridge, 1910.

Brainerd, G. W., The Maya Civilization, *Southwest Museum,* Los Angeles, 1954.

——, The Archaeological Ceramics of Yucatan, Univ. Calif., *Anthropological Records,* Vol. 19, Berkeley, 1958.

Carnegie Inst. of Washington, *News Service Bull.,* Buried Temple Discovered at Site of Ancient Maya Capital, Vol. 1, No. 1, July 24, 1926.

————, Colonel and Mrs. Lindberg Aid Archaeologists, Pt. 2, Aerial Survey of the Maya Region, Vol. 1, No. 50, Dec. 1, 1929.

————, The Great White Ways of the Maya, Vol. 3, No. 9, Sept. 24, 1932.

————, The Ruins of Quirigua, Vol. 3, No. 19, Dec. 16, 1934.

————, The Caracol—A Perplexing Maya Ruin, Vol. 3, No. 27, Dec 15, 1935.

————, Important Maya Discovery in the Guatemalan Highlands, Vol. 4, No. 6, Aug. 23, 1936.

Carr, R. F., and Hazard, J. E., Map of the Ruins of Tikal, El Peten, Guatemala Tikal Report No. 11, *Museum Monographs,* The Univ. Museum, Phila., 1961.

Carreno, Alberto Maria, Don Fray Juan de Zumarraga, Pioneer of European Culture in America. *The Americas: A Quarterly Rev. of Inter-American Cultural Hist.,* Academy of Am. Franciscan Hist., Washington, D.C., Vol. 6, No. 1, 1949.

Caso, Alfonso, Monte Alban, Richest Archeological Find in America, *National Geographic Mag.,* 487–512, Oct., 1932.

Castenada Pacanini, Ricardo, *Tikal. La ciudad arqueologica mas grande de la civilizacion maya,* Ministerio de Educacion Publica, Guatemala, 1958.

Cather, Willa, *Death Comes for the Archbishop,* Alfred A. Knopf, N.Y., 1927.

Catherwood, F., *Views of Ancient Monuments in Central America, Chiapas and Yucatan,* N.Y., 1844.

Cerezo Dardon, H., Breve historia de Tikal, *Antropologia e Historia de Guatemala,* Vol. 3, No. 1, Guatemala, 1951.

Codex Dresdensis, Die Maya—Handschrift der Königlishen Bibliothek zu Dresden; herausgegeben von Prof. Dr. E. Förstemann, Leipzig, 1880.

Codex Peresianus, Manuscrit hieratique des anciens Indiens de l'Amerique Centrale Conserve a la Bibliotheque Nationale de Paris, avec une introduction par Leon de Rosny, Publie en couleurs, 2d ed., Paris, 1887.

Codex Tro-Cortesianus, Codice Maya denominado Cortesiano que se conserva en al Museo Arqueologico Nacional (Madrid), Reproduccion fotocromolitografica ordenada en la misma forma que el original hecha y publicada bajo la direccion de D. Juan de Dios de la Rada y Delgado y D. Jeronimo Lopez de Ayala y del Hierro, Madrid 1897.

Coe, W. R., Two carved lintels from Tikal, *Archaeology,* Vol. 11, No. 2, 75–80, Cambridge, 1958.

————, Tikal 1959, *Expedition,* Vol. 1, No. 4, 7–12, Phila., 1959.

————, Stela 29, Tikal, Guatemala, *Phila. Anthropological Soc. Bull.,* Vol. 13, No. 1, 1–3, Phila., 1959.

————, A Tikal summary, *Phila. Anthropological Soc. Bull.,* Vol. 14, No. 2, 16–17, Phila., 1961.

————, Maya Mystery in Tikal, *Natural Hist.,* N.Y., Pt. 1, Vol. 71, No. 7, 10–12, Aug.–Sept., 1962. Pt. 2, Vol. 71, No. 8, 44–53, Oct., 1963. Reprinted in Guatemala, 23–30, Consulate-General of Guatemala, N.Y., 1962 and 1963.

————, Priestly power and peasant corn: Excavations and Reconstructions at Tikal, *Illus. London News,* London, Pt. 1, Vol. 240, No. 6390, 103–106, Jan. 20. Pt. 2, Vol. 240, No. 6391, 135–137, Jan. 27, 1962.

————, A Summary of Excavation and Research at Tikal, Guatemala: 1956–1961, *Am. Antiquity,* Vol. 27, No. 4, 479–507, Salt Lake City, 1962.

———, Current Research (Tikal), *Am. Antiquity*, Vol. 28, No. 3, 417–419, Salt Lake City, 1963.

———, A Summary of Excavation and Research at Tikal, Guatemala: 1962, *Estudios de Cultura Maya*, Vol. 3, 41–64, Mex., 1963.

———, Current Research (Tikal), *Am. Antiquity*, Vol. 29, No. 3, 411–413, Salt Lake City, 1964.

———, Tikal, Guatemala, and Emergent Maya Civilization, *Science*, 147, 1401–19, Mar. 19, 1965.

———, Ten Years of Study of a Maya Ruin in the Lowlands of Guatemala, *Expedition*, University of Pennsylvania, Vol. 8, No. 1, 1965.

Coe, W. R., and Broman, V. L., Excavations at the Stela 23 Group, No. 2 in Tikal Reports 1–4, *Museum Monographs,* The Univ. Museum, Phila., 1958.

Coe, W. R., and McGinn, J. J., The North Acropolis of Tikal and an Early Tomb, *Expedition*, Vol. 5, No. 2, 24–32, Phila., 1963.

Coe, W. R., Shook, E. M., and Satterwaite, L., The Carved Wooden Lintels of Tikal, Tikal Report No. 6, *Museum Monographs,* The Univ. Museum, Phila., 1961.

Cole, Fay Cooper, and Deuel, Thorne, *Rediscovering Illinois,* Univ. of Chicago Press, 1937.

Cooke, C. Wythe, Why the Mayan Cities of the Peten District, Guatemala, Were Abandoned, *Jour. of the Wash. Acad. of Sci.,* Vol. 21, No. 13, 283–87, Washington, 1931.

Corbett, D. S., The Art of the Mayas, *Art and Archaeology,* Vol. 18, No. 4, 145–53, Balt., 1924.

Coursin, David Baird, M.D., Undernutrition and Brain Function, *Review of Nutrition Research,* Borden Company, N.Y., Vol. 26, No. 1, Jan.–Mar. 1965.

Covarrubias, Miguel, *The Eagle, the Jaguar, and the Serpent: Indian Art of the Americas,* Knopf, N.Y., 1954.

Culbert, T. P., Ceramic Research at Tikal, Guatemala, *Ceramica de Cultura Maya,* Vol. 1, Nos. 2 & 3, 34–42, Cambridge, Mass., 1963.

Cummings, Byron, Ruins of Cuicuilco, May Revolutionize Our History of Ancient Am., *National Geographic Mag.,* 203–220, Aug., 1923.

De Terra, Helmut, Comments on Radiocarbon Dates from Mexico, *Am. Antiquity,* Vol. 17, No. 1, Pt. 2 (Memoir No. 8), 33–38, Salt Lake City, 1951.

———, *Man and Mammoth in Mexico,* Hutchinson of London, 1957.

Demarest, Donald, and Taylor, Coley, *The Dark Virgin, The Book of Our Lady of Guadalupe,* Academy Guild Press, 1959.

Deuel, Thorne, Hopewellian Communities in Illinois, *Ill. State Museum Scientific Papers,* Vol. 5, Springfield, Ill., 1952.

———, *American Indian Ways of Life,* Ill. State Museum, Springfield, 1958.

Douglass, Andrew Ellicott, Secret of the Southwest Solved by Talkative Tree Rings, *National Geographic Mag.,* 737–770, Dec., 1929.

Drucker, Philip, *Ceramic Sequence at Tres Zapotes, Veracruz, Mexico,* Smithsonian Inst., *Bureau of Am. Ethnology,* No. 140, Washington, 1943.

———, *Ceramic Stratigraphy at Cerro de las Mesas, Veracruz, Mexico,* Smithsonian Inst., Bureau of Am. Ethnology, No. 141, Washington, 1943.

———, *Some Implications of the Ceramic Complex of La Venta,* Smithsonian Misc. Coll., Vol. 107, No. 8, Washington, 1947.

———, La Venta, Tabasco: A Study of Olmec Ceramics and Art, Smithsonian Inst., Bureau Am. Ethnology, Bull. 153, Washington, 1952.

Drucker, Philip, and Heizer, Robert F., Gifts for the Jaguar God, *National Geographic Mag.,* 367–375, Sept., 1956.

Dyal, Paul, *Empress of America, Auto Viajes Internacionales,* Mex., 1959.

Dyson, R. H., Jr., The Tikal Project—1962, *Archaeology,* Vol. 15, No. 2, 131–32, N.Y., 1962.

Elson, B. F., ed., *Mayan Studies,* Univ. Book Exchange, 1961.

Estrada Monroy, A., Tikal—Estudios sobre probable uso de Grupo E., *Anales de la Sociedad de Geografía e Historia,* Vol. 34, 45–56, Guatemala, 1961.

Fleischer, R. L., and Price, P. B., Techniques for Geological Dating of Minerals by Chemical Etching of Fission Fragment Tracks, Report No. 64-RL-3635 M, *General Electric Research Lab.,* Schenectady, N.Y., 1964.

Galloway, A. C., An Interesting Visit to the Ancient Pyramids of San Juan Teotihuacan, *National Geographic Mag.,* 1041–1049, Dec., 1910.

Gamio, Manuel, y Otros, *La poblacion del Valle de Teotihuacan,* 3 vols., Mex., 1922.

Gates, William, An Outline Dictionary of Maya Glyphs, *Maya Society Pub. No. 1,* Balt., 1931.

Greater St. Louis Archaeological Society, *Cahokia Brought to Life,* St. Louis.

Greene, Virginia, and Moholy-Nagy, H., A Teotihuacan-style Vessel from Tikal: A Correction, *Am. Antiquity,* 1965.

Griffin, James B., *Archaeology of Eastern United States,* Univ. of Chicago Press, 1952.

Haviland, W. A., A "Miniature Stela" from Tikal, *Expedition,* Vol. 4, No. 3, 2–3, Phila., 1962.

———, Prehistoric Settlement at Tikal, Guatemala, *Expedition,* Vol. 7, No. 3, 1965.

Henry, Thomas R., and Durenceau, Andre, Ice Age Man, the First American, *National Geographic Mag.,* 781–806, Dec., 1955.

Hewett, E. L., The Excavations at Quirigua in 1912, *Bull. of the Archaeological Inst. of Am.,* Vol. 3, 163–71. (Reprinted as The Third Season's Work in Guatemala, Paper No. 22, School of Am. Research, Archaeological Inst. of Am., Santa Fe, 1912.)

———, *Latest Work of the School of Am. Archaeology at Quirigua,* Holmes Anniv. Vol. 157–62, Washington, 1916.

Holmes, W. H., A Quirigua Mystery, *Art and Archaeology,* Vol. 4, No. 6, 340, Washington, 1916.

———, Masterpieces of Aboriginal Am. Art, 5, The Great Dragon of Quirigua, Pt. 1, *Art and Archaeology,* Vol. 4, No. 6, 271–78, Washington, 1916. Pt. 2, Vol. 5, No. 1, 39–49, 1917.

Ill. Archaeological Survey, Indian Mounds and Villages in Ill., *Univ. of Ill. Bull. No. 2 of Ill. Archaeological Survey,* Univ. of Ill., Urbana, 1960.

Instituto de Antropologia e Historia de Guatemala, *Arqueologia guatemalteca,* Con un prologo de Ernesto Chinchilla Aguilar. Guatemala, Ministerio de

Educacion Publica, 204 p. ilus. (Biblioteca guatemalteca de cultura popular "15 de septiembre", v. 20), 1957.

Judd, Neil M., "Pyramids" of the New World, *National Geographic Mag.*, 105–128, Jan., 1948.

Kempton, J. H., Maize, the Plant-Breeding Achievement of the Am. Indian, *Old and New Plant Lore*, Vol. 11, Smithsonian Inst., Washington, 1931.

———, Maize—Our Heritage from the Indians, *Smithsonian Inst. Annual Report, 1937*, 385–408, Washington, 1938.

Kempton, J. H., and Popenonoe, Wilson, Teosinte in Guatemala, *Contrib. to Am. Archaeology*, Vol. 4, No. 23, Carnegie Inst. of Washington Pub. 483, 199–217, Washington, 1937.

Kidder, Alfred V., A Program for Maya Research, Carnegie Inst. of Washington, 1—10, Washington, 1937.

———, Kaminaljuyu, Guatemala: Addenda and Corrigenda, *Carnegie Inst. of Washington, Notes on Middle Am. Archaeology and Ethnology*, No. 89, Washington, 1948.

Kidder, A. V., Jennings, J. D., and Shook, E. M., Excavations at Kaminaljuyu, Guatemala, *Carnegie Inst. of Washington*, Pub. 561, Washington, 1946.

Kidder II, Alfred, and Samayoa Chinchilla, Carlos, *The Art of the Ancient Maya*, Photographs by Reuben Goldberg, N.Y., Thomas Y. Crowell, 1959.

Kidder, A. V., and Thompson, J. Eric S., The Correlation of Maya and Christian Chronology, *Co-operation in Research*, Carnegie Inst. of Washington, Pub. 501, 493–510, Washington, 1938.

Knorozov, Jurij V., The Writing of the Ancient Mayans: A Study of Deciphering, Sovjetskaja Etnografia, No. 1, *Acad. of Sciences of the Union of Soviet Socialist Republics*, 1955.

Koshetz, Herbert, Dyes Used by Indians in Mexico May Be Clue to Early Migration, *New York Times*, 53, Sun., Aug. 1, 1965.

Kulp, J. Lawrence, Feely, Herbert W., and Tryon, Lansing E., Lamont Natural Radiocarbon Measurements, I, *Science*, Vol. 114, 565–568, Washington, 1951.

Kulp, J. Lawrence, Tryon, Lansing E., Eckelman, Walter R., and Snell, William A., Lamont Natural Radiocarbon Measurements, II, *Science*, Vol. 116, 409–414, Washington, 1952.

Landa, Diego de, *Relacion de las cosas de Yucatan*, Merida, 1938.

Laws, W. D., An Investigation of Temple Plasters from Tikal, Guatemala, with evidence of the use by the ancient Maya of plant extracts in plaster making, Wrightia, Vol. 2, No. 5, 217–228, *Texas Research Foundation*, Renner, 1962.

Lazo de la Vega, Luis, *Hvei Tlamahuicoltica omonexiti in ilhuicac cihuapilli Santa Maria totlaconantzin Guadalupe in nican hvei altepenahuac Mexico itocayocan Tepeyacac*, Mex., en la Imprenta de Juan Ruyz, 1649.

Lincoln, J. Steward, The Maya Calendar of the Ixil of Guatemala, *Contrib. to Am. Anthropology and Hist.*, Vol. 7, No. 38, Carnegie Inst. of Washington, Pub. No. 528, Washington, 1942.

Long, R. C. E., The Age of the Maya Calendar, *Jour. of Royal Anthropological Inst.*, Vol. 54, 353–62, London, 1924.

Los Mayos Antiguos, *Coleccion de monografias de arqueologia, etnografia y linguistica mayas publicadas con motivo del Centenario de la exploracion de Yucatan por John L. Stephens y Frederick Catherwood en los anos 1841–42,* 1941.

Lothrop, S. K., *Metals from the Cenote of Sacrifice, Chichen Itza, Yucatan,* Cambridge, 1952.

——, Atitlan, an Archaeological Study of Ancient Remains on the Borders of Lake Atitlan, Guatemala, *Carnegie Inst. of Washington, Pub. 444,* Washington, 1933.

Makemson, Maud W., *The Book of the Jaguar Priest: a Translation of the Book of Chilam Balam of Tizimin* with commentary, Henry Schuman, N.Y., 1951.

Maudslay, Alfred Percival, *Biologia-Centrali-Americana,* 4 Vols. of text and plates, London, 1902.

Miller, Carl F., Life 8,000 Years Ago Uncovered in an Alabama Cave, *National Geographic Mag.,* 542–558, Oct., 1956.

——, Russell Cave: New Light on Stone Age Life, *National Geographic Mag.,* 427–438, Mar., 1958.

Moholy-Nagy, H., A Tlaloc Stela from Tikal, *Expedition,* Vol. 4, No. 2, 27, Phila., 1962.

Morley, Sylvanus Griswold, The Inscriptions of Naranjo, Northern Guatemala, *Am. Anthropologist,* Vol. 2, No. 4, 543–62, Lancaster, 1909.

——, A Group of Related Structures at Uxmal, Mexico, *Am. Jour. of Archaeology,* 2d ser., Vol. 14, No. 1, 1–18, Norwood, 1910.

——, The Correlation of the Maya and Christian Chronology, *Am. Jour. of Archaeology,* 2d ser., Vol. 14, No. 2, 193–204, Norwood, 1910.

——, Ancient Temples and Cities of the World, Chichen Itza, *Bull. of the Pan-Am. Union,* Vol. 32, 453–68, Washington, 1911.

——, The Historical Value of the Books of Chilan Balam, *Am. Jour. of Archaeology,* 2d. ser., Vol. 15, No. 2, 195–214, Norwood, 1911.

——, Excavations at Quirigua, Guatemala, *National Geographic Mag.,* 339–361, Mar., 1913.

——, Ancient Temples and Cities of the New World; Uxmal, the City of the Xius, *Bull. of the Pan-Am. Union,* Vol. 32, 627–42, Washington, 1911.

——, Quirigua, an Ancient Town, 1,400 Years Old, *Scientific Am.,* Vol. 107, 96, 105, N.Y., 1912.

——, Introduction to the Study of Maya Hieroglyphs, *Bureau of Am. Ethnology, Bull. 57,* Washington, 1915.

——, Rise and Fall of the Maya Civilization in the Light of the Monuments and the Native Chronicles, *Proceedings of the Internat. Congress of Americanists,* 19th Session, Washington, 140–49, Washington, 1915.

——, The Supplementary Series in the Maya Inscriptions, *Holmes Anniv. Vol.,* 366–96, Washington, 1916.

——, Archaeological Research at the Ruins of Chichen Itza, Yucatan, *Carnegie Inst. of Washington,* No. 200, 61–91, Washington, 1913.

——, The Ruins of Tuloom, Yucatan, *Am. Museum Jour.,* Vol. 17, No. 3, 190–304, N.Y., 1917.

——, The Hutun as the Principal Chronological Unit of the Old Maya Empire, *Proceedings of the Internat. Congress of Americanists,* 19th Session, Washington, D.C., 1915, 195–201, Washington, 1917.

——, The Inscriptions of Copan, *Carnegie Inst. of Washington,* Pub. 219, Washington, 1920.

——, The Foremost Intellectual Achievement of Ancient America, *National Geographic Mag.,* 109–30, Feb., 1922.

——, The Earliest Mayan Dates, *Congres International des Americanistes, Compte-rendu de la XXI Session,* Goteborg, 1924, Pt. 2, 625–67, Goteborg Museum, Goteborg, 1925.

——, Chichen Itza, an American Mecca, *National Geographic Mag.,* 63–95, Jan., 1925.

——, New Light on the Discovery of Yucatan and the Foundation of the New Empire, *Am. Jour. of Archaeology,* Archaeological Inst. of Am., 2d ed., Vol. 31, No. 1, 51–69, Concord, 1927.

——, Un jarro Maya pintado, *Forma,* Vol. 1, No. 5, 22–24, Mex., 1927.

——, Unearthing America's Ancient History, *National Geographic Mag.,* 99–126, July, 1931.

——, *Guia de las ruinas de Quirigua,* Traducida del ingles por Adrian Recinos, Washington, 1936.

——, Yucatan, Home of the Gifted Maya, *National Geographic Mag.,* 590–644, Nov., 1936.

——, The Inscriptions of Peten, *Carnegie Inst. of Washington,* Pub. 437, 5 Vols., Washington, 1937–38.

——, The Maya New Empire, Cooperation in Research, *Carnegie Inst. of Washington,* Pub. 501, 533–65, Washington, 1938.

——, *The Ancient Maya,* Stanford Univ. Press, Calif., 1947. 3d. ed. rev. 1958.

——, Guide Book to the Ruins of Quirigua, 1935; 2d printing, Octavo, viii plus 205 pp., frontispiece, 48 figs., *Carnegie Inst. of Washington,* Pub. 16, Washington, 1947

Morley, S. G., and Morley, Frances R., The Age and Provenance of the Leyden Plate, *Contrib. to Am. Anthropology and Hist.,* Vol. 5, No. 24, Carnegie Inst. of Washington, Pub. 509, Washington, 1939.

Morris, Earl H., Charlot, Jean, and Morris, Ann Axtell, The Temple of the Warriors at Chichten Itza, Yucatan, *Carnegie Inst. of Washington,* Pub. 406, Washington, 1931.

Munoz, Jaoquin, *Guatemala, From Whence the Rainbow Takes Its Color,* Tipografia Nacional de Guatemala, 3d ed., 1952.

Orozco y Berra, Manuel, *Historia antigua y de la conquista de Mexico,* 4 Vols., Mex., 1880.

Palacios, Enrique Juan, Maya-Christian Synchronology or Calendrical Correlation, *Middle Am. Papers,* Dept. of Middle Am. Research, No. 4, 147–180, Tulane Univ., New Orleans, 1932.

Parson, M. J., Maya Temple Adventure, *Lore,* Vol. 14, No. 2, 64–69, Milwaukee, 1964.

Pearse, A. S., Creaser, Edwin P., Hall, F. G., and collaborators, The Cenotes of Yucatan: A Zoological and Hydrographic Survey, Quarto, iii plus 304 pp.,

19 pls., 246 figs., *Carnegie Inst. of Washington,* No. 457, Washington, 1936.

Phillips, P., Ford, J. A., and Griffin, J. B., *Archaeological Survey in the Lower Mississippi Valley,* Peabody Museum, Harvard Univ., 1951.

———, The Casa Redonda at Chichen Itza, Yucatan, Contrib. to Am. Archaeology, Vol. 3, No. 17, *Carnegie Inst. of Washington,* Pub. 456, 129–54, pls. 1–8, Washington, 1937.

Pollock, H. E. D., et al., Mayapan, Yucatan, *Carnegie Inst. of Washington,* Pub. 619, Washington, 1962.

Proskouriakoff, Tatiana A., An Album of Maya Architecture, *Carnegie Inst. of Washington,* Pub. 558, Washington, 1946.

———, A Study of Classic Maya Sculpture, *Carnegie Inst. of Washington,* Pub. 593, Washington, 1950.

———, Mayapan, the Last Stronghold of a Civilization, *Archaeology,* Vol. 7, No. 2, 1954.

———, Death of a Civilization, *Scientific American,* Vol. 192, No. 5, 1955.

———, An Albumn of Maya Architecture, University of Oklahoma, 1963.

Ralph, E. K., Review of Radiocarbon Dates for Samples from Tikal Related to the Mayan Calendar Correlation Problem, *American Antiquity,* 1965.

Recinos, Adrian, Translator, *Popul Vuh, The Sacred Book of the Ancient Quiche Maya,* University of Oklahoma, Norman, Oklahoma. English version by Sylvanus G. Morley and Delia Goetz, 1950.

——— and Goetz, Delia, *The Annals of the Cakchiquels,* Univ. of Okla. Press, Norman, Okla., 1953.

Roys, Ralph L., Personal Names of the Maya of Yucatan, *Carnegie Institution of Wash.,* Pub. No. 523, 31–48, 1940.

Ruppert, Karl, The Temple of the Wall Panels, Chichen Itza, *Carnegie Institution of Wash.,* No. 403, 117–40, 1931.

———, The Caracol at Chichen Itza, Yucatan, Mexico, *Carnegie Institution of Wash.,* Pub. No. 403, 1935.

———, The Mercado, Chichen Itza, Yucatan, Mexico, *Carnegie Institution of Wash.,* Pub. No. 546, 1943.

———, Chichen Itza, Architectural Notes and Plans, *Carnegie Institution of Wash.,* Pub. No. 595, 1952.

Ruz Lhuillier, Alberto, Exploraciones en Palenque, *30th Internat. Congress of Americanists,* London, 1954.

Samayoa Chinchilla, Carlos, *The Emerald Lizard,* The Falcons Wing Press, Indian Hills, Colorado, 1957.

Satterthwaite, Linton, Jr., Piedras Negras Archaeology: *Architecture,* Pt. 1, No. 1, Introduction, Univ. Museum, Univ. of Penn., Phila., 1943.

———, Maya Long Count Numbers, *Expedition,* Vol. 2, No. 2, 36–37, Phila., 1960.

Satterthwaite, L., and Broman, V. L., and Haviland, W. A., Miscellaneous Investigations: Excavation near Fragment 1 of Stela 17, with Observations on Stela P34 and Miscellaneous Stone 25; Excavation of Stela 28, Fragment 1; Tikal Report No. 8, *Museum Monographs,* The Univ. Museum, Univ. of Penn., Phila., 1961.

Satterthwaite, L., and Ralph, E. K., New Radiocarbon Dates and the Maya

Correlation Problem, *Am. Antiquity,* Vol. 26, No. 2, 165–184, Salt Lake City, 1960.

Shook, Edwin M., Investigaciones Arqueologicas en las Ruinas de Tikal, Departmento de El Peten, Guatemala, *Antropologia e Historia de Guatemala,* Vol. 3, No. 1, 9–32, Guatemala, 1951.

———, The Temple of the Red Stela, *Expedition,* Vol. 1, No. 1, 26–33, Phila. (Spanish trans. in *Antropologia e Historia de Guatemala,* Vol. 11, No. 2, 7–14, Guatemala), 1958.

Shook, Edwin, Coe, William R., Broman, Vivian L., and Satterthwaite, Linton, *Tikal Reports 1–4,* Univ. Museum, Univ. of Penn., Phila., 1958.

Shook, Edwin M., and Kidder, A., II, The Painted Tomb at Tikal, *Expedition,* Vol. 4, No. 1, 2–7, Phila., 1961. (Spanish trans. in *Antropologia e Historia de Guatemala,* Vol. 14, No. 1, 5–10, Guatemala, 1962.)

Smith, A. Ledyard, Uaxactun, Guatemala: Excavations of 1931–1937, with intro. by A. V. Kidder, Quarto, xii plus 108 pp., frontispiece, 143 figs., *Carnegie Inst. of Washington,* Pub. 588, Washington, 1950.

Spinden, Herbert J., The Question of the Zodiac in America, *Am. Anthropologist,* Vol. 18, No. 1, 53–80, Lancaster, 1916.

———, Central American Calendars and the Gregorian Day, *Jour. of the National Acad. of Sciences,* Vol. 6, 56–59, Washington, 1920.

———, The Reduction of Mayan Dates, *Papers of Peabody Museum of Am. Archaeology and Ethnology,* Harvard Univ., Vol. 6, No. 4, Cambridge, Mass., 1924.

———, Ancient Mayan Astronomy, *Scientific Am.,* Vol. 138, No. 1, 8–12, N.Y., 1928.

Stephens, J. L., *Central America, Chiapas and Yucatan,* 2 Vols., N.Y., 1841.

———, *Incidents of Travel in Yucatan,* 2 Vols., N.Y., 1843.

———, *Incidentes de viaje en Centro America, Chiapas y Yucatan,* traducida por Benjamin Mazariegos Santizo, revisada por Paul Burgess, 2 Vols., Quetzaltenango, Guatemala, 1939–40.

Stirling, Matthew W., Discovering the New World's Oldest Dated Work of Man, *National Geographic Mag.,* 183–218, Aug., 1939.

———, Great Stone Faces of the Mexican Jungle, *National Geographic Mag.,* 309–334, Sept., 1940.

———, Stone Monuments of Southern Mexico, Smithsonian Inst., *Bureau of Am. Ethnology,* No. 138, Washington, 1943.

Stromsvik, Gustav, Substela Caches and Stela Foundations at Copan and Quirigua, *Contrib. to Am. Anthropology and Hist.,* Vol. 7, No. 37, Carnegie Inst. of Washington, Pub. 528, 63–96, Washington, 1942.

Szecsy, Janos de, Santiago de los Caballeros de Goathemala, en Almolongo (Investigaciones del ano 1950), Guatemala, Editorial del Ministerio de Educacion Publica, Publicaciones del Instituto de antropologia e historia de Guatemala, 1953.

Teeple, J. E., Maya Astronomy, *Carnegie Inst. of Washington,* Pub. 403, Contrib. 2, Washington, 1930.

Thomas, Cyrus, Mayan Calendar Systems, Bureau of Am. Eth., *Smithsonian Inst. 19th Ann. Report,* 1897–98, Pt. 2, 693–819, Washington, 1900.

——, Mayan Calendar Systems, Bureau of Am. Eth., *Smithsonian Inst. 22nd Ann. Report,* 1900–01, Pt. 1, 197–305, Washington, 1904.

Thompson, J. Eric S., The Civilization of the Mayas, *Field Museum of Natural Hist., Anthropology Leaflet 25,* 1st ed., Chicago, 1927.

——, A Correlation of the Mayan and European Calendars, *Field Museum of Natural Hist., Pub. 241, Anthropological Series,* Vol. 18, No. 1, Chicago, 1927.

——, The Solar Year of the Mayas at Quirigua, Guatemala, *Field Museum of Natural Hist., Anthropological Series,* Vol. 17, No. 4, Chicago, 1932.

Thompson, J. Eric S., *The Rise and Fall of Maya Civilization,* Univ. of Oklahoma Press, Norman, 1956.

——, *Maya Hieroglyphic Writing,* Univ. of Oklahoma Press, Norman, 1962.

Tozzer, A. M., Landa's relacion de las cosas de Yucatan, ed. with notes, Papers of the *Peabody Museum of Am. Archaeology and Ethnology,* Harvard Univ., Vol. 18, Cambridge, Mass., 1941.

Trik, Aubrey S., The Splendid Tomb of Temple I at Tikal, Guatemala, *Expedition,* Vol. 6, No. 1, Univ. Museum, Phila., 1963.

United Fruit Company, Middle Am. Information Bureau, Zaculeu, *Restoration,* N.Y., 1947.

Vaughn, T. W., Geological History of Central America and the West Indies during Cenozoic Time, *Bull. Geol. Soc. of Am.,* Vol. 29, 615–30, Washington, 1918.

Vela, David, *El Hermano Pedro en la Vida y en las Letras,* Union Tipografica, Guatemala, 1935.

Villa, R. Alfonso, The Yaxuna-Coba Causeway, *Contrib. to Am. Archaeology,* Vol. 2, No. 9, *Carnegie Inst. of Washington,* Pub. 436, 187–208, Pls. 1–9, Washington, 1934.

Villacorta Calderon, Jose Antonio, *Codices Mayas,* Sociedad de Geografia e Historia de Guatemala, Guatemala, 1930.

——, *Prehistoria e historia antigua de Guatemala,* Sociedad de Geografia e Historia de Guatemala, Guatemala, 1938.

Villagra, A., *Bonampak, la ciudad de los muros pintados,* Mex., 1949.

Vinson, G. L., Two Important Recent Archaeological Discoveries in Esso Concessions, Guatemala, *Exploration News Letter,* Standard Oil Co. (N.J.), N.Y., Mar., 1960

Wauchope, Robert, Implications of Radiocarbon Dates from Middle And South America, *Middle Am. Research Reports,* Vol. 11, No. 2, Tulane Univ., New Orleans, 1954.

Webster, H. T., Tikal Graffiti, *Expedition,* Vol. 6, No. 1, 36–47, Phila., 1963

Willson, Robert W., Astronomical Notes on the Maya Codices, *Papers of the Peabody Museum of Am. Archaeology and Ethnology,* Harvard Univ., Vol. 6, No. 3, Cambridge, Mass., 1924.

Wray, Donald E., and Mac Neish, Richard S., Hopewellian and Weaver Occupations of the Weaver Site, Fulton County, Ill., *Ill. State Museum Sc. Papers,* Vol. 7, No. 2, 1961.

INDEX